Using Microcomputers
in Physical Education
and the
Sport Sciences

Using Microcomputers in Physical Education and the Sport Sciences

Edited by
Joseph E. Donnelly, EdD
Kearney State College

Human Kinetics Publishers, Inc.
Champaign, Illinois

Library of Congress Cataloging-in-Publication Data

Donnelly, Joseph E.
  Using microcomputers in physical education and the sport sciences.

  Includes index.
  1. Physical education and training--Study and
teaching. 2. Computer-assisted instruction. 3. Computer
managed instruction. 4. Sports sciences--Data processing.
5. Microcomputers. I. Title.
GV362.D66   1987   613.7'028'5   86-20096
ISBN 0-87322-083-8

Senior Editor: Gwen Steigelman, PhD
Production Director: Ernie Noa
Assistant Production Director: Lezli Harris
Copy Editor: Steve Davenport
Assistant Editor: Kathy Kane
Proofreader: Jennifer Merrill
Typesetter: Theresa Bear
Text Layout: Denise Mueller
Cover Design: Jack Davis
Printed By: Braun-Brumfield

ISBN: 0-87322-083-8

Copyright © 1987 by Joseph E. Donnelly

Printed in the United States of America

10 9 8 7 6 5 4 3 2

Human Kinetics Books
A Division of Human Kinetics Publishers, Inc.
Box 5076, Champaign, IL 61825-5076
1-800-DIAL HKP
1-800-334-3665 (in Illinois)

Contents

Preface

The Digital Equipment Corporation introduction of the minicomputer to the business world in 1957 was considered a landmark development. The minicomputer was considered the first "affordable" system that could be interfaced with the outside world and sold for $120,000! The initial minicomputer had about 64 kilobytes of random access memory or RAM, which is equivalent to the memory found in typical modern microcomputers. The minicomputer subsequently evolved through several changes, which improved the general architecture and the ability to accept peripherals. Perhaps the most significant change was the decrease in the price to about $10,000.

The Apple microcomputer was introduced to the general public in 1979 and marked the beginning of widespread availability. For about $3,000, computer users were able to buy a new system. The use of BASIC language allowed for relatively easy programming, which could be adapted to the user's unique situation. Soon software outlets began to appear, and a wide variety of custom and generic programs were developed and made available.

The small size and simple construction of the microcomputer allows it to be moved from place to place. The portability of the microcomputer is a feature that allows the user to bring the microcomputer to various work sites rather than having to bring the work or work site to the microcomputer. Educational institutions find multiple uses for the microcomputer, thereby making justification of cost relatively easy. Data base management, word processing, spreadsheet calculations, and computer-assisted instruction are examples of some of the typical jobs the microcomputer performs in the educational environment. In physical education, the cost of a microcomputer looks quite good beside such traditional items as wrestling mats, motorized treadmills, or gymnastic equipment.

Unfortunately, many physical educators and coaches appear hesitant to invest the time and effort necessary to become skilled microcomputer users. Perhaps it is the difficulty that was once associated with computer programming that makes some individuals wary. The aura of electronic wizardry may prevent other potential users from investigating microcomputers. Regardless of the reason, microcomputers are here to stay and represent a powerful tool. Physical educators have a responsibility to their profession to have a working knowledge of the capabilities of microcomputers and how they may help students and athletes.

This book represents an effort to inform physical educators and coaches about the general configurations and capabilities of the microcomputer. It provides the information necessary for them to become informed microcomputer users. Many examples of microcomputer hardware, data management, and applications are illustrated to show physical educators and coaches what their colleagues have already done and to encourage further accomplishments. It is trite to say that the use of the microcomputer is limited only by the user's imagination; however, it is also quite true.

Part I explains computer hardware and data management. The standard components of a microcomputer system are illustrated, and various peripheral devices are explained. Basic programming is presented to help readers understand how software works instead of how to become computer programmers. Part II is devoted to the illustration of microcomputer applications specific to physical education and sports. Chapters in part II include the topics of computer-assisted instruction, managing administrative functions, motor learning and control, graded exercise testing, exercise physiology, sport psychology, and biomechanics.

The authors trust that this book will help physical educators and athletic coaches develop a more confident attitude toward the use of microcomputers in their teaching, coaching, and research, an attitude that will facilitate the design and implementation of new microcomputer systems to serve unique individual needs.

Joseph E. Donnelly

Computer Hardware and Data Management

The starting point for all microcomputer systems is the understanding of basic hardware (physical components) and data management systems (software). Few effective microcomputer applications can occur if the user does not have a clear idea of the hardware and data management necessary for the application that the microcomputer is to perform. Chapters 1 and 2 acquaint the reader with various hardware components frequently utilized in physical education and sports. Elements of a general microcomputer system are outlined in chapter 1, and peripherals that may be interfaced with the microcomputer to facilitate data acquisition are discussed in chapter 2. A variety of interfaces are presented. Examples illustrate the hardware that makes possible the communication between a peripheral and the microcomputer. Suggestions on how to accomplish the actual interfacing (attachment) of peripherals to the microcomputer are also provided. Chapter 3 discusses software and systems design. Tips on purchasing software, writing programs, and data storage are explained. Further, chapter 4 expands on the basic concepts of programming found in chapter 3 and provides information on syntax, files, and logic flow. Examples of computer software are presented to illustrate the utility of the microcomputer in physical education and sports.

CHAPTER 1

Elements of a General Microcomputer System

James G. Richards

A prospective new user of microcomputers may notice little in common among the various brands and styles of microcomputers that are currently available. They come in a variety of sizes, shapes, and colors, with or without built-in screens and detachable keyboards, and have a multitude of additional options. From a cosmetic standpoint, some microcomputers are very attractive, whereas others look like modified breadboxes. Yet, despite the differences in appearance, level of sophistication, and overall unit cost, most microcomputers have a great deal in common, especially when their basic components or building blocks are considered.

The functional building blocks of virtually all microcomputer systems include (a) the central processing unit, (b) the main memory unit, (c) the auxiliary memory unit, and (d) the input/output unit. All of these units are connected by a series of wires, which is referred to as a *bus*. In addition, the microcomputer system must have its own power supply.

The Central Processing Unit

The *central processing unit* (CPU) is the heart of the microcomputer system and, for the most part, determines the capabilities and limitations of the microcomputer. The CPU itself consists of several parts, including an *arithmetic and logic unit* (ALU), a bus control unit, and several high-speed registers. The ALU is responsible for performing all arithmetic and logic operations, and the bus control unit is responsible for determining the locations in memory to be used or addressed by the ALU. The high-speed registers consist of nothing more than individual memory locations, which are contained in the CPU and can be used by the ALU and control unit for temporary storage of instructions, data, and results.

In most microcomputer systems, the CPU is contained on a single silicon wafer, referred to as a *chip*. The extremely delicate chip is

3

mounted inside of a rectangular section of black plastic that is approximately 0.16 inches thick and has a series of small metal pins protruding downward from both sides. This plastic packaging is known as a *dual in-line package*, or DIP, and may contain from 4 to 50 pins. The DIP containing the CPU is often referred to as a microprocessor and is usually larger than most other DIPs. Figure 1.1 shows the Synertek 6502 microprocessor DIP, which is used in the Apple II family of computers.

Before discussing some of the differences among the more popular microprocessors, an explanation of the means by which computers process information is in order.

To begin with, a computer processes information in binary form. A *binary digit* is one that can take on one of two possible values. In the case of computers, these values are either zero or one (called *logical 0* or *logical 1*), and the binary digit is usually referred to as a *bit*. In order to make more efficient use of bits, the computer groups a series of bits together, usually in multiples of eight. These groups are referred to as *bytes*. For most machines, such as the Apple and TRS 80, bits are manipulated in groups of eight. Other machines, such as those in the IBM PC family, utilize 16-bit units. The functional unit of a computer's memory is measured in bytes, rather than bits. A computer system that has 48K of random-access memory (RAM) actually has 48 kilobytes (K) of memory available to the user.

Figure 1.1 The Synertek 6502 microprocessor DIP. This chip is the heart of the Apple II line of microcomputers.

Several different microprocessors are found in today's microcomputer systems. For example, the Apple IIe uses a Synertek 6502 microprocessor, whereas the Radio Shack TRS-80 series of computers uses a Zilog Z-80 microprocessor. Both of these are 8-bit microprocessors, which means that both CPUs operate on data and addresses (locations) that are 8 bits in length. However, the microprocessors differ in the way in which they process the data and have a different set of commands governing their operations. In essence, the two microprocessors speak different languages.

The microprocessors found in the IBM family of computers (IBM PC and compatible computers) are the Intel 8086 and 8088 series of microprocessors, which process information in 16-bit units. The Apple Macintosh utilizes the Motorola M68000 microprocessor, which also operates on 16-bit units of information. Microcomputers operating with larger scale microprocessors have the advantage of being able to contain a much larger main memory for program and data storage. In addition, microcomputers that utilize the larger microprocessors typically operate at a faster clock rate than their smaller counterparts and have the ability to perform a series of operations at a much faster speed than the smaller microprocessors. They are also much more expensive than the smaller microprocessors.

Main Memory

Main memory can be thought of as that portion of memory directly accessible to the CPU. Each location in memory consists of a byte of information with a unique address. The maximum number of unique addresses that a microcomputer can access depends on the number of bits contained in the address. If a machine uses an 8-bit address, then only 256 memory locations can be addressed. A 16-bit address can be used to access 65,536 memory locations. Obviously then a computer with an 8-bit microprocessor will not be able to contain as much main memory as a computer with a 16-bit microprocessor.

There are two types of main memory: *read-only memory* (ROM) and *random-access memory* (RAM). The ROM section of memory contains information in the form of instructions that are used by the CPU in order to control the overall function of the microcomputer. This section of memory is not accessible to the user in the sense that the user cannot store information of any kind in this location. The remaining quantity of main memory constitutes the RAM section of memory. The RAM section is that memory directly accessible to the user for storage of programs or data. A computer with more RAM will handle larger programs and/or larger quantities of data than will a computer with less RAM. The term RAM stems from the user's ability to access indiscriminately any single memory location in this segment of memory.

Auxiliary Memory

In addition to main memory, most microcomputers make available to the user a means for mass storage of information. This is memory that is not directly accessible to the CPU but can be accessed through the use of specific input/output devices. In order to access a program or block of data stored on auxiliary memory, it must first be moved into main memory (RAM), where it is available to the CPU.

Many types of mass storage devices are available, but the two most frequently found on microcomputers are floppy-disk drives and hard-disk drives. A *floppy disk* is a magnetic storage device that looks something like a small brown phonograph record packaged inside a black plastic envelope. The "standard" size of the disks for microcomputers is 5.25 inches in diameter (see Figure 1.2), although the older 8-inch format disks are also available for most computers. The technology is currently moving toward smaller formats for floppy disks. The Apple Macintosh, which utilizes a 3.5-inch format disk, is one such ex-

Figure 1.2 The 5 1/4 inch floppy-disk drive that is supplied with the Apple II+ and IIe.

ample. Floppy disks can contain from 128K of information to as many as 1.2 megabytes (M). In concrete terms, a disk with 128K storage capacity can hold 128,000 characters (letters or single-digit numbers), the equivalent of approximately 35 pages of text. They are very popular at the current time, primarily because they can contain a relatively large amount of information and can move it to and from the computer very quickly. Also, floppy-disk drives are one of the least expensive forms of mass storage devices.

The hard-disk mass storage system is beginning to appear on a wide scale. The *hard disk* is a unit that has a permanently fixed disk inside the computer (the user cannot touch it) and has the capacity of storing very large quantities of data. A typical hard-disk system might be capable of storing 20M of information, or enough to contain the full volume of Tolstoy's *War and Peace* with room to spare. As one might expect, these devices are fairly expensive when compared to floppy-disk drives.

A new technology that may soon appear on a commercial basis involves the use of optics for purposes of mass storage. These devices will be capable of storing much greater quantities of information than those utilizing the current magnetic technology.

Input/Output Unit

In order for a computer to be functional, it must have a means of communicating with the outside world in a manner that is comprehensible to its users. *Input* and *output* devices accomplish this task and usually operate with the use of device controllers that allow such peripheral units as disk drives and printers to interact with the CPU in an orderly and organized manner.

An input device is responsible for obtaining information from the outside world and communicating it directly or indirectly to the CPU. The single most common input-only device is the *keyboard* (see Figure 1.3). When a key on the keyboard is pressed by the user, a binary code for that key is sent to the CPU. The CPU then determines from the sequence of keys what function it is supposed to perform.

The most common output-only device is the *monitor* (see Figure 1.4). This includes the screen and appears to the user as a simplified television set. The output hardware for the monitor is responsible for accepting binary data from the CPU and converting it to a character or series of dots that are then sent to a video generator. The *video generator* provides the signal to the monitor, where it is reproduced on the screen. In this manner, the computer can communicate to the user.

Certain hardware units have the capability of performing both input and output functions. One of these is the device controlling the

Figure 1.3 A Zenith Z-158 keyboard. This computer is an IBM-compatible. Note that the keyboard is removable from the remainder of the microcomputer.

Figure 1.4 A Zenith 1220 monitor. This is a composite monochrome (green) monitor capable of producing both graphics and text.

input and output of information to and from mass storage units, such as disk drives. This device, referred to as the *disk drive controller*, has the responsibility of reading specific sections of memory and transferring the contents of that memory to the correct locations on the disk. As might be expected, this process is also performed in the reverse order.

Finally, general types of input/output units are available in the form of *serial* and *parallel interfaces*. These interfaces are combination input/output devices that enable the computer to communicate with other computers as well as other types of equipment, such as printers, plotters, card punch units, and modems. These interfaces will be discussed in detail in later chapters.

Overall Structure

The overall structure of a typical single-bus system is presented in Figure 1.5. The bus controller contained in the CPU is responsible for determining which unit on the bus is being addressed by the CPU

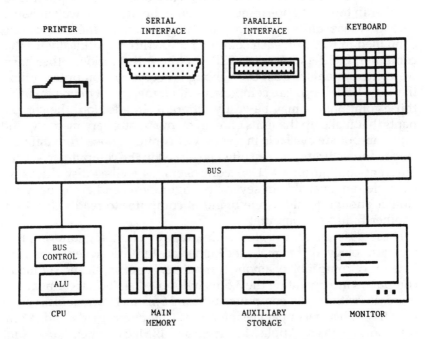

Figure 1.5 A schematic diagram of a single-bus system in which all components of the microcomputer are attached to the CPU via the bus.

and in which direction the information is moving. The CPU regularly checks the bus to determine whether any of the peripherals need its attention.

The actual physical layout of the various components inside a typical microcomputer system is generally such that almost all units are contained on a single printed circuit board, which is referred to as a *motherboard*. The motherboard will have connections or terminals whereby the power supply, the keyboard, the monitor, and other external units may be attached, but the actual hardware that controls these devices is usually contained on the motherboard. In addition to these units, the motherboard contains a series of DIPs that constitutes RAM and a series that constitutes ROM. As engineers continue to put more and more circuits onto a single chip, the size and density (number of chips per square inch) of the motherboards will decrease and the subsequent computing power will increase.

Compatibility

Virtually all microcomputers share the common functional units discussed in this chapter. What distinguishes one microcomputer from another in terms of appearance and compatibility is the way in which each of these units is controlled and packaged. The instructions contained in ROM on each computer are written specifically for that computer and define how the CPU is to use the various other hardware components. Thus, even though most microcomputers utilize the same basic hardware components, their method of operation using those components may be vastly different. In addition, the components that make up the units of main memory, auxiliary memory, and input/output are available in a variety of configurations from different chip manufacturers and can often be placed in the computer in several different configurations. Disk controllers, as well as disk drives for example, are available in several configurations and are usually not similar enough to allow one brand of computer to read a disk from another brand of computer.

These differences, coupled with a rapidly changing (and improving) technology, do not make the immediate future look very promising in terms of compatibility among computers. For example, newer model computers incorporating the 3.5-inch floppy-disk format cannot communicate with similar computers utilizing 5.25-inch format disks other than through serial or parallel interfaces. Computers made by different companies, such as Apple Macintosh and IBM, cannot exchange software even when the disk formats are the same because different microprocessors, and hence different instruction sets, are used. What may happen is that a polarization of standards will evolve; that is, two or possibly three standard formats of microcomputers may eventually dominate the market, as opposed to the numerous formats that currently exist. As far as the future is concerned, the only certainty is that the power contained in the microcomputer will continue to increase tremendously.

CHAPTER 2

Interfacing Peripherals for Data Acquisition and Control

James G. Richards

Interfacing refers to the "joining" of an external device with a microcomputer. The reasons for interfacing are varied and represent powerful avenues for expanding the role of the microcomputer. Most instruments that produce a voltage or current output can be joined to the microcomputer as long as applicable rules are followed. This joining or interfacing allows for communication between the instrument and the microcomputer. The communication may take the form of data acquisition and storage or instrument control by the microcomputer. General examples of interfacing will be presented in this chapter. Specific examples of interfacing will be presented in subsequent chapters of this text.

Basic Interfaces

Generally, four types of interfaces can usually be found: (a) parallel interfaces, (b) serial interfaces, (c) analog-to-digital converters, and (d) digital-to-analog converters. Before describing each of these interfaces in more detail, definitions of these terms are given. In addition, a distinction must be made between digital and analog signals.

A *digital signal* is one in which bytes are transmitted from one location to another, either inside or outside of the computer. The voltage can take on one of two possible values: 0 or 5 volts (V). No voltages other than these are allowed in most digital signal processing applications. An *analog signal* is one in which a continuous voltage is transmitted, that is, an electrical current that can take on any voltage value within a specified range (i.e., 0 to 10 V). A computer cannot deal with analog signals internally, but it may read them from or transmit them to the outside world through the use of devices that convert analog signals to and from digital signals. For example, a momentary analog signal of 2.5 V may be converted into a digital value of 128 (1000 0000 in binary).

Parallel Interfaces

A parallel interface allows the computer to send information to external devices in the form of complete bytes of information; that is, during every transmission, eight bits of information are simultaneously transferred from one unit to another. A parallel interface generally consists of 24 to 36 lines or wires that connect two units. Eight of these lines are data lines (the lines over which the bytes of information are actually transmitted), and eight of these lines are control lines. The control lines govern the exact time of data transfer, the rate of transfer, and the status of the data lines. The remaining lines are generally not used or are treated as grounds.

The maximum rate at which data can be transferred via a parallel interface is one megabit (1,000,000 bits) per second, or approximately 125,000 bytes per second. This is equivalent to transmitting 125,000 characters (i.e., letters or single-digit numbers) every second. Given an average word length of five characters, this means that about 25,000 words can be transmitted in only 1 second.

One of the most common applications of the parallel interface is transmitting information to printers. In the microcomputer world, the Centronics parallel interface is perhaps the most widely used for this purpose. Most dot matrix type printers are sold with Centronics ports (connectors) as standard equipment. The Centronics style interface utilizes a 36-pin connector and has become an unofficial standard interface for low-cost printers (less than $1,200).

Another type of parallel interface common among the more expensive microcomputers is the IEEE-488 parallel interface, also known as the HPIB (Hewlett Packard Interface Bus) or GPIB (General Purpose Interface Bus). This interface is somewhat more sophisticated than the Centronics interface in that it can support from 1 to 15 separate devices on the same bus, that is, the set of wires connecting the equipment. The wires can be in the form of a printed circuit board, typically used inside of a microcomputer, or in the form of a cable, which is usually used to connect the computer with external equipment. With the use of bus controllers, data can be sent along the bus in two directions: from a particular piece of equipment or to the piece of equipment. An interface of this type is usually available as an option on most types of peripheral equipment.

Cables needed to physically connect machines that have parallel interface ports are usually provided by or are available from the manufacturer of the peripheral equipment to be connected. Although it is possible for users to construct their own cables, it is recommended that the manufacturer's cables be used in order to eliminate any possible errors in wiring. The time and money saved in using a ready-made cable is well worth the cost.

The RS-232 Serial Interface

A serial interface is one that transmits information one bit at a time to or from one location. The rate at which this transfer can occur is measured in bits per second and is referred to as *baud rate*. The maximum rate of transfer is 20,000 baud, although more common rates are 300 or 1,200 baud.

The most widely used serial interface is the standard RS-232 serial interface. The term "standard" is somewhat misleading because the interface rarely functions without some modification. The actual connector for the RS-232 interface is a 25-pin subminiature type D connector, which may be either male or female. The configuration of this connector is shown in Figure 2.1. In its minimum configuration, only three lines need to be used by two communicating instruments. These

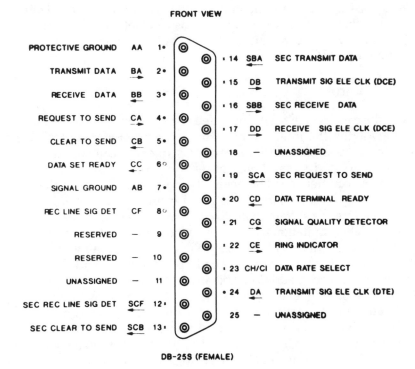

Figure 2.1 The RS-232 serial interface connector.

are lines 2, 3, and 7. In most cases, however, more than three lines are used.

It should be observed from Figure 2.1 that two peripheral units connected by this interface cannot simultaneously transmit and receive data on line 2. It seems logical that one of the units should, in fact, receive data on line 2 and transmit data on line 3. This discrepency constitutes the basic difference between the two types of RS-232 interfaces. The DTE (Data Terminal Equipment) type transmits data on line 2, and the DCE (Data Communications Equipment) type transmits data on line 3. In addition, several of the remaining lines that control the communications protocol are also switched. In most cases, the peripheral equipment manufacturers supply all of the information necessary to modify and interface a specific microcomputer to their device. In the event that this information should prove to be unsatisfactory, the manufacturer of the serial interface should probably be contacted.

Many microcomputers, such as the Epson Equity and the Zenith Z-100, provide an RS-232 serial port as standard equipment, whereas microcomputers such as the Apple II+ and IIe allow the user to add an RS-232 interface onto the internal bus via a plug-in card. It should be noted that many of the plug-in cards available for this type of application have the capability of being configured as DTE or DCE at the time of installation.

Data Control

Once the cables have been connected correctly, several other parameters involving the interface must be determined and controlled before a successful communications sequence can occur. These parameters—parity, baud rate, number of stop bits, and the number of bits transmitted per character of information—control the exact manner in which data are transferred from one unit to the other.

Parity refers to a system that allows the receiving unit to detect, within reasonable limitations, whether or not an error occurred during transmission of data. This is accomplished by counting within a byte the number of bits that are "turned on" (logical 1) and then determining whether one additional bit appended to the byte will be logical 1 or logical 0. In an even parity scheme, the total number of bits that are set to logical 1, including the parity bit, must be an even number. If the receiving unit detects an odd number of bits set to logical 1, then it may assume a transmission error has occurred. In an odd parity scheme, the total number of bits set to logical 1 must be an odd number in order to register as an error-free transmission. Parity will generally need to be set by the user as even, odd, or disabled (sometimes referred to as mark parity). In mark parity no error checking is performed by the receiving unit.

A short example may better illustrate how the parity scheme functions. Consider a unit that is about to transmit a byte with a binary value of 0010 1101 across a serial line. The total number of bits that are turned on in this byte is four. In an even parity scheme and in a mark parity scheme, this byte would be sent as it currently exists. However, if the parity were set to odd, the highest order bit (the bit on the far left) would be set to 1, to insure that the total number of bits transmitted would be odd. The altered byte would then appear as 1010 1101. After checking the number of bits that are turned on to insure that the byte was transmitted correctly, the receiver would then strip the parity bit to return the byte to its original form.

As was mentioned earlier in the discussion of serial interfaces, the baud rate of a device refers to the rate at which individual bits will be transmitted between devices. This rate must be precisely defined according to the manner in which the receiving unit handles incoming data. At the start of transmission, a single bit is generally transmitted by the sending unit, usually the computer, in order to alert the receiving unit that a byte of information is on the way. The receiving unit then checks for the logic level of each incoming bit at a precise rate until the entire byte of information has been read. If, for example, the receiver checks the incoming line the first time and finds a logical 1 signal level, then a logical 1 level is assigned to the first bit. It then checks the incoming line a second time and assigns the measured logic level to bit 2 and so forth. If the receiving unit is checking the line at a different rate than the sending unit is transmitting bits, the transmitted data are lost. For example, if the sending unit is transmitting information at a rate of 300 baud (300 bits per second) and the receiving unit is reading the data line at a rate of 1,200 baud, the receiving unit reads four bits when only one is present and the resulting transmission is garbled.

Fortunately, the acceptable baud rates have been standardized and can be selected by the user in many cases. The only precaution the user must take is to make sure that both pieces of equipment are set to the same baud rate and that the set baud rate is supported by each unit. For most microcomputers, baud rates of either 300 or 1,200 are normally used to communicate with peripheral equipment.

Once the receiving unit has accepted the byte, it must move it to another location in memory before it can accept a new byte of information. To allow for this delay, a specified number of *stop bits* are added to the end of the transmitted byte. These bits do nothing more than create a long enough delay to allow the receiving unit to store the most recently transmitted byte. Usually the user must specify either

1, 1.5, or 2 stop bits, the exact number of which will be dictated by the receiving unit.

The last parameter that the user must specify to the serial interface is the number of bits transmitted per character of information. This number will generally be 7 or 8 and will depend on the coding scheme of the receiving unit. The most common coding scheme for microcomputers utilizes the American Standard Code for Information Interchange, referred to as the ASCII scheme for short. This scheme is based upon assigning a character code (letter, number, etc.) to each unique combination of a 7-bit sequence. For example, the letter "A" is assigned the bit sequence 0100 0001, "B" is assigned the sequence 0100 0010, and so forth. Note that this scheme uses only the rightmost 7 bits of an 8-bit byte, thus leaving the remaining first bit free for use as a parity bit or special character assignment. If the receiving unit utilizes the standard ASCII code for character representation, then 7 bits will be sent. If other types of character representation are used, such as the IBM EBCDIC code, then 8 bits will be transmitted. In any case, the instructions for the receiving unit should specify the number of bits expected during transmission.

The RS-232 serial interface is used to communicate with virtually all types of peripheral equipment and will appear either as the standard interface or as an available option for a specific instrument. The user should pay very close attention to both the interface and equipment manuals, however, as it seems to be the exception rather than the rule that two instruments can communicate without intervention by the user. In any case, if the user is uncertain whether or not two units can be connected via a serial interface, either the manufacturer or someone knowledgeable in the area should be consulted.

Analog-To-Digital Converters

An *analog-to-digital* (A/D) *converter* is a device that transforms a continuous voltage signal into a binary digit that the computer can read. Continuous voltage signals are generally used to drive such equipment as chart strip recorders, oscilloscopes, and other types of recording equipment. An A/D converter allows the user to intercept the analog signal at a point between a specific piece of equipment and a recorder and to read the instrument's output directly into the computer. This process then allows the user to manipulate the data in any way desired and to do so without introducing human measurement error, which generally occurs when reading a recorder printout.

An A/D converter usually connects to the host computer internally as opposed to a serial or parallel output port. However, A/D converters are made to connect to RS-232 serial interfaces.

The most basic A/D converter operates on the assumption that the analog signal lies within the 0- to 5-volt (V) DC range; that is, the analog signal must be positive and must not exceed 5 V in magnitude. This usually means that the analog signal must be conditioned or transformed to fall within this range. As can be seen later in this chapter, this is usually not a problem.

To understand how a typical A/D converter works, assume that we have an A/D unit that converts a 0 to 5 V DC signal into an 8-bit binary digit. Understanding that each of the 8 bits can take on one of two values (logical 0 or logical 1), 256 unique combinations of bit patterns can occur, ranging from 0000 0000 to 1111 1111. Each of these bit patterns represents a decimal value. An example of this system is shown in Table 2.1.

Table 2.1 The Numeric Representation of Binary-Coded Decimals

Binary Code	Decimal Equivalent
0000 0000	0
0000 0001	1
0000 0010	2
0000 0011	3
•	•
•	•
•	•
0100 0101	69
0100 0110	70
•	•
•	•
•	•
1111 1100	252
1111 1101	253
1111 1110	254
1111 1111	255

The A/D converter consists of three primary components: (a) a binary counter, (b) a digital-to-analog converter, and (c) a comparator. The *binary counter* is an integrated circuit (IC) that counts sequentially in binary form from 0 to 255 or from 255 to 0. It has eight outputs, each of which represents 1 bit in the binary-coded digit. At any time then, we can read a binary-coded digit from the counter. The eight output lines from the binary counter are connected to eight input lines of a *digital-to-analog* (D/A) *converter*. This device, through a series of resistors, converts the binary digit into an analog signal that ranges from 0 to 5 V. A binary digit with a value of 0 will result in the D/A converter's outputting a voltage of 0. Consequently, a binary digit with a value of decimal 255 will result in the D/A converter's outputting a voltage of 5. As might be suspected, binary digit values between 0 and 255 result in D/A outputs of voltages between 0 and 5 V.

The analog output of the D/A converter is sent to a *comparator*, the same place where the external analog signal to be converted is sent. The comparator literally compares the output from the D/A converter to the external analog signal to determine which is greater. If the external analog signal is greater, the comparator directs the counter to count upward. If the D/A output signal is greater, the comparator directs the counter to count downward. This process occurs several thousand times every second until the D/A output is equal to the external analog signal. At this point, the computer reads the value of the binary digit on the output lines of the counter.

Although this is a simplified explanation of the inner workings of A/D converters, it is the method by which they function. Several properties of the A/D converter can now be described in light of the above explanation. First, it should be noted that the A/D is dividing a 5-V signal range into 256 parts. This produces a resolution of 0.00195 V per binary digit. Therefore, whatever units are actually being measured can be divided into 256 parts over its full scale. For example, if the peripheral is a carbon dioxide analysis unit that can measure from 0 to 10% carbon dioxide content in the air, the resolution that can be measured by an 8-bit A/D converter is 0.0313% CO_2. In other words, each binary unit represents a quantity of 0.0313% CO_2.

In many cases, dividing the measurement range into 256 parts provides enough resolution for accurate measures. However, if this resolution proves to be less than that which is required, then a 12-bit A/D converter, which has the ability to divide a 0 to 5 V DC signal into 4,096 parts, should be considered. In the case of the carbon dioxide analyzer example, each binary digit would represent 0.00195% CO_2. Twelve-bit A/D units are recommended for such uses as reading from force platforms, transducers, and any other units where extremely fine resolution is needed.

Commercially manufactured A/D converters usually have the capacity to handle 16 separate channels of information, that is, each channel connecting to a different peripheral unit. Not all channels can be read by the computer at the same time, although all 16 channels can generally be read inside of a millisecond if necessary. The typical maximum sampling rate of an off-the-shelf A/D converter is around 12,000 samples per second per channel.

Digital-To-Analog Converters

A D/A converter is a device generally used to output information from the computer to the environment. It works by adding the voltages from the individual bits of a byte to form an analog signal. Each bit puts out a 5 V DC signal when it is in a logical 1 state and 0 V DC when in a logical 0 state. A resistive network attached to the bits changes the output voltage of each bit to a lower value. The least significant bit will then output approximately 0.02 V DC, whereas the next most significant bit will output a voltage of approximately twice that value (0.039 V DC) and so forth. The most significant bit will then provide an output of approximately 2.50 V DC. When the output voltages from all of the individual bits are added together, an analog signal is produced. This signal will range from 0 V DC when all of the bits are logical 0 (binary digit value of 0) to 5 V DC when all bits are set to logical 1 (binary digit value of 255 decimal). Intermediate binary digit values produce intermediate output voltage levels.

D/A converters are commercially available in both 8-bit and 12-bit varieties and, like the A/D converters, usually connect directly to the internal bus of the computer. D/A converters are most frequently used to control peripherals such as motors, relays, lights, and so on. In some cases, D/A converters can be utilized to drive such equipment as plotters or external recording equipment if the need should arise.

Hardware for Interfacing

Interfacing the microcomputer to peripheral units often necessitates the use of additional hardware support in and around the microcomputer. For example, when utilizing an A/D converter to sample data in a real time situation (e.g., from a force plate or at 15 second intervals from an O_2/CO_2 unit), the user must know the exact rate of sampling in order to perform accurate calculations on the data. Although time base calculations can be estimated roughly by cross referencing the recorder output to the data collected on the computer, this method usually produces less than satisfactory results and essentially defeats one of the major reasons for using a microcomputer. A solution to this problem is to include a clock in the computer's arsenal of hardware.

Hardware clocks/calendars are available commercially from several manufacturers, the costs of which usually range from $150 to $300. A primary concern that the user should have when utilizing a hardware clock is the resolution with which the unit functions. Almost all available clocks will count in terms of hours, minutes, and seconds, but it is the subsecond range where the differences begin to emerge. Some clocks, for example, can count in increments of 1/60th of a second, whereas others can count in increments of 1/100th or 1/1000th of a second. The general rule is the higher the resolution, the more expensive the clock. When sampling from A/D units at 350 samples per second or higher, however, the millisecond resolution is a necessity and well worth the extra cost.

An additional hardware consideration that may prove to be a necessity as well as a tremendous convenience is the acquisition of a second disk drive. A second drive allows the user to minimize the amount of time spent switching between program and data disks. This is especially useful when a library of programs needs to access a stored data set one program at a time. If the user has to constantly swap disks in order to maintain the integrity of the programs, disasters will inevitably occur.

Another advantage to obtaining a second disk drive is the flexibility gained when using languages other than BASIC. Languages such as Pascal typically function more effectively on multiple drive systems, and again the convenience is well worth the investment.

Printer buffers and *graphics cards* constitute another family of hardware additions that enhance the operating capacity of the microcomputer. A printer buffer is a device that attaches between the microcomputer and the printer. Essentially, the microcomputer sends the information to the printer buffer instead of the printer. The printer buffer then controls the printing process. A standard serial or parallel interface will usually drive a printer, but there are advantages to using a printer buffer or graphics card instead of these bare interfaces. For example, the printer buffer can store most or all of the information sent to the printer from a computer. Generally, when the computer is sending information to the printer, the keyboard is locked; that is, the user cannot perform any other operations on the computer until the printing process has been completed. The process of sending the information to the printer buffer is as fast as storing information in the computer's memory. When all of the information has been transmitted to the printer buffer, the printer buffer card then takes control of the printer and returns control of the computer back to the user. This means that there is virtually no delay between the time the information is sent to the printer and the time when control of the computer is returned to the user.

A graphics card allows the user to send graphic output to the printer in the form of a single command. On computers such as the Apple II which can employ a standard serial or parallel interface, the user has to write software to allow the printer to handle the graphics. The graphics card eliminates this process; it provides the advantage of storing on the graphics card itself all of the subroutines required to produce graphic output for the printer. If this card is not available, then the user must write all of the software that will "convert" the graphic image to a code the printer can understand. This is, needless to say, more than a trivial task. The graphics card serves the function of eliminating this tedious process and saving quantities of memory at the same time. However, most graphics cards do not possess a large enough buffer to relieve the computer of the necessity of being temporarily dedicated to the printer and thus locking the keyboard. The graphic routines on the card, therefore, save valuable space in memory and make the programmer's life much easier. All that is needed to produce the output is a one-line command to the printer.

Some hardware units that combine the features of both of these printer interfaces are available. Capable of handling both text and graphics, this type of interface is referred to by at least one company as a pipeline. For those uses where a great amount of graphic and/or text printout is needed, this type of interface is ideal.

The *modem*, an add-on unit that fits into a somewhat miscellaneous category in terms of enhancing the microcomputer, enables the computer to communicate with other computers via a phone line. A modem, short for modulator/demodulator, is really a specialized type of serial interface that essentially converts the binary 0 and binary 1 signal levels into frequencies or sounds capable of being transmitted over telephone lines. The *modulator* is the unit that converts the logic levels to frequencies, whereas the *demodulator* converts the frequencies back to logic levels. Assuming that the character codes, baud rate, parity, and number of stop bits are compatible, the modem allows the microcomputer to behave as a terminal and communicate with another device virtually anywhere in the world. Of course, someone still has to pay for the phone call.

There are basically two kinds of modems currently available: *acoustic* and *direct connection*. An acoustic modem communicates directly through the telephone receiver by creating sounds that are transmitted in the same manner a voice is transmitted. The device has a cradle where the user actually places the receiver so that the computer can "talk" into the phone. The direct connect modem has a jack that plugs into the body of the phone at the same place where the receiver plug is normally located. The displaced receiver plug would then plug into the modem in order to maintain the capability to use the receiver. This type of modem is currently more popular, primarily because of the features that can be implemented on the computer as a result of this hardware configuration. For example, this type of modem usually has the capacity to dial and answer the phone by itself, which is extremely convenient when waiting for another computer to initiate a call.

Modems have a somewhat limited baud rate at which they can operate, with 1,200 baud currently being the most common. Modems that communicate at 300 baud are also available and relatively inexpensive compared to 1,200-baud modems, but the extra speed is worth the extra price.

Adapting Analog Devices

Earlier it was mentioned that an analog signal frequently has to be conditioned before it can be read by an A/D converter. The user should never attach a peripheral unit to an A/D board to see if it works without first testing to see that the output voltage of the unit is within the 0 to 5 V range. There are three basic situations that can occur when an analog signal does not fall into the specified 0 to 5 V range: (a) The signal range may be larger than the allowable 5 V range, (b) the signal range may be much smaller than the allowable 5 V range, and (c) the analog signal may be negative. It is also possible that the third situation may occur in combination with the first two.

Fortunately, the first two conditions are much more prevalent than the third. Modifying a voltage range is usually not a tremendous problem, especially when the objective is to make the range smaller. In this situation, all that is usually needed is a variable resistor, sometimes known as a *potentiometer*.

Figure 2.2 An assortment of variable resistors that are currently used in electronic applications.

Potentiometers come in a variety of sizes and shapes and in a variety of resistance values and precision levels. A few of the available types of resistors are shown in Figure 2.2. Note that all of the resistors shown have one feature in common: They all have three electrical contacts. The three contacts allow the user literally to tap any percentage of the full voltage range of a recorder output up to 100%. This has the effect of dividing the recorder output voltage range by any constant necessary to achieve a 0 to 5 V range for the A/D unit. Figure 2.3 illustrates how the potentiometer is oriented in order to achieve this effect. Turning the dial on the potentiometer has the effect of moving the pointer for pin C along the resistor between pins A and B. If the output of the hypothetical recorder shown in Figure 2.3 ranges between 0 and 10 V, then the output to the A/D will vary between a maximum of 10 V and a maximum of 0 V as the pointer moves from pin A to pin B. It is possible to set the pointer at pin C so that when the recorder output is at its maximum of 10 V, the A/D input is at its maximum of 5 V. In this case, when the recorder output drops to 6 V, the A/D input will drop to 3 V. There then exists a ratio of 2:1 between the recorder input and the A/D input.

The resistance values selected for this type of application are usually quite large. Generally, resistors in the range of 10,000 ohm and higher

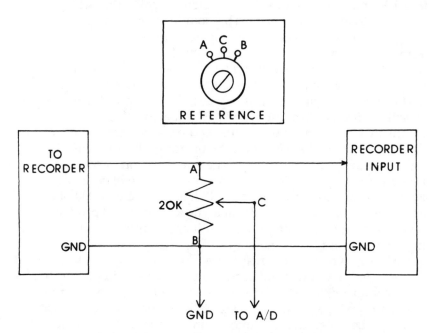

Figure 2.3   An electrical diagram of a potentiometer used as a voltage divider in a typical circuit.

are the most satisfactory. In addition, it is also recommended that multiple-turn (10- or 15-turn) potentiometers be used whenever possible as the accuracy with which these can be set is much greater than the 1-turn variety.

The situation in which the analog signal input to the A/D converter has a very small voltage range (much less than 5 V) is one that does not create any hardware problems but does create precision problems. Recall that a 5 V signal is divided into 256 parts by an 8-bit A/D converter. If the magnitude of the analog signal being converted can achieve a maximum value of 1 V, then the A/D converter can divide this signal into only 51 parts instead of the maximum 256 parts. For example, consider the carbon dioxide unit described earlier in this chapter. If the recorder output of the CO_2 unit ranged from 0 V to 0.1 V over a 0 to 7% CO_2 range, then the A/D resolution would be 0 to 5 binary digit units, producing an equivalent resolution of $\pm 1.37\%$ CO_2. This occurs because the range that the A/D converter can read, 0 to 0.1 V output of the CO_2 unit, constitutes 2% of the 0 to 5 V. Two percent of the corresponding digital output of the A/D converter is five units. Five units spread over a 7% range yield a resolution of $\pm 1.37\%$ CO_2. This is hardly an acceptable situation.

In this case, the solution to the resolution problem is to amplify the 0 to 1 V analog signal to a 0 to 5 V signal, which the A/D converter can then divide into 256 parts. This solution is not arrived at as easily as the previous one because it involves amplifying the voltage signal with what is known as an *operational amplifier* (op amp), an electrical device housed on an *integrated circuit* (IC). An IC is used for hundreds of circuits ranging from active filters to comparators.

The electrical diagram of the op amp is shown in Figure 2.4. The specific IC used in this case is an LM324 quad op amp package, which means that there are actually four separate amplifiers housed on the same chip. Here is basically how the op amp will work when it is configured according to Figure 2.4. The amplification factor, commonly referred to as "gain," is determined by the ratio of resistors R1 and R2 to resistor R1. For example, if R2 has a value of 1,000 ohms (1k) and R1 is set to a value of 500 ohms, the amplifier will produce a gain of 3. An input voltage of 1 V will produce an output of 3 V. By lowering the value of R1, the gain of the amplifier can be increased. Conversely, by increasing the resistance at R1, the gain can be lowered. For an amplifier system designed to produce a gain greater than 1, it is recommended that the maximum value of R1 be equal to the value of R2. Typically, a resistance value of 1k works for most applications. It should be noted that the maximum output of the op amp with a 5 V power supply is approximately 4.7 V.

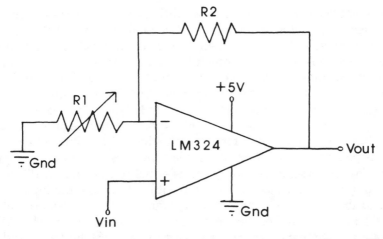

Figure 2.4   An electrical diagram of an LM324 op amp configured to amplify in the noninverting mode.

Consider the previous example wherein the output of the CO_2 analyzer ranged from 0 to 0.1 V. By using an LM324 op amp with a gain of 50 ([R1 + R2]/R1 = 50), the CO_2 output can easily be converted to a 0 to 5 V range, thus increasing the effective resolution of the A/D converter to $\pm 0.0027\%$ CO_2.

Op amp systems can easily be constructed with predrilled and etched circuit boards available at most electronic stores. When constructing the board, the user should employ a 14-pin socket instead of wiring the chip directly to the board. An LM324 op amp utilizing a 14-pin socket is shown in Figure 2.5.

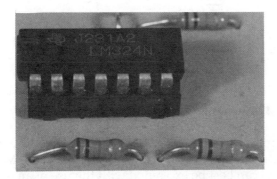

Figure 2.5   An LM324 DIP in a 14-pin low-profile socket.

The voltage transformation most difficult to make is the conversion of a negative analog signal to a positive analog signal. Although this problem does not occur frequently, it does deserve some attention. The problem is handled in much the same manner as the amplification of the analog signal was, but a different type of op amp is utilized. The one used in this situation is a type 741 op amp. The major differences between this unit and the LM324 discussed earlier is that the 741 requires a dual power supply (positive and negative voltage) and has the capability of internally adjusting the baseline voltage. The 741 is packaged in an 8-pin IC and is configured as shown in Figure 2.6. The gain factor as configured is equal to the ratio of R2 to R1, except that the gain factor is now negative; that is, if the input is -2 V and the gain is -1, the output is equal to 2 V. Resistance values for R1 and R2 should be the same as those recommended for the LM324 op amp. Note that this is called an *inverting amplifier* and will produce a positive output voltage only when the input voltage is negative.

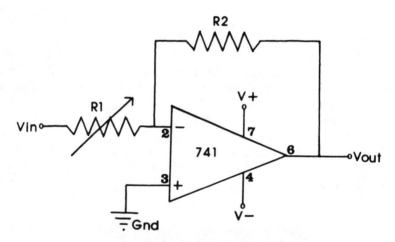

Figure 2.6 An electrical diagram of a 741 op amp configured to amplify in the inverting mode.

Control of Data Collection

There are a number of considerations that need to be accounted for when setting up the software to control data collection. Many of these considerations can best be explained with the use of an example such as sampling data from a force platform. For illustrative purposes, assume that we have a simple force platform consisting of four vertical transducers and four amplifiers. Our objective is to sample from each of the transducers at a specified rate and then analyze the data.

To begin with, a sampling rate needs to be determined. It is generally recommended that the sampling rate for such devices as transducers or strain gauges be at least 2 1/2 times the resonant frequency of the device on which the units are mounted. Assume also that our hypothetical force plate has a resonant frequency of 100 hertz (Hz). The sampling rate for the transducers should be approximately 250 Hz per transducer, which means that the A/D converter must sample at a rate of 1000 Hz (4 • 250). This means that the software code doing the actual sampling must be written in assembly or machine language because these are the only languages that can run fast enough to do this.

Once the sampling rate has been determined, a strategy to handle the data must be adopted. There are two basic ways in which the sampling interval can be handled. The first way, which we will call a *closed sampling interval*, involves sampling the data for either a specified period of time or for a specified number of samples. For example, we may start data collection when the user presses the ESCape key and stop data collection when 2,000 samples have been collected or 2 seconds have elapsed. In either case, the sampling interval lasts for a given duration regardless of what happens in the testing environment, and every data collection period will last for the same period of time.

The second method of handling the sampling interval, which we'll call an *open sampling interval*, involves sampling the data until a specific event occurs in the testing environment. In this type of situation, the sampling interval can differ for each trial. For example, we may design the software so that data collection is started when a load greater than 2 newtons is detected on one of the transducers and ended when a load less than 2 newtons is present on the same transducer.

Once the decision for handling the sampling interval has been made, a decision as to what to do with the collected data must be made. Is the data to be processed as it is collected, or should it be stored for analysis immediately following the collection period? The decision is actually based on what needs to be done with the data. If the purpose is to provide immediate feedback to the subject, then the data will need to be processed as it is obtained. For example, a user may be interested in monitoring the center of pressure under a subject's foot during a one-legged stance that lasts for 30 seconds. If the goal is to have the subject watch what is happening as the experiment progresses, then the data will have to be processed and perhaps graphically represented as it is collected. If the need to process the data immediately is not present, then the user may simply choose to store the data and process it at the end of collection.

This second option has some major advantages if it is, in fact, applicable to the situation. First, the assembly language program needed to collect the data can be reasonably short, making programming much simpler. Second, the data processing routines can be written in a higher level language, such as BASIC or Pascal. Higher level languages are much easier to manage than assembly language because they are simpler to change and debug. The ease in programming with these languages is offset, however, by slower execution speed.

If the actual data collection routine is written in assembly language, the typical data structures, such as arrays, are not readily available to the user for storage of the data. Perhaps the most convenient and efficient means of storing data from an assembly language routine is to utilize a stack format. To store data in a stack format, the user must establish a starting point and sufficient space for the stack in RAM at a location that does not interfere with the program. The starting point is referred to as the *base of the stack,* and a variable that contains the address of the base of the stack is referred to as the *stack pointer.* From an assembly language standpoint, this variable is usually nothing more than another memory location.

To utilize the stack structure from the data collection routine, the user must read in the data from the peripheral unit, store it at the location indicated by the stack pointer, and then increment the stack pointer to the next location in the stack. The whole process is then repeated until either a specific number of samples are collected or an event in the testing environment occurs that signals the end of data collection. At the completion of data collection, the stack pointer can be used to determine the number of data points collected by subtracting the value of the base address.

Analysis of the collected data can then be performed with a higher level language such as BASIC. This routine would start "looking" at the data at the base and then proceed sequentially through the stack. Through this process, it becomes relatively simple to integrate, plot, or perform calculations on the data.

The sample assembly language routine presented in Figure 2.7 is used to collect data from a three-transducer forceplate system and is designed to begin and end data collection with the detection of a load and the absence of a load, respectively. The data are stored in a stack format beginning at memory location $6300 hexadecimal, and the stack pointer is contained in memory locations $OA and $OB. Note that memory locations $OA and $OB when concatenated are equal to the base location of the stack. The jump to subroutine $FCA8, with a value in register A, determines the sampling rate of the routine. Thus the longer the delay, the slower the sampling rate will be.

```
6000-    A9 00        LDA    #$00
6002-    85 0A        STA    $0A        *Store stack base ($6300)
6004-    A9 63        LDA    #$63       *in $0A, $0B
6006-    85 0B        STA    $0B

6008-    A2 00        LDX    #$00
600A-    A0 00        LDY    #$00       *Zero registers, jump to A/D
600C-    20 12 60     JSR    $6012      *subroutine, jump to $6020
600F-    4C 20 60     JMP    $6020

6012-    8C 01 C3     STY    $C301
6015-    48           PHA
6016-    68           PLA              *Subroutine to read A/D converter.
6017-    2C 02 C3     BIT    $C302      *Channel to be read is contained
601A-    10 FB        BPL    $6017      *in the Y-register.
601C-    AD 00 C3     LDA    $C300
601F-    60           RTS

6020-    69 FC        ADC    #$FC       *Check for load. If none, goto $600C
6022-    90 E8        BCC    $600C

6024-    A0 02        LDY    #$02       *Get A/D value for channel 2.
6026-    20 12 60     JSR    $6012      *Store at $6300
6029-    81 0A        STA    ($0A,X)

602B-    E6 0A        INC    $0A        *Increment $0A. Increment $0B if
602D-    D0 02        BNE    $6031      *necessary. (new contents = $6301)
602F-    E6 0B        INC    $0B

6031-    A0 01        LDY    #$01
6033-    20 12 60     JSR    $6012
6036-    81 0A        STA    ($0A,X)    *Get and store contents for channel #1.
6038-    E6 0A        INC    $0A        *Increment $0A, $0B to $6302.
603A-    D0 02        BNE    $603E
603C-    E6 0B        INE    $0B

603E-    A0 00        LDY    #$00
6040-    20 12 60     JSR    $6012
6043-    81 0A        STA    ($0A,X)    *Get and store contents for channel #0.
6045-    E6 0A        INC    $0A        *Increment $0A, $0B to $6303.
6047-    D0 02        BNE    $604B
6049-    E6 0B        INC    $0B

604B-    69 FE        ADC    #$FE
604D-    B0 01        BCS    $6050      *Check for load. If none, exit.
604F-    60           RTS

6050-    A9 23        LDA    #$23
6052-    20 A8 FC     JSR    $FCA8      *Jump to delay subroutine.  Then
6055-    4C 24 60     JMP    $6024      *continue collection routine.
6058-    00           BRK
```

Figure 2.7 An Apple assembly language routine designed to collect information from three channels of a forceplate.

Enhancing Program Execution

An astute reader may have noticed the statement in the previous section concerning the location of the data stack in RAM. A question that may come to mind is how does the programmer know where to put this structure so that it does not interfere with program execution?

Writing a program in assembly language poses no problem because the programmer can choose the location of the program in memory and then place the stack elsewhere. But how does the programmer know what memory locations a program written in a higher level language will use? If the documentation is complete enough, it may contain a solution to this problem. If it is not, the burden falls onto the shoulders of the programmer.

For example, a compiled Pascal program may utilize sections of memory both above and below the blocks of memory reserved for graphics sections, whereas an interpreted BASIC program may use only the sections of memory below the graphics blocks. In the former case placement of a stack in memory may become tricky; in the latter it is relatively easy.

One solution to this problem involves the use of a software system referred to as *compiler*. It essentially translates a higher level program, or *source code*, into an assembly or machine language program, or *object code*. In doing this, the compiler fragments the source code into several components. For example, one component may consist of all of the array space needed by the program, whereas another may consist of the space necessary to contain all other variables and constants. A third component may contain the main code, whereas a fourth may contain what are called *library modules* (routines that instruct the computer as to the location and access requirements of variables and hardware components).

There are two primary advantages and one disadvantage to using a compiler. One advantage is that the programmer is informed as to the length of each module and has the option of placing the modules at any convenient location in memory. This means that the programmer has added flexibility in placing the stack and in making a maximum amount of memory available for data storage. A second advantage is that a compiled program will execute at a faster speed than an uncompiled program. Some of the available compilers for the BASIC language claim that program speed may increase by a factor of 20.

A major disadvantage to using compilers is that they tend to increase the size of the program; that is, the object code will require more memory to run than the source code. If the source code is extremely long, the compiler may not have enough space to create an object code. Also, if sections of memory need to remain reserved, as do sections for graphics, the amount of space available for the object code may be limited. A compiler may increase a program's size by as much as a factor of 2. All in all, if the compiler is used, the increase in programming speed is impressive.

CHAPTER 3

Software and Systems Design

Jerry L. Mayhew
Jon B. Broyles

Viewed as a tool for data management, the microcomputer can save vast amounts of time as well as perform tedious, complicated rote tasks more accurately than the individual can. The key to the usefulness of the microcomputer is its *software*, which may be defined as a set of instructions to be executed by the computer. Software may be stored on a floppy disk or a hard disk to be loaded into the computer when the user is ready for it. Software may also be the small *program*, a term often used interchangeably with software, typed into the computer for quick, temporary calculations. Programs may range from a simple print statement to a complex financial management analysis.

Before purchasing a computer, you should prioritize the tasks that you will want to perform. In so doing, consider not only your immediate needs but also your long-term requirements. For example, although it may be convenient to have a microcomputer to do your yearly equipment inventory, you might be wiser to spend some extra time making a list by hand if that is its only use. However, in some cases, even when the task is an infrequent one, it may be so big that only a computer can adequately handle the vast amount of data. Therefore, even though a basketball coach plans to use the computer only to summarize team statistics for evaluating the season, there is so much information that a clear, objective view of it is not possible. A computer has the advantage of quickly and objectively reducing the mountain of data to meaningful terms. Thus, instead of puzzling over stacks of game and player statistics for months, the coach can have the answers and be well on the way to implementing improvements before the next game.

If the survey of your needs reveals sufficient cause for puchasing a microcomputer, your software needs should be a paramount factor in the selection process. Software comes from three primary sources: (a) commercially available programs, (b) professionally developed programs, and (c) user-developed programs. All software is not the same.

People approach programming from different standpoints and prospectives; therefore, the same program may be written two different ways and yet arrive at the same answer. Moreover, all software will not run on all computers. Programs developed and stored in one computer's format will not necessarily run on another computer. The machine language, the inborn commands specific to each computer and used to build a programming language, may be different from one model to another.

Purchasing Software

Most people who seriously consider buying a computer do so because they have one or more computational tasks that they wish it to perform. Unfortunately, most of these people look first at the computer and later at the software to accomplish the desired tasks. Often they find that the particular model they purchased will not support the software to accomplish their tasks. Therefore, your first consideration in buying a computer should be your software needs.

You should identify the commercially available software to perform those tasks required of the computer. In some fields there may be several packaged, or "canned," programs to accomplish the same task. Each one will have unique features, and you must decide on the most satisfactory one. One important factor of a commercially available program is its *user friendliness*, that is, how easy it is to follow the directions given by the program. The decision concerning commercially available programs may not be too difficult because there are few programs to perform specific tasks in physical education. Such general tasks as record keeping, financial management, game scheduling, and tournament design are available. Specific tasks like calculating body fat percentage from skinfolds, estimating maximal oxygen uptake from ergometer performance, and projecting exercise prescriptions are rapidly becoming available. Thus, you should survey the market to find the software to perform as many of the necessary tasks as possible.

Computer specialty stores, computer journals, professional computer programmers, demonstrations at professional meetings, and colleagues are some of the possible sources of program information. You should be careful not to let professional computer personnel overwhelm you by speaking "computerese," the high-level, technical jargon that often leaves the average layperson totally lost. Do not be afraid to be direct in your questions and make sure you understand the answers because it is your money that is at stake.

After gathering as much information as possible, you may decide that the commercially available software is sufficient for your immediate and future needs. Commercially available software will designate which computer(s) will run that program. Be sure to check the manufacturer's listing for such information. As in many fields, physical education is experiencing a rapid expansion of the programs available to perform many tasks common to the profession. It is probable that over the next few years many programs will become available for use in the laboratory, in the classroom, and on the field of play. Although it is impossible to know which computers these programs will be written for, it is probable that only a few of the larger manufacturers will remain solvent in the next decade. Therefore, plan your purchase carefully.

After a thorough search of available programs, you may be ready to purchase a computer. However, more often than not, you find that the survey of commercially available programs produces little that is of use. High program costs, computer incompatibility, excessive computer memory requirement, and insufficient application are some of the reasons for this problem. Thus you may proceed to the next step, which is having your program needs satisfied by a professional computer programmer.

Custom Programs

Computer science has been a viable profession for some time, but only recently has there been an explosion in the number of individuals entering that profession. Because of the growing number of individuals with computer training, you may be fortunate enough to employ a professional computer programmer. Although the cost of a professional programmer may range from $10 to $50 or more per hour, you are almost certainly assured that your specific needs can be fulfilled by this individual. Most users can explain all their programming needs to a professional who, in turn, can develop excellent programs. Obviously the longer and more complicated the program, the more you will pay to have it developed. With the relatively inexpensive computers on the market today, it is conceivable that you could pay more for the professionally prepared software than you have invested in the hardware.

Competent programmers may be located in a number of places. More and more businesses are using computers, and many of them employ programmers. Almost all institutions of higher education use computers to keep their records and usually have one or more programmers in their employ. Larger high schools may even have a computer programmer on their staff. Nonprofessional but highly advanced amateurs may have excellent programming skills. These individuals may enjoy the challenge and the additional income from developing programs for your data management needs.

If you are fortunate enough to locate a competent programmer, the choice of a microcomputer may be based on factors other than software availability. However, if the programmer prepares and stores the custom designed software on a disk, you must be certain that it is compatible with his or her microcomputer. If it is not compatible, the programmer may have to provide a handwritten copy of the software so you can enter and store it on your computer. Because of the portability of most microcomputers, you can allow the programmer to take the computer for programming to avoid incompatibility.

When asking a professional programmer to custom design a computer program for you, you should be prepared to write up a contract for the work. It need not be an elaborate document but should state the name and nature of the program, the ownership rights, and the price. It is generally agreed that when the programmer is paid, the product becomes the property of the purchaser. To the contrary, commercially available programs cannot be resold by the purchaser because they are copyrighted.

If you cannot find a good programmer or if the cost of a programmer is beyond your budget, the next alternative is to write the program yourself. In this case, the choice of a microcomputer may be based on factors other than software availability. Such things as expandability, memory, video display, cost, and service should be considered.

Writing Basic Programs

For most people in physical education who wish to use a computer to simplify their data management tasks, there may be no commercially available programs. Without the convenience of inserting a preprogrammed disk into the computer, many people are intimidated or frustrated when dealing with a computer simply because they do not understand the fundamental steps of programming. Therefore, for the vast majority of users, the ability to develop simple programs will facilitate the usefulness of the microcomputer not only in physical education but in everyday tasks. However, some people fear that they will press the wrong keys, wipe out a program, or cause the whole unit to self-destruct. Others become frustrated when all their efforts are met with "error" messages.

Most microcomputers are programmed in BASIC (Beginners All-Purpose Symbolic Instructional Code). Although the thought of learning a computer language may seem intimidating, BASIC is actually a rather simple technique for programming microcomputers (see chapter 4). From a practical standpoint, BASIC computer programs are of two types: interacting and self-contained. The *interacting program* stops at various points through its execution to await informational input by the user. Once the information required is entered, the computer continues to execute until the final solution is derived. The *self-contained program*, as the name implies, contains all the elements necessary for the computer to complete its operation and provide a solution.

The process of writing most computer progams is usually not too difficult. The first step for the programmer is to define the task that the computer is required to perform. This may consist of such things as calculating percent body fat from skinfold measurements, estimating maximal oxygen intake from submaximal heart rate, or calculating target heart rate. Although some of these functions may be commercially available, they are not always collectively on a disk in the manner needed, or the formulae used are not those desired.

Once the task is defined, it can be broken down into its component parts. For example, to calculate percent fat from skinfold measurements, the user will have to supply the measurements, calculate body density, convert density to percent fat, and display the answer. Each step becomes a command in a computer program. These commands are ordered logically and then translated into computer or program language to construct the program.

Many textbooks are available to instruct the user in programming. Some of these are programmed texts; that is, they guide the user through the specific steps on the computer as he or she observes the results. Some programming books are excellent, whereas others are laden with computer jargon that may confuse the beginner. Unfortunately, there are no programmed texts developed strictly for physical education.

For those who prefer more formal guidance, numerous vocational schools and continuing education programs have beginning courses in rudimentary computer programming. In selecting a course, users should make sure that it fits their needs. Some courses may be survey courses designed to acquaint students with various aspects of a computer, its operation, and how to purchase one. Most computer users are more interested in learning to program and thus should enroll in classes specifically designed to accomplish that goal.

After you have learned to write programs, several helpful suggestions might facilitate your effectiveness and avoid frustration. Programs that will be used repeatedly should be stored on a floppy disk. A very wise procedure is always to keep a backup disk. Floppy disks do not last forever, and the first warning of disk failure is often too late to salvage hours or days of programming work. Furthermore, because disks are magnetic media, they can be easily erased by passing them too near a magnetic field. A common telephone may have enough of a magnetic field to erase your disk. Therefore, always keep a backup disk with a copy of all your programs. The backup disk should be kept in a separate location from your everyday working disks. In case of damage to the original disk, the backup will be readily available. It might also be wise to make hard (paper) copies of programs for quick referencing. If you continue to modify your programs, the hard copy may provide an excellent overview.

In summary, the microcomputer can greatly facilitate your data management capability. Selection of a computer will be based on many factors. The availability of software is a primary consideration in choosing the right computer. However, few commercially available programs may exist to perform the tasks you desire. In such cases you may have to develop some programming skills in order to take advantage of the computer's speed and accuracy. Various textbooks offer a means of self-teaching to allow you to develop programming skills. Once developed, your programs should be stored on floppy or hard disks for ready accessing, with copies stored on a backup disk for emergency use.

System Design

The popular saying "The computer is no smarter than the programmer" is true. Too often the computer is represented in the media as a quasi-intelligent device capable of making decisions or providing information on its own. Actually the computer has no more potential than the software that programs it. It is a convenient tool that can speed calculations, hasten multiple-choice decisions, and eliminate time-consuming distractions, but it can do all these things only if it is properly programmed to do so.

Once the beginner becomes familiar with the device and begins to develop software, he or she will quickly note the similarities between hand calculations and the computer. Anyone who has been required to add long columns of numbers, find the average of several groups of numbers, or derive the percentage of various items can appreciate the speed of the computer. For instance, if an individual is required to add five numbers (321, 489, 176, 226, 359), he or she usually does so in a particular order or pattern. It takes the average person 15.6 seconds to add these figures by hand (i.e., pencil and paper). Using a computer program to add the same figures, the average user requires only about 10 seconds (the program having already been written), a 32% savings of time. If the average of the five numbers is also required, virtually no additional time is required by the computer, but the hand-calculated time is increased by an average of 10 seconds or 85%. The only time the computer is not working is the time required for the user to enter the numbers.

The computer may offer only a small advantage over a hand calculator for such simple problems as adding five numbers. As the task becomes more complicated, however, it is more difficult and time-consuming for the calculations to be done by hand. In addition, the more conditional decisions added to the calculations, the longer it takes and the greater the potential for error when performing the maneuvers by hand.

Despite the great speed of the computer, it still performs the operations much as the user would by pencil and paper. When finding the average of five numbers, the user first sums them and then divides by five. The computer does the same thing but with much greater speed. Because the computer operates much like pencil and paper calculations, it is simplest to develop programs along the same lines.

Structured Programming

Programming is a logical set of instructions to accomplish a given task on the computer. This set of instructions may flow in a smooth, uninterrupted fashion, or it may be so jumbled that it is unreadable and, therefore, difficult to modify and debug. Structured programming is a simple set of rules to follow to make programs more readable.

There are three basic structures for programs: (a) sequential, (b) if-then-else, and (c) do-until or do-while. These three programs are constructed from two types of statements: imperative and conditional. *Imperative statements* are commands that must be executed by the computer, such as computational statements and input-output statements. *Conditional statements* depend on a logical condition to determine if they will be executed.

Flowcharts are diagrams or drawings of the way the program will perform. In flowcharts, an imperative command or group of commands appears in a rectangle. A conditional statement or group of statements appears in a diamond shape. These structures are connected via straight lines that are read from top to bottom of the flowchart. If there are any ambiguities in the chart, arrows on the lines should be used.

The *sequential program structure* consists of imperative statements where the execution of one command follows that of another (see Figure 3.1). There is one entry point to the structure and one end point, which is a characteristic common to all structured programs.

The *if-then-else program structure* is a combination of one conditional statement and two separate imperative statements or group of statements (see Figure 3.2). The conditional statement will determine which imperative statement(s) will be executed. After the execution of either group of imperative statements, the program returns to a common exit point.

INPUT

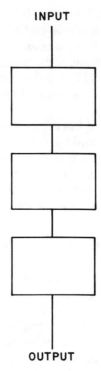

OUTPUT

Figure 3.1 Sequential program structure.

In other words, after information is input, it is evaluated. If the condition is true, the program is routed to the group of imperative statements on the left (see Figure 3.2). If the condition is false, the program branches to the statements on the right (see Figure 3.2). No matter which direction the program takes, it returns to a common output or exit point.

The *do-until structure* is a looping type program that consists of a conditional statement and an imperative statement or group of statements (see Figure 3.3). In a do-until structure, the imperative statement is executed first and then the condition of completeness is tested. If the condition is satisfied, the program is exited. If the condition is not satisfied, the imperative statement(s) is executed again. This process is repeated until the condition is satisfied, hence the name do-until.

The *do-while structure* is similar in nature to the do-until. In the do-while structure, however, the condition is tested before the imperative statement(s) is executed (see Figure 3.4). If the condition is not satisfied, the imperative statement is executed. The condition is then

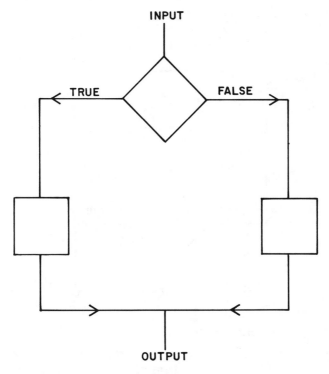

INPUT

TRUE

FALSE

OUTPUT

Figure 3.2 If-then-else program structure.

checked again, and this looping process continues while the complete-ness condition remains false, hence the name do-while.

Storage and Retrieval of Data

One of the big advantages of a computer is its ability to handle large qualities of data rapidly. Data may be stored in two types of files: in-ternal and external. *Internally stored data* coexist in the same file with the program to manipulate those data. It is, in essence, a one-shot program where the data and its format are dependent on the program. These data have no other function than that specified in the program. *Externally stored data*, however, may be run with more than one pro-gram; therefore, this file contains nothing but data. More than one program may access these data. When data are stored in an external file, care should be taken to code those data with proper indicators that clearly illustrate what each data point represents. When the pro-gram is executed, it will retrieve (access) the data file from the same disk or another disk (in a dual system) in order to run the program.

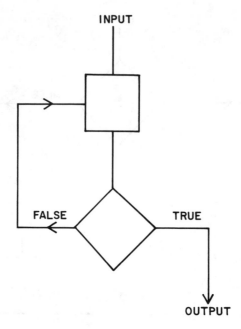

Figure 3.3 Do-until program structure.

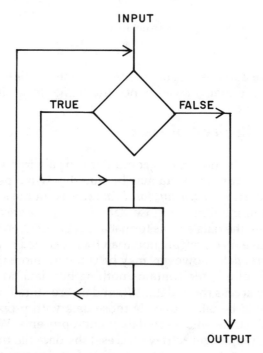

Figure 3.4 Do-while program structure.

Various computers have unique programming instructions (commands) for accessing external data files. The user should consult the manual to determine how the commands access the data. This should be done prior to establishing large external data files so that time will not be wasted constructing files that will not work.

CHAPTER 4

Developing Simple Programs

Jerry L. Mayhew
Jon B. Broyles

Many people are overwhelmed by computer technology and have difficulty believing the power of the desk-top microcomputer. Most of these same people are intimidated because they do not understand the fundamental steps in communicating with the computer.

Understanding some fundamental programming concepts and identifying key BASIC program commands will allow the user to begin constructing simple programs. As the user develops programming skills and confidence, more advanced procedures may be incorporated in the programs to handle almost all of the physical educator's data management needs.

Fundamental Programming Concepts

To understand BASIC programming, four simple concepts should be kept in mind to produce more successful programs. First, each line in a BASIC computer program should be complete within itself. A line should be made up of a line number and an operative statement (program command). Although some computer languages do not require each line to begin with a line number, the first five spaces of a BASIC line may be used for a line number. All five spaces need not be used, but they are there in case they are needed.

If a formula or calculation is too long to fit on one line, it should be terminated at a logical point and attached to the next line.

The subsequent line can then complete the calculation. For example, the following body composition prediction equation may be too long to be handled on one line:

10 D = 1.0571 − .00052*V1 + .00168*V2 + .00114*V3 + .00048*V4 − .00145*V5

Therefore, the calculation should be stopped or split at a point that would not violate the intended mathematical procedure (such as between multiplication or division steps) and the procedure continued on the next line. Thus, it might look like the following:

```
10 D=1.0571-.00052*V1+.00168*V2+.00114*V3
20 D=D+.00048*V4-.00145*V5
```

The second programming concept to consider is that BASIC programs, unless otherwise directed, follow a chronological sequence of execution. Thus, the computer begins computation at the lowest line number and proceeds in a stepwise fashion to the end of the program. Consequently, programming should follow a logical sequence of thought. To assist the programmer in defining the task the computer is to perform and in breaking that task into its logical component parts, a flowchart may be useful. Recall that the flowchart is a road map of key words that guides the computer through a task. A simple flowchart is shown in Figure 4.1

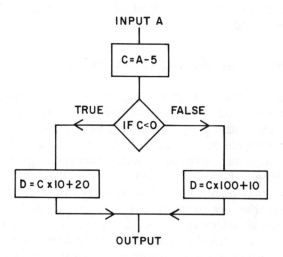

Figure 4.1 Simple flowchart.

It should be noted that the computer may be directed to deviate from the chronological order of execution if the need arises. Often this will be necessary to avoid incorrect calculations or error messages. In addition, such deviations may speed up the operation. For example, the program from the flowchart in Figure 4.1 might look like the following (see Example 4.1):

```
100 INPUT A
110 C=A-5
120 IF C<0 GOTO 200
130 IF C>0 GOTO 300
200 D=C*10+20
210 GOTO 400
300 D=C*100+10
310 GOTO 400
400 PRINT D
```

(4.1)

Although you really do not need line 310 because the computer naturally falls through to line 400, line 210 is necessary. If it were not there, the computer would recalculate D according to line 300, thus changing the answer it computed in line 200.

The third programming concept is that lines should be numbered in intervals of 10 throughout a program. This allows the user to insert lines as they are needed after having completed the program. Most computers will automatically place line numbers in chronological order no matter when they are typed into the program. This is very useful when the user discovers that a line has been left out in the middle of his or her program. It is a simple matter to give the required procedure a line number between two appropriate lines.

The fourth programming concept is that mathematical operations follow a hierarchy. The hierarchy of execution from highest priority to least is as follows:

1. Operations inside of parentheses,
2. Exponential operations,
3. Multiplication and division, and
4. Addition and subtraction.

Furthermore, computers usually perform operations on the same line from left to right following the hierarchy above. Thus, in Example 4.2 the answer (A) is 7.5 and not 5 because the first operation is multiplication, then division, and finally addition.

```
10 A=5+5*2/4
```

(4.2)

It is easy to see that parentheses can be very useful to achieve the order of calculation required.

Basic Syntax

There are seven fundamental operation statements or program directives in BASIC that give the user the capabilities necessary to develop computer programs. Additional BASIC commands may be used to add to the user's programming skills, but the seven fundamental commands are all that are required to construct interacting and self-contained programs.

LET

The LET statement assigns a value to a variable, such as LET X = 25 or LET Y = 2*X + 10, or to a string or literal, such as LET X\$ = "THE AVERAGE IS". A *string*, or *literal*, is a group of words enclosed in quotation marks. It is designated with a \$. Although the LET statement is still used, it is often dropped in favor of simply assigning a given value to a variable such as X = 5 or X\$ = "THE AVERAGE IS".

Variables may be designated by a single letter (A, B, X, Y, etc.), the combination of letter and a number (A1, B1, X2, Y5, etc.), or two letters (AA, BB, AB, BX, etc.). The latter, which may be dependent on the capacity of your computer, is not common to most microcomputers. At least 260 variables are possible with single letters and the letter-number combination (26 letters and 9 numbers). More than nine numbers can be used in this method, but the user must be careful to keep the parentheses in order.

String variables, designated with a \$ afterward, follow the same rules as numerical variables. Thus, string variables may be designated as A\$, X\$, C1\$, or Y5\$. When a string variable is designated, it is enclosed in quotation marks.

PRINT

The PRINT statement causes the computer to print or output to the video screen or a printer the literal enclosed in parentheses, the value assigned to a variable, or a combination of the two. Thus execution of the line in Example 4.3 would cause the computer to print what it sees enclosed in the quotation marks.

    10 PRINT "THE NUMBER IS"   (4.3)

Executing the lines in Example 4.4 would cause the computer to print the value 5.

```
10 A=5
20 PRINT A                                              (4.4)
```

A combination line such as that shown in Example 4.5 would cause the computer to print the literal in quotation marks followed by the value 5.

```
10 A=5
20 PRINT "THE NUMBER IS", A                             (4.5)
```

At this point the use of formatting punctuation is worth noting. The simplest and most common line formatting punctuations are a comma (,) and a semicolon (;). The video screen of a computer is usually divided into several zones made up of a given number of columns. The exact number of columns in each zone varies from model to model. Each successive comma on the same line causes the computer to output the variable in a subsequent zone. In Example 4.5, the computer will print the literal and, because of the comma, skip to the beginning of the next zone to print the value of A. If two commas had been used, the computer would have skipped over to the beginning of the third zone to print the value of A. A semicolon would have caused the computer to print the value immediately adjacent to the literal. Therefore, the three lines shown in Example 4.6 would cause the following output:

```
10 A=5
20 PRINT "THE ANSWER IS";A
30 PRINT "THE ANSWER IS",A
40 PRINT "THE ANSWER IS",,A                             (4.6)

THE ANSWER IS 5
THE ANSWER IS    5
THE ANSWER IS         5
```

When the PRINT statement is used without anything after it on the line, it causes the computer to print a blank line or, in essence, skip a line. This is useful in formatting an output for clarity and aesthetic appeal. It should also be noted that many computers use a question mark (?) to denote a PRINT designation. Therefore, PRINT A and ?A would produce the same results. Furthermore, many computers allow multiple line designations on the same line number when the statements are separated by a colon (:). Several PRINT statements can therefore be placed on a single line number, such as 10 PRINT: PRINT: PRINT, and have the same effect, notably skipping three lines.

INPUT

The INPUT statement is most often used in the interacting program and allows the user to insert a numerical value or string into the program at a given point. It allows a specific value to be assigned to a given variable. For example, the following line (see Example 4.7) would cause the computer to stop at this point and await the typing in of a given numerical value for A.

    10 INPUT A   (4.7)

If, instead of A in Example 4.7, the variable had been a string designated A\$, the computer would have waited for the entering of a word or group of words; however, it should be noted that a number could have been entered without the computer giving an error message. The fact that a number can be entered as a string variable is useful because it allows the use of both words and numbers as input variables. As will be illustrated later, this will allow the programmer to code the statements to do particular things on literal commands.

GOTO

The GOTO statement is always followed by a line number. When the computer reaches this directive in a program, it is routed to some other location in that program designated by the line number. The destination of the GOTO statement may be forward or backward in the program.

IF

The IF statement is often used in conjunction with the GOTO statement in order to stipulate when the computer will go to another destination in the program. In Example 4.8 the user enters the value 1 or 2, and the computer makes a judgment as to which calculation it will perform.

```
10 INPUT A
20 IF A=1 GOTO 100
30 IF A=2 GOTO 200
100 B=A*5
200 B=A*20                                    (4.8)
```

The IF statement can also be used to evaluate a string variable. Instead of entering the numbers 1 or 2, the user might want to enter M for male or F for female. As Example 4.9 shows, this can be done with a string variable.

```
10 INPUT S$
20 IF S$="M" GOTO 100
30 IF S$="F" GOTO 200                                    (4.9)
```

Line 100 and subsequent lines might contain sex-specific calculations for males, such as skinfold prediction of body fat. Line 200, of course, would have the sex-specific female equation.

Some programmers prefer to use an IF-THEN statement instead of an IF-GOTO directive. The outcome is the same; that is, the computer is routed to the line number specified after the THEN command. Using the IF-THEN statement, Example 4.9 can be shortened to the following (see Example 4.10).

```
10 INPUT A
20 IF A=1 THEN B=A*5
30 IF A=2 THEN B=A*20                                    (4.10)
```

Two other qualifier words can be used in an IF-THEN statement. If the user needs to meet two conditions in order to perform the calculation, the IF-AND command can be useful. If either condition is sufficient to warrant making the calculation, the IF-OR command can be used. Therefore, line 20 might require two provisions to be met before the calculation is done (see Example 4.11).

```
20 IF A=1 AND X=1 THEN B=A*5                             (4.11)
```

If both conditions are not met, the program falls through to the next line. If only one condition needs to be satisfied before performing the calculation, it might look like the one in Example 4.12.

```
20 IF A=1 OR X=1 THEN B=A*5                              (4.12)
```

Multiple qualifiers may be placed on the same line. Thus, a multiple line might include several limits within which a value must lie before the calculation is made. For example, if the user wished to perform the above calculation with A or X equal to or greater than 1 and less than 5, it would look like Example 4.13.

```
20 IF A>=1 AND A<5 OR X>=1 AND X<5 THEN B=A*5            (4.13)
```

READ-DATA

In the self-contained program, the READ and DATA statements are two separate commands that work together to function like an INPUT statement. The READ statement causes the computer to assign numeric or string values from the DATA statement to the respective variables in the READ command. Example 4.14 illustrates a READ-DATA tandem.

```
10 READ X
20 DATA 10
```
(4.14)

In Example 4.14 the computer assigns the value 10 to X. If line 10 had been READ X, Y, the computer would have taken the data in pairs and an additional value would have to appear on the DATA line. The READ-DATA statements are often used with the FOR-NEXT commands to handle large quantities of data.

FOR-NEXT

In both types of programs, a repeating loop may be created by FOR and NEXT statements. The FOR command sets the limits on how many times the computer will repeat the loop. Any number of calculation statements may be placed between the FOR and NEXT statements. As Example 4.15 shows, Example 4.14 can be expanded to illustrate the FOR-NEXT loop.

```
10 FOR I=1 TO 6
20 READ X
30 X1=X1+X
40 NEXT I
50 DATA 10,20,30,40,50,60
```
(4.15)

The computer will go through the loop six times, each time reading the next value of X in the DATA statement. Line 30 adds each new value to the preceding sum, thus totaling the values.

In some cases the programmer may wish the FOR-NEXT loop to calculate a series of values between two specific points. For instance, a coach may wish to develop a pace chart for the 400-meter run from the pace for the 100 meters (see Example 4.16). In this case, the FOR statement designates the fastest and slowest limits of the 100-meter times, and line 20 calculates the 400-meter times. Note that a PRINT statement inside the loop causes the computer to print the 100-meter and 400-meter times on each trip through the loop.

```
10 FOR I=12 to 20
20 T=I*4
30 PRINT I, T
40 NEXT I
```
(4.16)

With these fundamental BASIC commands, the novice programmer can manage most of his or her data needs. The best way to develop skill with these programming commands is to experiment with the various procedures. The more the user becomes familiar with the operating capabilities of the computer, the more his or her programming imagination will grow.

Files

A *computer file* is the term given to the storage of a program or data. Files are commonly stored on magnetic media such as hard disks or floppy disks. Data stored as files may be stored in one of two ways: for *serial access* or for *random access*. Most programs access information serially; that is, they read one piece of information after another. In other words, data point 1 must be read before data point 2. Most files stored by a programmer on floppy disks or cassette tapes are serial access.

Random access files allow reading of data in any order regardless of the physical order of its storage on the disk. Although it is a time-saving method, random accessing of information means that it must be stored in a particular order. Therefore, random access files are infrequently used by the beginner programmer.

The serial access file may be further divided into two types: internal data storage and external data storage. When the file contains both the program and the data, it is termed an *internal data storage file*. When the amount of data is modest, this form of program offers many advantages and is not inconvenient. However, when large amounts of data must be handled, it is more advantageous to store that data in an *external data storage file*. The program file is separate from the data and will access the particular data file when it is designated.

More detailed description of file handling is difficult because this is one of the microcomputer operations most dependent on a particular system or brand. Each model has unique features for handling an external data file. As the novice programmer becomes more adept in the use of the computer, procedures for handling external data files may be developed.

Advanced Syntax

The seven fundamental BASIC programming commands discussed previously will allow most individuals to develop highly functional software. However, there are additional commands inherent in most BASIC computer packages that will expand the programmer's capabilities to construct software. Although this section is not an exhaustive list of those additional commands, some of the more useful ones will be presented.

TAB

The TAB command works like the tab on a typewriter. It allows the programmer to designate the number of spaces the computer is to skip on a given line before outputting a value. The number of spaces is enclosed in parentheses immediately after the TAB command. The variable or string to be printed is placed immediately after the closing parenthesis.

In Example 4.17 the computer is instructed to skip over 10 spaces before beginning to print the literal.

$$10 \text{ PRINT TAB (10) ''THE ANSWER IS''} \tag{4.17}$$

If the programmer also wished to output the calculated answer, that variable would be placed immediately after the literal, or another TAB command might be used to place the value in a desired location (see Example 4.18).

$$10 \text{ PRINT TAB (10) ''THE ANSWER IS'' TAB(30)A} \tag{4.18}$$

SQR

At times the programmer may need to extract the square root of a number. The SQR function will take the square root of a variable immediately enclosed in parentheses. An entire computation may be enclosed within the parentheses and achieve the same results (see Example 4.19).

```
10 A=36
20 B1=SQR(A)
30 B2=SQR(5*5+11)
```
$$\tag{4.19}$$

In Example 4.19 the value for variable B1 would be the same as for B2, namely, the square root of 36 or 6.

Note that some programmers use the exponential or power function to extract the square root. Because the square root of a number is the same as raising it to the .5 power, the square root of 36 could be derived by raising it to the .5 power as shown in Example 4.20. Although the computer will usually produce the same answer for both the SQR and the .5 features, the SQR is probably more accurate when involving larger numbers.

$$10 \ B2 = (5*5 + 11)\uparrow .5 \qquad\qquad\qquad (4.20)$$

Note that most computers use an upward arrow ($\uparrow$) to designate an exponential; however, some may use a double multiplication sign (**).

INT

Often the programmer would like to output only the integer of a given variable. This can be achieved by the INT function. The computer outputs only the integer of the number denoted in parentheses following the INT command. Thus the program in Example 4.21 would output the numbers 20, 20, and 30.

```
10 DATA 20.1,20.556,30.9999
20 FOR I=1 to 3
30 READ X
40 PRINT INT(X)
50 NEXT I                                          (4.21)
```

Most computers output variables to six or eight decimal places. The INT function is sometimes used for rounding variables. The variable is multiplied by the power of 10 desired in the decimal place, added to .5, and divided by that same power of 10. Table 4.1 illustrates the most commonly used decimal roundings.

Table 4.1 **Rounding Numbers to Specific Decimal Places**

Decimal Place	Rounding Function
0.1	INT(X*10+.5)/10
0.01	INT(X*100+.5)/10
0.001	INT(X*1000+.5)/10
0.0001	INT(X*10000+.5)/10000

FN

As the programmer gains experience in programming, secondary objectives may be to save time and avoid duplication in the development of programs. When a specific function or procedure is to be repeated throughout the program, line space may be saved by using the function designation FN. Thus, the rounding procedures shown above could be assigned to a function such as FNA(X) or FNB(X). Example 4.22 shows a function to round a variable to one decimal place.

    10 FNA(X) = INT(X*10 + .5)/10   (4.22)

This line says that the function A of any variable designated by X will be equal to the rounding procedure. A further example (see Example 4.23) might help clarify the function command.

    5 INPUT R
    10 FNA (X) = INT(X*10 + .5)/10
    20 C = 3.1416*R2
    30 D = R*2
    40 PRINT FNA(C),FNA(D)   (4.23)

The program in Example 4.23 calculates values for C and D and outputs those values for each variable to the nearest decimal place.

Most models of microcomputers require that the function command be preceded by a ''define'' or DEF designation. Initially the programmer would DEF FNA(X) to equal some procedure and henceforth in the program would have to use only the FNA(X) command to have that function executed.

Trigonometric Functions

Most computers have the standard trigonometric functions included in their programming language. Such commands as SIN, COS, and TAN will give the trigonometric value of the angle (1 radian = 57.29578°) and must be converted to degrees for most uses.

The conversion of trigonometric functions from radians to degrees can be accomplished using the FN designation. These functions would be designated as follows:

    sin FNS(X) = SIN(X*3.1416/180)
    cos FNC(X) = COS(X*3.1416/180)
    tan FNT(X) = TAN(X*3.1416/180)

Therefore, after defining the function for converting the trigonometric operations to degree values, the user need only use the function designation for the operations desired throughout the program. For instance, once the cosine function has been defined in a program, the user needs only to designate the desired angle within parentheses, such as FNC(30). This would cause the computer to output the cosine of 30° or 0.8660.

GOSUB

In some programs the user may reach a point where the need to stop the present procedure and perform other calculations becomes evident. In other words, the programmer may need to leave the present routine without losing that place to go to a subroutine before returning to the regular routine. This can be accomplished by the GOSUB command.

The GOSUB command is always followed by a line number designating the location of the subroutine. In addition, every subroutine must be ended by the command RETURN in order for the computer to resume its regular routine on the line immediately following the GOSUB statement. In many cases it is more advantageous for the computer to branch to a subroutine if some condition is met. Therefore, the ON-GOSUB statement can be used in some computers. If the conditional element is met in the ON portion of the statement, the computer goes to the subroutines beginning with the line number designated after the GOSUB portion of the statement (see Example 4.24).

```
10 PRINT "WHAT PROGRAM WOULD YOU LIKE?"
12 PRINT"1-%FAT"
14 PRINT"2-TARGET HEART RATE"
16 PRINT"3-CALORIC EXPENDITURE"
20 INPUT P
30 ON P GOSUB 100,200,300
40 PRINT"WOULD YOU LIKE ANOTHER?"
50 INPUT A$
60 IF A$="Y" THEN 10
70 IF A$="N" THEN 900
100 PRINT"SUBSCAPULAR & THIGH SKINFOLDS",
110 INPUT S1,S2
120 D=1.1043-.0013*S1-.0013*S2
130 F=457/D-414.2
140 PRINT"%FAT IS",F
150 RETURN
200 PRINT"TYPE AGE AND RESTING HEART RATE",
210 INPUT A,H
220 M=220-A
230 T=(M-H)*.6+H
240 PRINT"EXERCISE TARGET HEART RATE IS",T
250 RETURN
```

(Cont.)

```
300 PRINT"CALORIC EXPENDITURE FOR RUNNING"
310 PRINT"HOW MUCH DO YOU WEIGH?",
320 INPUT W
330 PRINT"HOW MANY MILES DID YOU RUN?",
340 INPUT M
350 C=1.5*(W/2.2)*M
360 PRINT"YOU BURNED"C"CALORIES"
370 RETURN
900 END                                           (4.24)
```

The program in Example 4.24 also illustrates the use of an ON-GOSUB command for a menu of program selection. One program allows the user to select from among various smaller computational procedures without having to load each one into the computer memory.

DIM

The DIM statement allows the programmer to establish space for a table to be included in a program. Often the user finds that a value from a table must be input into a program, a procedure that not only is time consuming but also carries the potential for additional errors in calculations. Therefore, it would be advantageous for the programmer to include the table within the program and have the computer search the table for the appropriate value each time.

The DIM statement establishes the limits of the table with the values given in parentheses. For example, DIM A(2,6) would provide for Table A to be two items wide by six items long. Such a table would appear as

$$1,1000$$
$$2,2000$$
$$3,3500$$
$$4,4700$$
$$5,5500$$
$$6,6600$$

The first step is to read the table into the program. This is done only once for each table in the program, and a GOTO statement should not route a continuous loop program back to a DIM statement or else an error message will be printed. Example 4.25 illustrates the reading of a table designated T1 into a program.

```
10 DIM T1(2,6)
20 FOR I=1 TO 6
```

```
30 READ T1(1,I),T1(2,I)
40 NEXT I
50 DATA, 1,1000,2,2200,3,3500,4,4700
60 DATA 5,5500,6,6600                                    (4.25)
```

Therefore, Table T1 is dimensioned for two and six items, and each pair of items is read into the program.

When the program gets to a point where a value from the table is needed, the computer searches that table for the appropriate value. This can be done with the following statements (see Example 4.26).

```
100 INPUT C
110 FOR I=1 to 6
120 IF C=T1(1,I) THEN D=T1(2,I):GOTO 200
130 NEXT I
200 PRINT D                                              (4.26)
```

In line 120 note that after the appropriate value is located, the computer is directed to go to line 200 using the multiple line designation (:). This saves the time of searching the entire table each time a value is needed, a valuable feature when large tables are used.

REM

There are many occasions when the programmer will wish to leave a note within the program as a reminder of what has been done. Most computers allow the programmer to insert remarks using the REM statement. These remarks are not part of the calculations and serve only as notes for the user. Example 4.27 shows the use of REM statements to keep track of what has been done throughout the program.

```
10 REM***THIS PROGRAM CALCULATES AVERAGES**
20 REM**LINES 40-50 DETERMINE HOW MANY NUMBERS**
40 PRINT"HOW MANY NUMBERS",
50 INPUT N
60 REM**LINES 70-100 TOTAL THE NUMBERS**
70 FOR I=1 to N
80 INPUT A
90 T=T+A
100 NEXT I
105 REM**LINES 110-140 CALCULATE AND SHOW THE AVERAGE**
110 B=T/N
120 PRINT:PRINT:PRINT
130 PRINT"AVERAGE",B
140 PRINT:PRINT:PRINT
150 GOTO 70                                              (4.27)
```

The preceding sections are not an exhaustive treatment of programming commands. Only the fundamental BASIC commands have been explained; however, these should be sufficient for the physical educator to develop programs to solve many data management needs.

As much as one is able to read about programming, there is nothing like practical experience to become comfortable and proficient with a computer. Do not be afraid to try different programming approaches; experiment with PRINT and TAB statements to get a desirable output format. Only through experimenting with various programming techniques can the beginner become proficient in having the computer handle data management problems.

PART II

Microcomputer Applications for Physical Education and Sport Sciences

The term *microcomputer applications* refers to various specific uses to which the microcomputer may be part. It must be emphasized that although specific applications are illustrated, they serve as examples of how microcomputers can be used to perform certain tasks and not the limit of the application. A complete illustration of every microcomputer application would be voluminous, unfeasible, and quickly outdated. Readers are encouraged to study the examples, recognize patterns and generalities of usage, and apply the basic principles to the situation and circumstances they experience.

Part II begins with a discussion of the concept of computer-assisted instruction (CAI) in chapter 5. The historical background is provided to help the reader understand how main frame computers have evolved to microcomputers. Suggested uses of CAI are discussed as well as common problems and shortcomings. Classroom applications for CAI, including fitness test standards, on-line testing, and simulations, are presented in chapter 6. Chapter 7 is devoted to the use of the microcomputer as a management tool for information systems, office management, scheduling, and data security.

Microcomputer applications in the sports sciences are presented in chapters 8 to 13. Motor learning and control are introduced in chapter 8 with a discussion about potential hardware and software useful in typical laboratory studies. Chapter 9 illustrates various applications in motor learning and control, including performance timing, memory, attention, and electromyography. Exercise physiology and the microcomputer is explored in chapters 10 and 11. Chapter 10 provides an in-depth look at graded exercise testing controlled by microcomputer. It is an example of a complex task made relatively simple by using a microcomputer. Chapter 11 illustrates use of the microcomputer in various data-gathering and reduction tasks frequently encountered by physical educators and exercise physiologists. Among the applications presented are fitness prescription, body composition, and diet analysis. Chapter 12 presents microcomputer applications in sport psychology including such topics as motivation, anxiety, self-assessment diaries, biofeedback, and relaxation techniques. Finally, microcomputer usage in biomechanics is presented in chapter 13. An introduction to the common hardware components, which may be used in conjuction with the microcomputer, is followed by bio-mechanical applications in the areas of film analysis, simultaneous data gathering from multiple instruments, motion sensing, timing, and classroom teaching.

CHAPTER 5

Computer-Assisted Instruction

Roger Volker

Whenever anyone uses the computer to learn something, there is a tendency to refer to the process as *computer-assisted instruction* (CAI). Elementary schoolchildren brush up on their multiplication tables with a computer. High school students use a computer to learn word processing and then use the same computer to write papers for language arts classes. Adults complete income tax returns with the computer.

Although instruction is part of each of these examples, they are more acccurately categorized as uses of tool software rather than CAI. Tools of this sort allow work to be done more quickly, accurately, and easily. However, you may not necessarily acquire new information by using tool software.

In this chapter we will focus on the use of the computer in physical education primarily as a teaching device. You will acquire an understanding of the characteristics of CAI and its use in physical education. The differences between CAI and other uses of the computer are emphasized. In addition, you will learn to design lessons that may be taught efficiently with the microcomputer and to evaluate commercially available CAI.

A wide variety of CAI is available, in part because so many sizes of computers are on the market. Because computers are frequently classified by size, a brief explanation may be helpful. Computers are often categorized into three groups based on the amount of memory they contain. If a computer can handle 16K, or 64K, or even 512K, it is called a *microcomputer*. Remember that "kilo" (K) is used for 1,000 bytes and that "mega" (M) is used for 1,000,000 bytes. *Minicomputers* range from a thousand to a few hundred thousand bytes, and a *mainframe* serving an entire campus, business, or industry may be many hundreds or thousands of megabytes. Computer memory capacity is increasing all the time, and these numbers may quite possibly be far too low to describe computers in the next few years.

CAI can be programmed on all three types of computers, but we will highlight the microcomputer in this chapter because it is more universally available to teachers and students. Because the Apple microcomputer is by far the most widely used in schools, illustrations and examples will be given with the Apple in mind.

Roots from the Past

Although microcomputers are relatively new, many of the tasks they are performing are not so new. The principles of instructional design, the teaching strategies, and learner characteristics that are considered when designing CAI have been in use for 50 years or more. Psychologists E.L. Thorndike, Sidney Pressey, and B.F. Skinner provided the groundwork for learning theory that helped formulate CAI. These psychologists were concerned with stimulus-response relationships, the effects of positive and negative reinforcement, and the need for immediate feedback in learning situations. Those ideas gave rise to the method of learning and teaching called *programmed instruction*. Programmed instruction allows the teacher to organize a lesson into small, sequential steps and provides reinforcement every time a step is learned. Lessons with very small, simple steps linked into a single chain are known as *linear programs*. Those lessons that have loops off the main program are termed *branched programs*. Early work by educational psychologists, followed by a great deal of interest in programmed instruction, provides a framework within which CAI can be considered. You can see that the frame-by-frame presentation of information is a natural task for a computer. The computer can also ask a question after each frame. The answer that the student chooses can be judged by the computer and remedial loops or skipping ahead can be handled very nicely. Computer graphics, color, and sound effects can be built into the program to add interest or further clarify ideas.

Based on a long history of systematic development that includes learning theory, CAI appears to be an excellent solution to some fundamental educational problems. However, there are advantages and disadvantages to consider. Before proceeding with the balance of this chapter, pausing to consider some of the strengths and weaknesses of CAI shown in Table 5.1 may be helpful. Clearly, CAI will not solve all the instructional problems encountered in the learning environment. Furthermore, realize that there is no consensus that CAI offers a better learning situation than traditional instruction.

Table 5.1   **Strengths and Weaknesses of CAI**

User	Strengths	Weaknesses
Student	• Offers self-pacing • Is effective for review • Branches to remediate difficult sections or to skip easy sections	• May be dull, boring • May not be sufficiently individualized, either too simple or too complex
Teacher	• Provides release from routine, repetitive instruction • Meets a variety of student needs • Assists in creating a richer, more varied instructional setting • Provides simulations and problem-solving experiences not available otherwise	• Requires extensive time for development • Requires programming skills by instructor or support staff • May not provide programs that closely correlate to curriculum or the individual needs of the students • Requires specialized equipment

What CAI Is and Is Not

Various efforts to classify CAI into categories have resulted in the following descriptions:

- Drill and Practice—repetition to perfect a skill or to memorize information
- Tutorials—introduction of a new concept followed by interactive instruction: question, answer, reinforcement, branching
- Simulation—representation of real events, requiring decision making and methods of handling random events
- Educational Games—skill-building activities, usually with very definite rules and a means of keeping score to increase a spirit of competition even if the opponent is oneself
- Problem Solving—presentation of information and data that can be manipulated by the student to explore answers to problems or to determine the consequences of certain actions

The single element that these categories have in common is that a computer is used. It is not necessarily true that each category is a form of instruction because the definition of "instruction" varies from person to person. Notice that a computer is not absolutely necessary either; any of these could be carried out without a computer. Thus although seeming to be useful at the outset, this list of CAI classifications fails to characterize CAI with any kind of uniqueness. A more useful approach often suggested by instructional technologists is to base the classification system on the unique qualities of the medium. What can computers do and what qualities do they possess that set them apart from other educational media? A description of some computer capabilities may be helpful.

- Can interface to other media
- Speed
- Variety in questions, information, responses
- Record-keeping capability
- Multifunctional: provide information, calculate answers, print out results
- Can update programs
- Low cost of production of software
- Artificial intelligence

After considering these features of the computer and comparing the computer to other types of instructional technology or to traditional teacher-based instruction, you may conclude that our earlier list of CAI classifications might be more meaningful it if were expressed in another way. Thomas and Boysen (1984) of the Computation Center at Iowa State University have proposed a different scheme because they feel that such categories are not continuous and do not focus on the student's learning needs. For example, no guidance is provided to understand where a lesson fits into the instructional sequence. Thomas sees the need for a taxonomy in which the categories correspond to steps in the learning process. His classification system is described as follows:

- *Experiencing*—programs that set the stage for future learning. They often involve the model of a concept but are easy to use, are high in student interest, and stimulate curiosity, thus enticing students to develop a deeper understanding. Experimental programs often precede formal instruction.
- *Informing*—programs to provide information, sometimes by replacing the text or lecture. Many informing programs are tutorial in nature, resembling programmed instruction.

- *Reinforcing*—programs used to strengthen learning that has already occurred. They adjust to the student's level of knowledge and maintain a record of the student's progress. This is the most common form in CAI and is easy to produce. Drill-and-practice programs are often used at this level.
- *Integrating*—programs that require application of previously learned ideas to solve problems. Simulations are examples of integrating programs.
- *Utilizing*—programs that serve as tools to solve real-life problems that are complex. Manipulations of words, ideas, numbers, and factors that are related to each other permit a focus on the content because the computer handles the mechanical details and furnishes answers rapidly and accurately.

Making CAI Effective

Classification systems permit us to organize types of CAI, but what about characteristics of the CAI itself? What makes instruction effective? CAI should contain characteristics that increase its acceptance among students. Some of these elements are based on fundamental traits of human nature. Common sense indicates that they are a part of our everyday lives and enhance traditional classroom instruction as well. Examples include the following:

- Fantasy
- Challenge
- Mystery
- Competitiveness

It is tempting to compare CAI to traditional classroom instruction, even though it is based on a different instructional delivery system. Many new developments in instructional technology suffer from a lack of acceptance on the part of teachers and students. CAI is subject to the same criticisms that have been used against films, television, programmed instruction, the overhead projector, teaching machines, and other media. Computers have been described as inhuman, mechanical, unthinking, and unable to accommodate to individual needs. It is important to consider these negative characteristics when promoting the use of computers in instruction or when substituting CAI for live instruction. However, the underlying reason for the lack of good will that students and teachers may feel for computers may be based on more fundamental reasons.

Students and teachers are gradually becoming used to instruction through technology, but many years of conditioning in classrooms have led students and teachers to expect and accept that teaching and learning will be carried out on a human-to-human basis. Lectures, class discussion, laboratory work, individual tutoring, and other aspects of schooling have always been teacher-based. However, learning can take place without a teacher being present, through books, television, and the computer. Studies continue to show that effective instruction is possible through technology. In some cases it is even preferred by students. Over the long haul, after development costs are paid, instructional systems using contemporary media turn out to be less expensive than the costly, labor-intensive teacher-based instruction. Regardless, some feel such instruction is incomplete and unfulfilling and that a teacher is needed as an instructional focal point.

A key to achieving acceptance of the computer by students as an instructional tool may lie in its introduction, promotion, and incorporation into the classroom. These activities are most clearly the responsibility of the teacher. Computer anxiety is a very real, measurable phenomenon and can be reduced by a teacher and by practice with the computer. Clear and appropriate uses of the computer for instruction have to be explained to the students. Emphasis on computer literacy may assist in helping students and teachers approach CAI in an orderly and systematic fashion so that it gradually becomes integrated into the classroom. This integration process, with careful attention to natural fears and criticism that accompany technological change, is important if CAI is to be accepted. To be effective, of course, the programming of the material is paramount. If CAI is boring, unattractive, and simplistic, the best material will be ruined and the student will not gain the intended benefit.

How to Use CAI

A distinction must be made between CAI (or computer-based instruction) and computer management of information. Computers are used a great deal to manage information, keep track of inventories, schedule tournaments, and maintain records that relate to people, money, and events. Standard software can be purchased reasonably to set up spreadsheets, create data bases, or carry out word processing. These uses, however, are not instructional in nature, even though they simplify some of the activities associated with instruction. Direct instruction, for which behavioral objectives can be written, pre- and posttests given, and cognitive, affective, or psychomotor skills measured, is called CAI or CBI (computer-based instruction) when a computer is used as the delivery system. For example, a student may learn the rules of a game, the method of keeping score, and the many do's and don'ts via a computer. A computer-based lesson may teach a technique, such as the operation of a device to measure breathing rate. An understanding and application, through sample problems, of Boyle's Law might be the basis of a CAI lesson for SCUBA trainees. A number of gaming programs are available to improve one's game of golf, or basketball, at least when played on the computer.

Earlier in this section two schemes for classifying and organizing the varieties of CAI were described. Although such systems are helpful in sorting and categorizing, they do not provide much assistance to the physical education instructor who wishes to solve specific instructional needs through the use of CAI. Instructional needs, or more accurately the selection of instructional materials to meet behavioral objectives, can be approached by considering the following questions:

- Is it important to simulate a real situation (playing a game, refereeing a game, judging contestants)?
- Is it necessary that information be memorized absolutely and completely?
- Is it appropriate to lead to the solution through a series of small steps that form a specific sequence?

Recall the definitions of simulation, drill and practice, and tutorial from the CAI classifications listed earlier. These three types of CAI may be chosen to meet instructional needs suggested by the three questions. Examples of the uses of computers in the classroom are discussed in the following chapter. Table 5.2 outlines some of the expectations that can be fulfilled when each of these types are incorporated into classroom instruction.

Strengths and weaknesses of the various forms of CAI provide some basis for judging the extent to which they may be used. In addition, the packaging also is important. The use of color, graphics, sound, support materials, clear instructions, and other elements often cause a lesson to be accepted or rejected by teachers and students. A checklist that is useful in evaluating software is described later in this chapter. For the time being, let us make the assumption that you want to base a portion of your instruction on the computer, have conducted a search for software, and have evaluated what you have found. If you are unable to identify suitable material, you have two alternatives: either drop the idea or write your own software. But how practical is it to become a computer programmer? Is there a payoff beyond your own classroom? And what kind of investment in time and effort will be required?

Table 5.2   Strengths and Weaknesses of Different Categories of CAI

Category	Strengths	Weaknesses
Simulations	• Compress time • Simplify circumstances in order to highlight special conditions • Create a problem-solving environment that approaches realism	• May be oversimplified because some detail might need to be omitted • May provide a false sense of accomplishment (a high score on a simulation does not guarantee a high score in real life)
Drill/Practice	• Provides endless repetition • Can keep time if this is a necessary measure of success • Can keep score as an indication of success	• Can be boring, trivial • Is not effective for building high-level competencies • Is effective at skill building
Tutorials	• Provide branching for greater individualization • Adjust to educational level of the student • Keep records of success/failure rate for self-diagnosis	• May be dull if too simplistic • May not provide sufficient branching to provide rich variety of alternatives • Are convenient; can be used when student wants

Writing Your Own Software

A somewhat dreary prospect awaits the classroom teacher who wants to become an author of computer software, yet probably no one is in a better position to design and produce the material. Only teachers know the subject matter, the pedagogy, and the needs of students. Drawing on experience and the intuition that effective teachers have, it is entirely possible to create your own programs, particularly if you have access to students who can provide assistance in programming, debugging, and field testing. The following considerations may be helpful in assessing your capabilities and resources if you are attracted to the idea of writing CAI. It is particularly crucial that a realistic and practical appraisal be made at the outset so that you do not find yourself trapped in a project at the midpoint, when the investment of time and energy makes it unwise to discontinue.

Instructional Design

The body of knowledge contributing to what is known about the design and development of effective instruction is vast, fairly inclusive, and accurate. If you follow the rules, the resulting instruction will work well and be accepted by students as an alternative to live instruction or the text. The overall process of instructional development consists of these steps:

1. Identify goals
2. Conduct instructional analysis
3. Identify entry behaviors and characteristics of students
4. Write objectives
5. Develop criterion-referenced tests
6. Develop instructional strategy
7. Select and produce instructional materials
8. Field test and revise
9. Conduct summative evaluation

Specific Features of CAI

Specific features that must be considered when writing CAI software include the following:

- Screen layout designed for interest and clarity
- Graphics for the purposes of teaching design, and fun
- Input and output variations including the mouse, joystick, light pen, touch screen, keyboard, and voice recognition

Time

Time necessary to write a CAI program is a consistently underestimated factor in CAI production. Production ratios of several hundred to one, or a few thousand to one are usually cited. This means that, for 1 minute of a CAI lesson, several hundred or a few thousand minutes are needed to produce it. A lesson that takes a student 20 minutes to work through might take the producer 100 to 300 hours to create. Because the teacher/producer would not be able to work full 40-hour weeks on the project, many months would be involved.

Programming Skill

With the increasing availability of simple programming languages, little or no skill is required to put the lesson on the computer. What is necessary, however, is careful choice of the language in the first place and some contact with others (e.g., staff, students, vendors of computers and computer software, manufacturers of the software) so that quick answers can be obtained to resolve difficulties. Complete authoring instructions, a reference manual, and sample programs are essential accessories.

Program Language

If the support materials for a language are effective and complete, attention may be focused on the language itself. Some of the characteristics to look for are as follows:

- Ease of use
- Number of commands
- Graphics
- Ability to incorporate numerical calculations
- Versatility

Generally the more powerful languages are more complicated, a characteristic that is true also of spoken languages. A large vocabulary helps to articulate ideas. However, big words do not necessarily convey more complicated thoughts. Nearly 50 authoring languages are in current use because of the variety of computers that are available and the levels of sophistication at which programming authors choose to work. Although it is beyond the scope of this chapter to discuss characteristics of the major languages, one of the most popular, useful, and user-friendly languages will be used as an example. That language is PILOT, available for the APPLE and IBM microcomputers. Although there are over 20 commands in the PILOT language, suitable programs can be constructed with only 4, as shown in Figure 5.1.

Note the absence of line numbers, if-then statements, do loops, and string variables. These terms, familiar to anyone who has programmed in FORTRAN or BASIC, are not needed in PILOT. The language is simple and straightforward, allowing the programmer to concentrate on the content and the organization of the lesson.

Lesson Organization

Lesson organization is important and follows accepted psychological principles that stem from the early days of programmed instruction

```
t: Studying superheroes can tell us a     (Display this text.)
 : lot about our own culture.            (Continue text display.)
t:                                        (Insert blank line.)
t: Have you heard of Wonder Woman?        (Display this text.)
t:                                        (Insert blank line.)

a:                                        (Accept answers.)
m: yes!yeah!sure!yep!uhhuh               (Match to these answers.)
ty:Name one superhuman quality that       (If a match is found,
 :she exhibits.                          display this text.)
jy:part1                                 (If a match is found,
                                          jump to the label
                                          named part1.)

t: Have you ever heard of a different     (If no match is found,
 : superhero?                            display this text.)
a:                                        (Accept answers.)
m: yes!yeah!yep!sure!uhhuh               (Match to these answers.)
ty:Name a superhuman quality associated   (If a match is found,
 :with that hero.                        display this text.)
jy:part1                                 (If a match is found,
                                          jump to the label named
                                          part1.)

t: I'll bet you don't watch much TV or    (If no match is found,
 : read many comic books! Since you've   display this text.)
 : never heard of a superhero that
 : someone else has made up, make up your
 : own! Then name a superhuman quality
 : he or she possesses.

*part1                                    (This is the label named
                                          part1.)
a:                                        (Accept answers.)
t: Would you like to have that            (Display this text.)
 : superhuman quality?
a:                                        (Accept answers.)
```

Figure 5.1 Example of PILOT Language Segment. *Note.* From *Super PILOT Editor's Manual* (p. 42-43) by Apple Computer, Inc., 1982.

in the 1960s. The concept of frames of information, followed by questions, a student's answer, knowledge of results, and reinforcement, is the basis for effective verbal programs (i.e., those that consist of words on a screen). But if the computer merely delivers words and makes predetermined responses to student answers, why not use programmed instruction on paper? CAI on PILOT differs from workbooks of programmed instruction in the following ways:

- Free responses, not just multiple choice, can be accepted.
- Graphics can be constructed by the computer, with additions or deletions made on them as conditions of student responses.
- A wide variety of responses can be accepted, with each one leading to different levels of new information. (In a sense the computer "learns" how capable the student is and adjusts by providing appropriate material suited to the level of learning being exhibited.)
- Diagnostic information that can be kept by the computer can help in further program development (wait time, the number of tries before a correct answer is obtained, and the branching pattern a student uses to get through the program).

Inexperienced writers of CAI tend to create simplistic programs in which the computer is used as little more than an electronic page turner. Writers of more elegant programs, often those people who are inherently good teachers to start with, design lessons that contain a wide variety of contingencies. Sounds and graphics, the layout of material on the screen, and the use of many different ways of providing reinforcement are capabilities unique to the computer.

The preceding information pertains largely to tutorial lessons. The traditional relationship between a teacher and student is a tutorial one, as compared to two other forms of CAI (a) simulation and (b) drill and practice. As such, tutorial CAI, at least as we know it today, is patterned after traditional teacher/student interactions and roles. The authoring of simulations requires a set of skills that are different from those used in tutorials. A greater emphasis on a carefully constructed scenario, or hypothetical situation, is necessary. A determination must be made about the essential elements in the simulation, and unimportant details must be excluded. Once the central event or setting is established, variables can be manipulated so that students can respond to the outcomes. The design and production of drill-and-practice lessons is by far the easiest because it consists primarily of repetitive question/answer routines.

Interactive Video

Students quickly discover that the computer communicates by printing words on a screen or on a paper printout. Graphs, charts, and diagrams may also be used from time to time. Recent developments have made possible the use of videotape or videodisk players in conjunction with microcomputers. Laser videodisks are more versatile than videotape because the access time to any position on the disk surface (i.e., any frame of information) is less than 3 seconds. To find a specific location on videotape, however, it is necessary to run the tape in either the FAST FORWARD or REWIND mode, the process taking a minute or two if the information is on the other end of the tape. The role of the computer is to find and play the tape or disk, as called for in the lesson. A number of systems are available to connect computers to videodisk or videotape players, and the lessons that are designed to be used with a computer/videoplayer system are called interactive video lessons. Instead of student-computer interaction, there may be student-videotape interaction. Suppose, for example, that you wished to design tutorial CAI on proper golf technique. Some background information is necessary and could be delivered effectively in a programmed format. But a point might be reached at which words no longer are adequate. Students need to view a demonstration or become involved in a demonstration provided by the tape or disk.

Evaluating CAI

Various checklists are available to facilitate the evaluation of CAI. These are often brief, frequently not more than a page in length. They can be completed in a few minutes (after viewing the program) and usually incorporate a five-position rating scale:

Poor	Fair	Average	Good	Excellent
X	X	X	X	X

Quantitative ratings such as these may be compared from one rater to another or across programs that are being rated. Objective rating scales are more usable because they reduce the amount of variation that might occur if open-ended questions were used. A generalized evaluation for computer software is provided in Figure 5.2. Note the balance between the mechanical aspects of the program (i.e., technical quality, type of documentation, instructional design) and the treatment of content.

MICROCOMPUTER SOFTWARE EVALUATION
(Adapted from NSTA Instrument – 1984)

Title of Program _____ Special Characteristics _____

Evaluator _____ Date _____ Instructional Quality _____

Subject Matter _____

Technical Quality _____

General Characteristics

	1	2	3	4	5	
The program makes the computer act as little more than a page turner or workbook.	!	__!	__!	__!	__!	The program exploits the computer's special capabilities (e.g., graphics animation) to provide a learning experience not easily possible by other means.
The program is wasteful of the limited time available for students to use the computer.	!	__!	__!	__!	__!	The program makes good use of the student's limited time on the computer.
The software package is in conflict with or irrelevant to the goals of the school's instructional program.	!	__!	__!	__!	__!	The software package is compatible with the goals and theoretical base of the school's instructional program.
The program expects one student to work on the computer and not to interact with anyone.	!	__!	__!	__!	__!	Two or more students are encouraged to interact with one another while using the computer program.

Continued

There is little or no evidence that students attain the learning objectives of the software package.	! __! __! __! __!	The evidence that students attain the software package's learning objectives is convincing.
The software package is incompatible with the learning objectives and instructional materials of a current course.	! __! __! __! __!	The software package fits in well with other instructional materials already being used in particular courses or classes.
The software package's cost is exorbitant for what it delivers.	! __! __! __! __!	The total cost of this package is reasonable compared to its instructional value.

===

Instructional Quality

<u>1</u> <u>2</u> <u>3</u> <u>4</u> <u>5</u>

The student is given very few choices that control how he/she works in the computer program's environment.	! __! __! __! __!	The program offers the student several options about the content to work on, the level of difficulty, and the rate of presentation.
The student using the program is passive and does little more than punch keys occasionally.	! __! __! __! __!	The student is actively involved in interacting with the computer's program.
The instructional strategies used in the computer program do not take pertinent research results into account.	! __! __! __! __!	The program's instructional strategies are based on relevant educational or psychological research findings.
The program cannot easily adapt to differences in students' ability, prior knowledge, or learning style.	! __! __! __! __!	The program has options that allow it to accommodate students' individual differences.
The software package fails to inform students about its learning objectives or the available activities.	! __! __! __! __!	Directions in the software package tell students where they will be going and what they will be doing.
The software package's instructional strategies and evaluation procedures ignore pertinent pedagogical principles.	! __! __! __! __!	The instruction used in the software incorporates good sequences, motivating features, and evaluation procedures.
The software package expects that all students will attain the same level of achievement.	! __! __! __! __!	Students using the software experience success in attaining objectives at several levels of sophistication.
The software package makes no provision for managing various instructional resources in a classroom.	! __! __! __! __!	The software package incorporates a management scheme for deploying available instructional resources.

===

Subject Matter

<u>1</u> <u>2</u> <u>3</u> <u>4</u> <u>5</u>

The package presents topics that are irrelevant to the needs of the intended students.	! __! __! __! __!	The topics included in the package are very significant in the education of intended students.
The content is very inaccurate.	! __! __! __! __!	The content is free from errors.
Racial, ethnic, or sex-role stereotypes are displayed.	! __! __! __! __!	The presentation is free of any objectionable stereotyping.

(Cont.)

Biased or distorted information is paraded as factual information.	! __! __! __! __!	Well-balanced and representative information is presented.
The package includes information that is greatly outdated.	! __! __! __! __!	The content presented in the package represents current knowledge.
The presentation of the content is confusing.	! __! __! __! __!	The content is clearly presented.
The package gives no attention to the processes of inquiry.	! __! __! __! __!	Inquiry processes are well integrated into this software package.

==

Technical Quality

1   2   3   4   5

Students require an unacceptable amount of guidance by teachers to operate the program successfully.	! __! __! __! __!	Students can easily and independently operate the program after a modest period of orientation.
Feedback given by the program to student responses is inappropriate and confusing.	! __! __! __! __!	The program's feedback to student responses is appropriate, informative, and timely.
The program's graphics displays are crude and cluttered.	! __! __! __! __!	Graphics displays are crisp and clear.
The program's stance is callous and insulting.	! __! __! __! __!	The program is "user sensitive."
The program has uncorrected "bugs" that cause it to behave inconsistently under certain circumstances.	! __! __! __! __!	All possible combinations or user input and variable ranges are anticipated by the program.
Program documentation is incomplete, confusing, and inconsistent with the observed behavior of the program.	! __! __! __! __!	Program documentation is comprehensive, clear, and consistent with the observed program behavior.
Teacher's materials are shabby, incomplete, and written in "hacker's" vernacular.	! __! __! __! __!	Teacher's guide materials are attractive, comprehensive, and suitable for the teacher-user who has little technical computer knowledge.
Student instructional materials other than the computer program are poorly organized, unattractive, and inappropriate.	! __! __! __! __!	Instructional materials other than the computer program are well designed and appropriate for the students who will use them.
The software package is physically flimsy and easily sabotaged.	! __! __! __! __!	The package's components are designed to survive classroom conditions.

Figure 5.2   Microcomputer software evaluation form.

The appropriate balance between the message and the delivery system is difficult to achieve. What should be done, for example, if the subject matter is accurate, vital to the course in which it is used, and well targeted for the students' ability, but the packaging is poor? On the other hand, the best written documentation and instruction manual, the finest graphics, and the most effective instructional design are of little use if the content they deliver is trivial. The most ideal CAI consists of proper content that is well executed.

If programs are marginal, you may have the option of modifying them to fit your needs. Some programs, after minor alterations, can be customized for local circumstances. Certain technical considerations must be taken into account, but frequently it is possible to change some aspects of the program design if the lesson is written in a familiar language. Graphics, the nature of the questions and reinforcement, and verbal information present on the screen can be modified unless the information is protected by scrambling or written in assembly language. Consult locally with people knowledgeable about computer programming, or contact the manufacturer for information about the process of modifying programs.

Many lessons are adopted on the basis of word-of-mouth recommendations. At conferences, professional meetings, and through informal contact with others in the field, you may obtain information about the strengths and weaknesses of certain programs. Computer magazines and professional journals are another source of information because they serve as a forum of opinion. The final decision to select and use a certain type of CAI is the result of the synthesis of opinion from all of these sources.

Future of CAI

When asked about the future of computing, someone has jokingly characterized the standard response from people who work with computers as ''Wait just six months, a significant breakthrough is just about to occur.'' Although truthful, this answer is not very practical. The use of computers in all phases of our lives is increasing, and changes are accepted as fundamental operating procedures. Computer equipment has become more powerful and less expensive at a more rapid pace than in any other area of technology. Changes in hardware have served only to make it better and more effective, and the trend is likely to continue. Configurations of computerized areas for work, for education, and for business and industry may be as different 10 years from now as they were 10 years ago.

Concern for the future is more appropriately focused on the computer user instead of the computer. The human relations of computer applications, propensity of people to adapt to technology and its uses, and particularly the infusion of computers into the educational enterprise are very real concerns. If one were to draw up a list of reasons that explain why there has been resistance to technology in education, some of the items might include the following:

- Lack of time to work with it
- Perceived resistance by students to use it
- Inhuman, machine-like qualities that are not suitable for interactive, tutorial instruction
- Lack of formal training in its use
- Cost of acquisition and use

These may be valid reasons to justify maintaining the status quo. It is important to realize that there is no convincing evidence that people learn more, learn more effectively, or retain information longer when CAI is used. Physical education by its very nature does not lend itself as well to CAI as other academic fields do.

Another reason may exist, however. Teachers and technology may be philosophical opposites. Teachers teach because they feel students have a need for human instructors. Technology shifts the focus from human-centered instruction to machine instruction. The future of computers as instructional tools is dependent on the degree to which teachers are willing to enhance live instruction with appropriate technology.

The outlook for the future of CAI might be characterized as bright but cautious. Although it is easy to become caught up in trendy technology, thoughtful teachers know that some consideration must also be given to the dark side. But computers are here and will remain. It is likely that they will eventually settle into an appropriate niche alongside overhead projectors, slide sets, film and TV, the chalkboard, and the book. Certainly the increasing sensitivity of teachers, manufacturers, and software producers is apt to result in increasingly useful materials.

Reference

Thomas, R.A., & Boysen, J.P. (1984). A taxonomy for the instructional use of computers. *AEDS Monitor*, **22** (11,12), 15-17, 26.

CHAPTER 6

Classroom Applications for Microcomputers

Richard Engelhorn

In addition to computer-aided instruction, the microcomputer can be used in a variety of ways to enhance teaching and learning in the physical education classroom and laboratory and to aid the teacher in several administrative tasks. This chapter illustrates the use of the microcomputer in several situations commonly encountered by the physical education professional. Detailed software and flowcharts are provided for some tasks, whereas others are described as potential applications. The functions of record keeping, report generation, grade calculations, test construction, laboratory simulations, and statistical analyses will be discussed. The physical education professional can expand the traditional approach to teaching many concepts by employing the computer in one way or another. This chapter illustrates a few of these applications and provides examples of software for certain of these functions.

Physical Fitness Assessment

Physical fitness and conditioning classes are very popular offerings at the college level, and fitness testing is often an important component of the courses. The software in Listings 6.1 and 6.2 at the end of the chapter were developed to provide students in physical fitness classes with a report outlining their test results and providing percentile data related to previous student fitness scores in the same course. The software, written in Applesoft BASIC for a 48K Apple II+, provides input and data storage routines for two testing periods (see Listing 6.1) and an output routine that gives percentile data and brief interpretations of the scores (see Listing 6.2).

The five input screens are shown in Figure 6.1 and the printed output is illustrated in Figure 6.2. The percent fat scores are calculated from the YMCA norms (Golding, Myers, & Sinning, 1982) using three or five sites for women and four or six sites for men. Ideal weights for individuals were calculated according to body fat percentages of

81

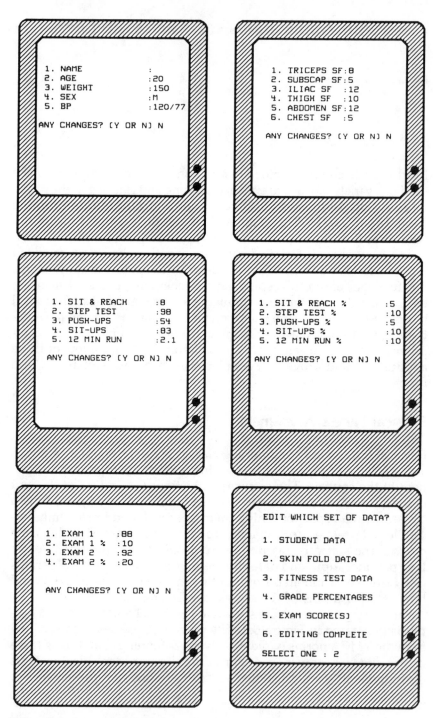

Figure 6.1 Input screens for fitness test results.

```
                        IOWA STATE UNIVERSITY
             PE 163/165 PHYSICAL FITNESS/AEROBIC DANCE

FITNESS ASSESSMENT FOR      DATA RECORDED SEPTEMBER 1985.

AGE : 20    WEIGHT : 150 POUNDS

USING THE SKINFOLD MEASUREMENTS, YOUR PER CENT BODY FAT IS 7.4 %
BASED UPON NATIONAL NORMS FOR YOUR AGE GROUP, YOUR PERCENTILE SCORE
      FOR THE PER CENT FAT DATA IS   97.

THE AVERAGE PER CENT BODY FAT FOR YOUR AGE AND SEX IS 13 %.
BASED UPON THE PER CENT FAT CALCULATIONS, YOUR IDEAL
      BODY WEIGHT IS 150 POUNDS.
THIS RESULT WAS BASED ON IDEAL PER CENT FAT VALUES
      OF 15 AND 23 FOR MEN AND WOMEN RESPECTIVELY.

THE STEP TEST WAS USED TO ESTIMATE YOUR MAXIMUM
            CAPACITY TO USE OXYGEN DURING EXERCISE.  THIS IS
            RECOGNIZED AS THE BEST INDICATOR OF CARDIOVASCULAR FITNESS.
THE SCORE IS THE MAXIMUM VOLUME [IN MILLILITERS] OF OXYGEN
            YOUR BODY CAN USE PER KILOGRAM OF BODY WEIGHT PER MINUTE.

YOUR SCORE WAS 45 ML/KG/MIN.
BASED UPON NATIONAL NORMS FOR YOUR AGE GROUP, YOUR PERCENTILE SCORE
      FOR THE MAXIMUM OXYGEN CONSUMPTION TEST WAS   84.

YOUR ESTIMATED MAXIMUM ATTAINABLE HEART RATE BASED UPON YOUR AGE
      IS 200 BEATS/MINUTE.
YOUR BLOOD PRESSURE WAS 120/77

FOLLOWING ARE YOUR RAW SCORES AND PERCENTILE
      SCORES FOR THE PUSH-UP, SIT-UP, AND 12 MINUTE
      RUN FITNESS TESTS.  THE PERCENTILE SCORES WERE
      CALCULATED FROM ISU STUDENT DATA.

                  T1 SCORE       T1 %     T2 SCORE      T2 %

FLEXIBILITY            6           70         8           88
STEP TEST [HR/MIN]   117           90        98           99
PUSH-UPS              42           50        54           85
SIT-UPS              78           81        83           90

* * * * * * * *  EXERCISE PRESCRIPTION  * * * * * * * *

DURING YOUR EXERCISE ACTIVITY YOU NEED TO KEEP YOUR HEART
      RATE AT APPROXIMATELY 167 BEATS PER MINUTE FOR
      OPTIMUM EFFICIENCY IN IMPROVING CARDIOVASCULAR FITNESS.

THE MINIMUM EXERCISE HEART RATE NECESSARY TO IMPROVE
      YOUR FITNESS IS 148, WHEREAS YOU SHOULD NOT EXCEED A
      HEART RATE OF 180 DURING EXERCISE.

THE EXERCISE HEART RATE SHOULD BE MAINTAINED FOR 20
      MINUTES FOR THE MAXIMUM TRAINING BENEFIT.
```

Figure 6.2 Output of program for fitness class results.

15 and 23 for men and women, respectively. If the students' percent fat was less than 15 or 23, their ideal weight was given as their present weight. The percentile scores were based upon data collected over several years from fitness and aerobic dance classes at Iowa State University.

The ease of program modification, in addition to efficient data entry and editing facilities, makes this program easy to apply to a wide range of applications. The data base can be easily modified or replaced to make use of other fitness tests and/or data bases. At the end of the semester, the output reflects the two test periods and percent change information. Written exam scores and the weightings used for both the fitness tests and exams are also input in this example so that course grades can be determined for each student. Instructors have the option of including the grading utility in the individualized fitness report. A flowchart for this program is illustrated in Figure 6.3.

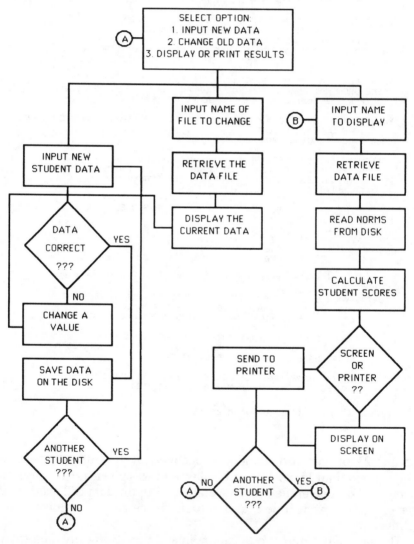

Figure 6.3 Flowchart for physical fitness assessment.

One very important advantage to using the computer for the storage of fitness data is the ability to update quite easily the percentile scores for each of the tests at the end of a semester or testing period. A third program would be used to perform the data base updating and calculation of new percentile scores. Whether the software is used for motivational purposes, for prescribing exercise intensity, or for grading, both the instructor and student benefit from this application of the microcomputer.

AAHPERD Fitness Test Reports

Another fitness-related application for the microcomputer provides support for elementary and secondary school physical educators using the AAHPERD Health-Related Fitness Test. The software in Listing 6.3 at the end of the chapter provides for the input, storage, and results output for one period of fitness testing. Figure 6.4 illustrates the input screen and the data types collected. The input function is easy to use and provides an efficient storage, editing, and retrieval system. Once the data have been stored on disk, the user may change any incorrect entries prior to printing or displaying the results. The program uses the data base provided by AAHPERD for the percentile calculations, but local data bases could be substituted or used in addition to the national norms. The normative data are stored in several files on floppy disk and are read by the program when needed. To be of maximum use as a fitness guide, individualized evaluations could

```
              HEALTH RELATED PHYSICAL FITNESS
                          TEST

       1 - LAST NAME  :
       2 - FIRST NAME  :
              3 - GROUP NUMBER  :
              4 - AGE [MONTHS]  :
              5 - SEX  :
              6 - HT  :    WT  :

                  7 - MILE RUN [MIN.SEC]  :

                  8 - 9 MIN RUN [YARDS]  :

                  9 - SITUPS  :

                  10 - TRICEPS SF  :
                  11 - SUBSCAPULAR SF  :

                  12 - SIT AND REACH  :

       DATA CORRECT  ??
       CORRECT WHICH DATA POINT  ?
```

Figure 6.4   Input screen for health-related physical fitness test.

be provided on the printout, commenting on the strengths and weaknesses of the student scores. The present software does not include this option; however, adding this feature should be easy for anyone with BASIC programming skills. The program output in its simplest form is shown in Figure 6.5. The test items used in this software could be modified to use any fitness test item as long as data for the percentile calculations are available.

```
                    BRADLEY SUMMER YOUTH FITNESS 1984

HEALTH RELATED PHYSICAL FITNESS TEST

* * * * * * * * * * * * * * * * * * * * * * * * * * * * * * * * * * * * * * * *

     NAME              SEX  AGE  HT   WT   DATE
     ----              ---  ---  --   --   ----
MARIE ENGELHORN         F    9   50   65   9/10/85

                  EVENT                 SCORE      PERCENTILE
                  -----                 -----      ----------

                  MILE RUN              8:46          89

                  SIT-UPS                40           87

                  SKIN-FOLDS             17           50

                  SIT & REACH            35           95

* * * * * * * * * * * * * * * * * * * * * * * * * * * * * * * * * * * * * * * *
```

Figure 6.5 Sample program output for health-related physical fitness test in simple format.

The microcomputer can be used by the physical educator for many purposes, but the ease of data handling and report generation may increase the use of regular fitness testing and, therefore, provide a vehicle for teaching fitness concepts. There are other fitness-related programs being used in schools, universities, and fitness centers. Most perform similar tasks but may be based upon different data sets. The two programs described previously are but two examples of using the microcomputer for fitness-related activities.

Grading and Record Keeping

Teachers often have a time-consuming task confronting them in the storage and calculation of student scores and grades. By employing software that allows for the storage and processing of student records, a teacher can save considerable time and energy. For the physical educator these may be fitness scores, sport skill test results, or written exam scores of various types. Daily attendance scores could even be entered so that a rapid summary of student attendance could be generated when needed.

There are three types of software in general use for grading and record-keeping activities. The least flexible is the program written specifically to handle grades and student records. Such programs may be very easy to learn, but they may provide limited options in terms of the types of records and the calculations that can be performed on the records. A more flexible system for this task makes use of one of the various data base management programs. The data base software allows for the efficient storage and retrieval of student data, but the types of calculations that can be performed on the data are often limiting. In this software, data are input to various fields of a file that can be stored on disk. Data can be recalled from a group of files based upon the data in any one field. For a more complete description of this type of software, see the administration applications chapter.

For maximum efficiency, although requiring a greater learning time, the spreadsheet software is essential. The spreadsheet allows the user to design a system specifically suited to the user's needs. In addition to being able to easily input, retrieve, display, and output student records, a wide range of mathematical and statistical calculations can be performed on the stored data. Numerous spreadsheet programs are readily available for a wide range of microcomputers. These commercial programs are somewhat similar, their cost varying with speed and ease of use. The latter two software packages can also be used for other functions in addition to grading and student records, making for a wise investment.

The spreadsheet programs, several of which are available for all types of microcomputers, are very efficient because of their design. The user is able to structure the physical makeup of the spreadsheet to fit individual needs. Names, numbers, or other information can be stored in a cell. Cells in rows or columns can be searched and/or sorted to achieve almost any purpose. Cells also can contain mathematical formulas that calculate the numerical value of the cell based upon other cells in the matrix. Figure 6.6 provides an example of the output from a spreadsheet-based program on the Macintosh microcomputer. This software, as is so with the spreadsheet software for other microcomputers, provides for a gradebook unique to the instructor. The instructor determines the weightings for each of the factors used in determining the course grade and uses those multipliers in a formula that will calculate the value of the item in the "total %" column. The exact format for the formula will vary among the different spreadsheet packages; however the effect is the same, an efficient and accurate method for storing and calculating student grades.

	1	2	3	4	5	6	7	8	9	10	11	12	13	14	15	16
1		SOC.	Exam1	Grade	Sched.	Curric.	Grade	Exam2	Grade	Quiz	Budget	Attn.	Final	Grade	Total	Final
2	NAME	SEC.	100pt	15%	Proj.5%	Proj.	15%	100pt	15%	5%	15%	5%	Exam	15%	%	Grade
3	TOMMY	5947	98	14.7	5	85	21.3	66	9.9	3.5	14	4	51	12.34	84.69	B
4	ANN	1620	83	12.5	5	93	23.3	97	14.6	5	14	4	59	14.27	92.52	A
5	FRED	7442	95	14.3	5	55	13.8	63	9.45	5	12	3	56	13.55	76.00	C
6	ALAN	6302	98	14.7	5	85	21.3	87	13.1	4	14	5	52	12.58	89.58	A-
7	DAVID	4297	54	8.1	5	78	19.5	71	10.7	5	13	2	45	10.89	74.14	C
8	NANCY	6313	94	14.1	5	85	21.3	80	12	4	14	5	54	13.06	88.41	B+
9	HEIDI	3645	76	11.4	5	83	20.8	75	11.3	4	12	4	41	9.92	78.32	C+
10	BOB	3097	94	14.1	5	85	21.3	90	13.5	4	14	5	55	13.31	90.16	A-
11	PENNY	6055	65	9.75	5	88	22	68	10.2	5	12	4	53	12.82	80.77	B-
12	MARCUS	4417	83	12.5	5	88	22	93	14	4	14	5	55	13.31	89.71	A-
13	SUSIE	6680	92	13.8	5	93	23.3	81	12.2	4	14	4	53	12.82	89.02	B+

Figure 6.6 Electronic gradebook utilizing a spreadsheet.

Test Construction

Test constuction is yet another area in which any teacher, physical education or otherwise, can make use of the microcomputer. Two possible avenues of software utilization are possible: (a) programs designed specifically for multiple-choice or other objective item tests and (b) general word processors. In this application the word processor provides far more flexibility and ease of use than any test generation program. All microcomputers now have sophisticated word processors that are easy to learn and use, allowing the user to create and print the text of almost any format. The instructor can even add graphics to the text with some software packages.

Several programs are available to allow for the input and printing of tests, and some provide for a variety of question types. However, to illustrate the essentials of such software, the flowchart in Figure 6.7 details the functions performed. A simple program that would handle multiple-choice or true-false questions could be written in BASIC, using the flowchart as a guide. This software would independently prompt for questions or choices, store the questions until all are in, save them on disk, and print the exam on a printer.

The major problem associated with this program would be that of formatting the printing of the test. The program would need to keep track of the lines printed per page and then advance the page when the available space was less than that required for a complete question. Such software would be easy to use, but the test writer's flexibility in terms of interspersing various types of questions or graphics may be sacrificed. Basically, it seems a poor investment to purchase specialized test construction software when powerful word processors are available for the microcomputer. The instructor using a word

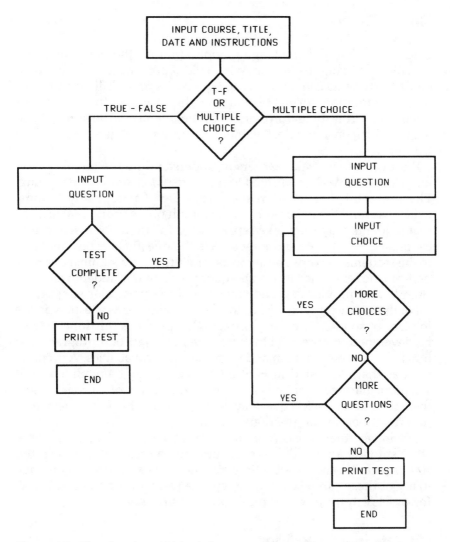

Figure 6.7 Flowchart for multiple-choice or true-false test construction.

processor with the capability of including graphics has unlimited flexibility in structuring the exam without loss of time or efficiency. In addition, the instructor or school also has the word processing software for use with other text-processing tasks, such as letters or research articles. The test construction software cannot provide the power or flexibility of the word processor.

On-Line Testing

One interesting and challenging application for the microcomputer is in the area of on-line testing. With a file of potential questions stored on disk, students can be presented questions for a drill-and-practice setting or for more formal testing. In either situation the computer's novelty and control features enhance the interest of the student and provide for considerable flexibility in presenting questions to the learner.

Practice tests that aid learners in understanding the limits of their knowledge are easily presented to the student in a one-on-one setting. The instructor first must create a large file of potential questions, usually several times larger than the length of the individual tests so that students may then take repeated tests without excessive duplication. The software randomly selects the questions, presents them to the students, records the answers, and provides a summary of their performance after each test. Subsequent tests for the student will differ slightly and provide a broad coverage of the particular subject.

For the instructor who wishes to use the computer as a testing device in place of an in-class exam, software that provides this function can be developed. Figure 6.8 illustrates the flowchart of a program that fulfills the text presentation and record-keeping capabilities. A program such as that illustrated in Figure 6.8 could easily be modified to fit the particular needs of an instructor. The addition of a program segment to randomly select questions would provide the practice test function described in the previous section.

Obviously, there are certain problems in using a microcomputer to test a student; among these are identifying the student, test security, results security, and possible time constraints for system use. Although many of these can be overcome, on-line testing may be most useful for practice testing where these problems do not exist.

Simulation and Modeling

For illustrating specific concepts in a classroom, lab, or activity setting, it is possible to apply the microcomputer to simulate situations that otherwise could not be observed or to test the effects of mathematical models on various movement situations. Of the many situations that can be simulated on the microcomputer, two examples are provided from the areas of exercise physiology and biomechanics. The first relates to cardiovascular dynamics and arterial pulse pressure, whereas the second uses shot putting to illustrate the effect of gravity on objects projected into the air.

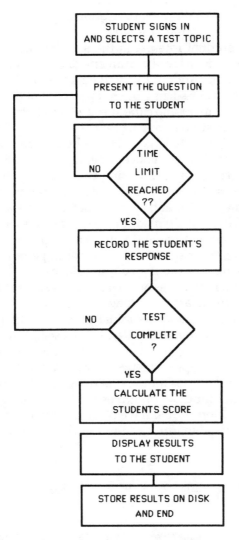

Figure 6.8 Flowchart for on-line testing and record keeping.

In general, all computer simulations are based upon a mathematical model. There are many sport and exercise science areas in which a model can be developed based upon laws of physics or physiologic functioning. Such models may have one or possibly several independent variables that affect the value of the dependent variable of interest. Through the interactive manipulation of these variables and observation of subsequent changes in the dependent variable, students are able to gain an understanding of relationships among the factors that affect the variables being studied.

To enhance student interest in the simulations, it is important to use creative graphics as well as numeric displays. Visual displays that do not use graphics are not likely to be as interesting to the student and may fall short of realizing the full potential of the microcomputer. It is also necessary to optimize the speed at which the program executes and to occupy the student during delays in reading the disk or during particularly long calculations. One method often used is to display information related to the concept being illustrated so that the student has something to read during these delays. BASIC programs should be compiled in order to execute commands most rapidly and reduce idle time for students. A compiler converts a BASIC program into machine language, which then executes anywhere from 2 to 20 times faster than the original BASIC. The higher execution speed of a compiled program also enhances the rapid generation of graphics.

The first example of the use of a simulation is taken from Randall (1980). The model calculates arterial pulse pressure during the cardiac cycle based upon heart rate, length of systole, aortic compliance, peripheral resistance, and the initial pressure. The program listing, which is included in the text by Randall, was slightly modified to provide on-screen labeling of the curves and was compiled to decrease execution time. The input screen is illustrated in Figure 6.9. Suggested values are in parentheses for the first three variables, whereas the last two variables are input as multiples of the normal values. Students using the simulation should have prior knowledge of the physiologic range of each variable input to the model. The program could also

```
               MECHANICS OF AORTIC PRESSURE

                    - - - - - - -


          HEART RATE (75?) - 75    BEATS/MIN

             CARDIAC CYCLE - .8    SEC

      DURATION OF SYSTOLE - ?.3    SEC

      STROKE VOLUME (75?) - ? 75   ML

        AORTIC COMPLIANCE - ? .9   X NORMAL

    PERIPHERAL RESISTANCE - ? 1.1X NORMAL


         INITIAL PRESSURE - ? 80   MM HG
```

Figure 6.9   Input screen for mechanics of aortic pressure modified from Randall (1980).

be designed to prompt for another value if the input value was outside the physiologic range.

For example, because these factors are often changed due to cardiovascular disease, the instructor may want to illustrate to the students the impact that changes in aortic compliance and the peripheral resistance to blood flow have on blood pressure. Instead of inputting a 1 for aortic compliance, the student may use a number less than one to reflect the loss of elasticity or compliance that occurs with cardiovascular disease. The student could also use a value greater than one for peripheral resistance because that is also the direction of change of that variable with cardiovascular disease. The output screen (see Figure 6.10) would then indicate the potential impact these changes had on cardiac output and blood pressure.

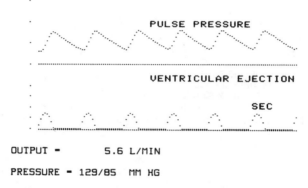

Figure 6.10   Example output screen from arterial pulse pressure simulation program.

To encourage the student to rerun the program using a different combination of independent variables, the program recycles automatically after each run. Figure 6.10 provides an example of the output from one program run. After the student has viewed this screen, any key press causes the input screen to reappear and the program can then be executed again.

From a teaching standpoint, it may be useful to structure the student's use of the software rather than having free experimentation by the student. By providing guidelines for the sequence of independent variable input, the instructor can illustrate specific concepts related to an issue and provide greater insight into an area than may be obtained through random variable input.

Projectile motion is the topic of the second simulation program. This software was used as a laboratory experience in a kinesiology class that students completed on their own time rather than at the designated class time. The projectile motion simulation illustrates the relationships among release height, angle, and velocity on the horizontal distance achieved by a shot putter. The input and display features are on a single screen, and the projectile path can be erased or maintained as the student replicates the task with different input values.

The graphics and input screen is shown in Figure 6.11. In addition to illustrating the relative path of the projectile, the time in flight and

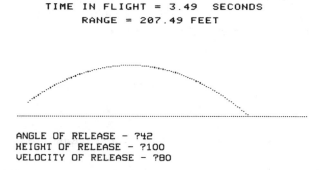

```
TIME IN FLIGHT = 3.49  SECONDS
       RANGE = 207.49 FEET
```

```
ANGLE OF RELEASE - ?42
HEIGHT OF RELEASE - ?100
VELOCITY OF RELEASE - ?80
```

Figure 6.11 Combined graphics and input screen for projectile motion simulation program.

horizontal range are displayed after each trial. The software for this program is provided in Listing 6.4 and is in Apple II+ BASIC. After the student has input all three variables to the program, an equation using the data for release height, velocity, and angle calculates the location of the projectile at approximately 0.01 second increments. The process continues until the projectile reaches ground level. Equations are also used to calculate the time in flight and horizontal range, both of which are displayed on screen after each trial. These equations are found in lines 1100, 1200, 1400, 2200, 2300, and 2400 of Listing 6.4. The program documentation explains the function of each line of the software.

Kinesiology students, by systematically varying the three parameters, are able to gain an understanding of the relative effect that takeoff angle, velocity of takeoff or release, and height of release have on projectile motion. The student could observe the effect that changing running velocity or takeoff angle would have on long jumping success. A shot putter's performance could also be varied by experimenting with all three variables. Because the pathways of each trial can be superimposed, the student can gain a visual image, as well as quantitative information, of the changes in projectile motion resulting from modifications in velocity, height of release, and release angle.

The two simulation applications described are but two of the many that could be used in physical education and sports teaching environments. The creative instructor, with an available mathematical model related to a particular concept, can design software based upon the model that simulates the physical or physiological mechanisms of interest. An enriched learning environment will be the result of quality simulations on the microcomputer, and the sports science student will be the beneficiary.

In addition to computer-only simulations for the lab setting, the microcomputer interfaced with a videotape or disk system can provide visual displays simulating real experiences. Just as the flight simulator is useful in training pilots for real flights, the microcomputer and videotape display can aid in the preparation of physical educators. The previous chapter introduced the concept of using videotape or disk players interfaced to the microcomputer to provide realistic illustrations of movement patterns, sport skills, or teaching behaviors in conjunction with interactive learning software. Programs such as these are currently in use and will continue to be used to enhance student learning. In this situation the student is led through a series of informational screens or displays on the computer. At various points in the session, the videotape system is activated by the computer software to provide a visual image of an event or activity. The student may then be requested to respond to questions concerning the videotape display.

One example of an application of this system is to use it to illustrate rules that referees of various sports are asked to interpret and enforce. Critical situations involving such rules from basketball, soccer, or other sports would be videotaped and displayed with a teaching and/or testing goal in mind. In the learning setting, the software could be used to prepare sports officials with the videotape system supplying realistic examples to go along with the descriptions and interpretations of rules provided by the microcomputer. The same taped information may be useful in a program designed to evaluate or certify sports officials. The videotape system could present various situations from sports competition and ask the observer or computer user to make appropriate judgments.

Another example for physical educators to consider comes from the area of movement analysis. Students in sport skill classes or biomechanics are learning how to diagnose movement errors based upon their knowledge of intended movement goals, sport strategies, and biomechanical and anatomical constraints. In the classroom setting it is very difficult to simulate situations that allow the student to test their diagnostic abilities or to learn from these opportunities. The videotape interfaced to the microcomputer has the potential to aid students of sport skills in learning to analyze movement performances. The computer software provides the tutorial and testing aspects with the videotape system displaying the controlled movement setting for analysis. The reader may at this point be visualizing other similar applications of this system for his or her particular situation. Creative physical educators with the time, knowledge, and dedication to the enhancement of the teaching-learning process can create interesting and educational experiences for their students. As indicated in the previous chapter, the development of quality educational software is a time-consuming task, but the videotape-aided simulation is one area in which the physical education student could significantly benefit.

Microcomputers have a place in the physical education classroom and laboratory and can fulfill a multitude of roles. The applications provided in this chapter are designed to serve as examples of what can be done and how these functions are implemented. Many more applications are currently in use by physical educators throughout the country. The microcomputer provides an interesting change of pace for the student, and through its use the student gains computer literacy as well as the particular concepts being taught. Physical educators should actively seek ways of using microcomputers in their classes and labs, whether it be for CAI or other applications. The task of designing computer-aided learning materials for the teaching environment is not an easy one; but as physical educators begin to see the benefits derived from microcomputer use and become more computer literate, an increased volume of software will likely become available for the physical education teacher.

References

Golding, L.A., Myers, C.R., & Sinning, W.E. (1972). *The Y's Way to Physical Fitness*. Chicago: YMCA of the USA.

Randall, J.E. (1980). *Microcomputers and Physiological Simulation*. Reading, MA: Addison Wesley.

Listing 6.1 Input program for fitness class results.

```
100   REM  *  *  *  *  *  *  *  *  *  *  *  *  *  *  *  *  *  *  *
102   REM  *  *   INPUT PROGRAM FOR FITNESS CLASS RESULTS
104   REM  *  *  *  *  *  *  *  *  *  *  *  *  *  *  *  *  *  *  *
120   D$ =  CHR$ (4)
140   DIM SD$(5,2,35),SF$(6,2,35),FT$(5,2,35),FP$(5,35)
160   DIM WT$(4,35)
180   HOME
200   GOSUB 720: GOSUB 300
220   INPUT "IS THIS A NEW FILE?? : ";Y$
240   IF Y$ < > "Y" AND Y$ < > "N" THEN 220
260   IF Y$ = "Y" THEN 2840
280   GOTO 520: REM  IF NOT NEW SUBJECT SKIP NEXT SECTION
290   REM  SET ALL ARRAYS = TO 999, WHICH IS NO DATA FLAG
300   FOR I = 1 TO 35
320   FOR J = 1 TO 2
340   FOR L = 1 TO 5
360 SD$(L,J,I) = "999":FT$(L,J,I) = "999"
380   NEXT L
400   FOR M = 1 TO 6:SF$(M,J,I) = "999": NEXT M
420   NEXT J
440   FOR P = 1 TO 5:FP$(P,I) = "999": NEXT P
460   FOR R = 1 TO 4:WT$(R,I) = "999": NEXT R
480   NEXT I
500   RETURN
520   ONERR  GOTO 5880
530   REM  DISPLAY MENU OF FUNCTIONS
540   HOME : VTAB (10)
560   PRINT  TAB( 7)" 1.  INPUT NEW DATA"
580   PRINT  TAB( 7)" 2. INPUT NEW DATA FOR POST-TEST"
600   PRINT  TAB( 7)" 3.  CHANGE DATA"
620   PRINT  TAB( 7)" 4.  END"
640   Z1 = 0: REM  Z1=1 FOR PRE-TEST, Z1=2 FOR POST-TEST
660   VTAB 20: INPUT "WHAT IS YOUR CHOICE?";M
680   ON M GOSUB 800,3000,3080,4660
700   GOTO 540: REM  REDISPLAY MENU
720   VTAB (20): HTAB (1): PRINT "INPUT CLASS AND SECTION NUMBER": INPUT
      "SUCH AS 16X-X : ";SN$
740   FI$ = "F85" + SN$
760   COUNT$ = "CT" + FI$
780   RETURN
800   GOSUB 300: REM  RESET ARRAYS FOR NEXT DATA INPUT
820   GOSUB 6140
840   Q = 1
850   REM  READ # OF FILES ON DISK
860   PRINT D$;"OPEN";COUNT$
880   PRINT D$;"READ";COUNT$
900   INPUT K
920   PRINT D$;"CLOSE";COUNT$
940   K = K + 1: REM  INCREMENT FILE COUNTER K
960   HOME : VTAB 2
980   IF Z1 = 2 THEN Q = 2: REM  SET Q=2 FOR POST-TEST DATA
990   REM  PRESENT SERIES OF INPUT SCREENS
1000  PRINT "TYPE 999 FOR MISSING DATA"
1020  VTAB (6)
1040  INPUT " 1.  NAME?          :";SD$(1,Q,K)
1060  INPUT " 2.  AGE?           :";SD$(2,Q,K)
1080  INPUT " 3.  WEIGHT?        :";SD$(3,Q,K)
1100  INPUT " 4.  SEX?           :";SD$(4,Q,K)
1120  INPUT " 5.  BP (SYS/DIAS)? :";SD$(5,Q,K)
1140  GOSUB 5180
1160  IF C$ = "N" THEN 1200
1180  VTAB (16): GOTO 1140
1200  HOME
1220  VTAB (2): PRINT "TYPE 999 FOR MISSING DATA"
1240  VTAB (6)
1260  INPUT " 1.  TRICEPS? :";SF$(1,Q,K)
1280  INPUT " 2.  SCAPULA? :";SF$(2,Q,K)
```

(Cont.)

```
1300    INPUT " 3.    ILIAC?    :";SF$[3,Q,K]
1320    INPUT " 4.    THIGH?    :";SF$[4,Q,K]
1340    INPUT " 5.    ABDOMEN? :";SF$[5,Q,K]
1360    IF SD$[4,Q,K] = "F" THEN 1400
1380    INPUT " 6.    CHEST?    :";SF$[6,Q,K]
1400    GOSUB 5320
1420    IF C$ = "N" THEN 1460
1440    VTAB [12]: GOTO 1400
1460    HOME : VTAB [2]: PRINT "TYPE 999 FOR MISSING DATA"
1480    VTAB [4]: PRINT "IF MODIFIED PUSH-UP TYPE 'XX MOD'"
1500    VTAB [6]
1520    INPUT " 1.    SIT AND REACH? :";FT$[1,Q,K]
1540    INPUT " 2.    STEP TEST HR?  :";FT$[2,Q,K]
1560    INPUT " 3.    PUSH-UPS?      :";FT$[3,Q,K]
1580    INPUT " 4.    SIT-UPS?       :";FT$[4,Q,K]
1600    INPUT " 5.    12 MIN RUN?    :";FT$[5,Q,K]
1620    GOSUB 5460
1640    IF C$ = "N" THEN 1680
1660    VTAB [16]: GOTO 1620
1680    HOME : INPUT "DO YOU HAVE THE TEST PERCENTAGES? :";Y$
1700    IF Y$ = "N" THEN 1920
1720    HOME : VTAB [2]: PRINT "TYPE 999 FOR MISSING DATA"
1740    VTAB [6]
1760    INPUT " 1.    SIT & REACH % [10-20]:";FP$[1,K]
1780    INPUT " 2.    STEP TEST % [10-20] : ";FP$[2,K]
1800    INPUT " 3.    PUSH-UPS % [10-20]   :";FP$[3,K]
1820    INPUT " 4.    SIT-UPS % [10-20]    :";FP$[4,K]
1840    INPUT " 5.    12 MIN RUN % [10-20] :";FP$[5,K]
1860    GOSUB 5600
1880    IF C$ = "N" THEN 1920
1900    VTAB [16]: GOTO 1860
1920    HOME
1940    VTAB [4]
1960    INPUT "DO YOU HAVE EXAM SCORES TO INPUT? :";C$
1980    IF C$ < > "Y" THEN 2220
2000    INPUT "HOW MANY WRITTEN EXAMS? :";WE
2020    IF WE < 1 OR WE > 2 THEN 2000
2040    VTAB [6]: INPUT "TEST 1 SCORE :";WT$[1,K]
2060    INPUT "TEST 1 %       :";WT$[2,K]
2080    IF WE = 1 THEN 2140
2100    INPUT "TEST 2 SCORE :";WT$[3,K]
2120    INPUT "TEST 2 %       :";WT$[4,K]
2140    VTAB [10]
2160    GOSUB 5740
2180    IF C$ = "N" THEN 2220
2200    VTAB [16]: GOTO 2160
2210    REM   SAVE DATA TO DISK
2220 Z = K
2240    PRINT D$;"OPEN ";FI$;",L400"
2260    PRINT D$;"WRITE ";FI$;",R";Z
2280    I = 2
2300    FOR S = 1 TO 2
2320    FOR L = 1 TO 5
2340    PRINT SD$[L,S,I]
2360    NEXT L
2380    FOR M = 1 TO 6
2400    PRINT SF$[M,S,I]
2420    NEXT M
2440    FOR N = 1 TO 5
2460    PRINT FT$[N,S,I]
2480    NEXT N
2500    NEXT S
2520    FOR R = 1 TO 5
2540    PRINT FP$[R,I]
2560    NEXT R
2580    FOR P = 1 TO 4
2600    PRINT WT$[P,I]
2620    NEXT P
2640    PRINT D$;"CLOSE ";FI$
```

(Cont.)

```
2650   REM   CLEAN UP MEMORY
2660   X9 - X9 + 1: IF X9 - 10 OR X9 - 20 THEN X -  FRE [0]
2680   IF SET - 1 THEN  RETURN
2690   REM  ANOTHER SUBJECT ? ?
2700   HOME : VTAB 12
2720   PRINT "DO YOU WANT TO ENTER MORE? ";
2740   INPUT G$
2760   IF Q - 2 AND G$ - "N" THEN 540
2780   IF Q - 2 THEN 3080
2800   IF G$ <  > "Y" THEN 2860
2820   GOTO 940
2830   REM  UPDATE FILE # COUNTER ON DISK
2840   COUNT$ - "CT" + FI$
2860   PRINT D$;"OPEN";COUNT$
2880   PRINT D$;"DELETE";COUNT$
2900   PRINT D$;"OPEN";COUNT$
2920   PRINT D$;"WRITE";COUNT$
2940   PRINT K
2960   PRINT D$;"CLOSE";COUNT$
2980   GOTO 520
3000   Z1 - 2
3020   GOTO 3080
3040   K - C
3060   GOTO 960
3070   REM  CHANGE DATA ROUTINE
3080   PRINT D$;"OPEN";COUNT$
3100   PRINT D$;"READ";COUNT$
3120   INPUT K
3140   PRINT D$;"CLOSE";COUNT$
3160   POKE 216,0
3180   PRINT D$;"OPEN ";FI$;",L400"
3190   REM  DISPLAY LIST OF NAMES IN FILE
3200   HOME : VTAB 1
3220   B - 0
3240   FOR M - 1 TO K
3260   B - B + 1
3280   PRINT D$;"READ ";FI$;",R";M
3300   INPUT SD$[1,1,M]
3320   PRINT M".";  TAB[ 5]SD$[1,1,M]
3340   IF B < 20 THEN 3500
3360   PRINT D$
3380   VTAB 22: PRINT
3400   Q - 0
3420   PRINT "PRESS ANY KEY TO CONTINUE!"
3440   GET L$: PRINT ""
3460   HOME : VTAB 1
3480   B - 0
3500   NEXT M
3520   PRINT D$;"CLOSE ";FI$
3540   VTAB 22: PRINT "PRESS ANY KEY TO CONTINUE!"
3560   GET G$
3580   HOME : VTAB 12
3600   INPUT "WHICH ONE WOULD YOU LIKE TO EDIT? ";C
3620   Z - C
3640   GOSUB 4720
3660   IF Z1 - 2 THEN 3040
3680   HOME : VTAB 5
3700   HOME : VTAB [10]: INPUT "IS THIS TEST DATA 1 OR 2? : ";Q: IF Q < 1
       OR Q > 2 THEN 3700
3720   GOTO 5920
3740   PRINT " 1. NAME            :";SD$[1,Q,2]
3760   PRINT " 2. AGE             :";SD$[2,Q,2]
3780   PRINT " 3. WEIGHT          :";SD$[3,Q,2]
3800   PRINT " 4. SEX             :";SD$[4,Q,2]
3820   PRINT " 5. BP              :";SD$[5,Q,2]
3840   GOSUB 5180
3860   GOTO 5920
3880   HOME : VTAB [6]
3900   PRINT " 1. TRICEPS SF:";SF$[1,Q,2]
```

(Cont.)

```
3920    PRINT " 2. SUBSCAP SF:";SF$[2,Q,2]
3940    PRINT " 3. ILIAC SF  :";SF$[3,Q,2]
3960    PRINT " 4. THIGH SF  :";SF$[4,Q,2]
3980    PRINT " 5. ABDOMEN SF:";SF$[5,Q,2]
4000    PRINT " 6. CHEST SF  :";SF$[6,Q,2]
4020    GOSUB 5320
4040    GOTO 5920
4060    HOME : VTAB [6]
4080    PRINT " 1. SIT & REACH     :";FT$[1,Q,2]
4100    PRINT " 2. STEP TEST       :";FT$[2,Q,2]
4120    PRINT " 3. PUSH-UPS        :";FT$[3,Q,2]
4140    PRINT " 4. SIT-UPS         :";FT$[4,Q,2]
4160    PRINT " 5. 12 MIN RUN      :";FT$[5,Q,2]
4180    GOSUB 5460
4200    GOTO 5920
4220    HOME : VTAB [6]
4240    PRINT " 1. SIT & REACH %        :";FP$[1,2]
4260    PRINT " 2. STEP TEST %          :";FP$[2,2]
4280    PRINT " 3. PUSH-UPS %           :";FP$[3,2]
4300    PRINT " 4. SIT-UPS %            :";FP$[4,2]
4320    PRINT " 5. 12 MIN RUN %         :";FP$[5,2]
4340    GOSUB 5600
4360    GOTO 5920
4380    HOME : VTAB [6]
4400    PRINT "1. EXAM 1    :";WT$[1,2]
4420    PRINT "2. EXAM 1 %  :";WT$[2,2]
4440    PRINT "3. EXAM 2    :";WT$[3,2]
4460    PRINT "4. EXAM 2 %  :";WT$[4,2]
4480    GOSUB 5740
4500    GOTO 5920
4520 SET - 1: GOSUB 2240
4540    HOME : VTAB 12
4560    PRINT "DO YOU WISH TO EDIT MORE? ";
4580 Q - 1
4600    INPUT G$
4620    IF G$ - "Y" THEN 3180
4640    GOTO 540
4660    HOME : VTAB 12: HTAB 14: PRINT "HAVE A NICE DAY!"
4680    PRINT D$;"RUN HELLO"
4700    END
4720    REM  INPUT FOR EDITING
4740    REM
4760    PRINT D$;"OPEN ";FI$;",L400"
4780    PRINT D$;"READ ";FI$;",R";C
4800    FOR J - 1 TO 2
4820    FOR L - 1 TO 5
4840    INPUT SD$[L,J,C]
4860    NEXT L
4880    FOR M - 1 TO 6
4900    INPUT SF$[M,J,C]
4920    NEXT M
4940    FOR N - 1 TO 5
4960    INPUT FT$[N,J,C]
4980    NEXT N
5000    NEXT J
5020    FOR P - 1 TO 5
5040    INPUT FP$[P,C]
5060    NEXT P
5080    FOR R - 1 TO 4
5100    INPUT WT$[R,C]
5120    NEXT R
5140    PRINT D$;"CLOSE ";FI$
5160    RETURN
5170    REM  CHANGE DATA ROUTINES FOR EACH INPUT SCREEN
5180    VTAB [12]: INPUT "ANY CHANGES? [Y OR N] ";C$
5200    IF C$ - "N" THEN  RETURN
5220    VTAB [16]: INPUT "CHANGE WHICH ONE? : ";C$
5240 C - VAL [C$]
5260    IF C < 1 OR C > 5 THEN 5180
```

(Cont.)

```
5280   VTAB [C + 5]: HTAB [22]: INPUT "";SD$[C,Q,Z]
5300   RETURN
5310   REM    *     *     *
5320   PRINT : INPUT "ANY CHANGES? [Y OR N] ";C$
5340   IF C$ = "N" THEN  RETURN
5360   VTAB [16]: INPUT "CHANGE WHICH ONE? : ";C$
5380   C =  VAL [C$]
5400   IF C < 1 OR C > 6 THEN 5320
5420   VTAB [C + 5]: HTAB [16]: INPUT "";SF$[C,Q,Z]
5440   RETURN
5450   REM    *     *     *
5460   VTAB [12]: INPUT "ANY CHANGES? [Y OR N] ";C$
5480   IF C$ = "N" THEN  RETURN
5500   VTAB [16]: INPUT "CHANGE WHICH ONE? : ";C$
5520   C =  VAL [C$]
5540   IF C < 1 OR C > 5 THEN 5460
5560   VTAB [C + 5]: HTAB [22]: INPUT "";FT$[C,Q,Z]
5580   RETURN
5590   REM    *     *     *
5600   VTAB [12]: INPUT "ANY CHANGES? [Y OR N] ";C$
5620   IF C$ = "N" THEN  RETURN
5640   VTAB [16]: INPUT "CHANGE WHICH ONE? : ";C$
5660   C =  VAL [C$]
5680   IF C < 1 OR C > 5 THEN 5600
5700   VTAB [C + 5]: HTAB [28]: INPUT "";FP$[C,Z]
5720   RETURN
5730   REM    *     *     *
5740   VTAB [12]: INPUT "ANY CHANGES? [Y OR N] ";C$
5760   IF C$ = "N" THEN  RETURN
5780   VTAB [16]: INPUT "CHANGE WHICH ONE? : ";C$
5800   C =  VAL [C$]
5820   IF C < 1 OR C > 4 THEN 5740
5840   VTAB [C + 5]: HTAB [15]: INPUT "";WT$[C,Z]
5860   RETURN
5870   REM    *     *     *
5880   IF  PEEK [222] < > 5 THEN  PRINT "ERROR # "; PEEK [222]: END
5900   GOTO 800
5920   HOME : VTAB [2]: PRINT "EDIT WHICH SET OF DATA?"
5940   VTAB [6]: PRINT "1. STUDENT DATA"
5960   VTAB [8]: PRINT "2. SKIN FOLD DATA"
5980   VTAB [10]: PRINT "3. FITNESS TEST DATA"
6000   VTAB [12]: PRINT "4. GRADE PERCENTAGES"
6020   VTAB [14]: PRINT "5. EXAM SCORE[S]"
6040   VTAB [16]: PRINT "6. EDITING COMPLETE"
6060   VTAB [20]: INPUT "SELECT ONE : ";C$
6080   C =  VAL [C$]: IF C < 1 OR C > 6 THEN 6060
6100   HOME : VTAB [6]
6120   ON C GOTO 3740,3880,4060,4220,4380,4520
6140   HOME : VTAB [6]
6160   PRINT "PLEASE BE CAREFUL IN TYPING IN YOUR DATA": PRINT
6180   PRINT "ALWAYS PUT '999' IN WHERE YOU DO NOT"
6200   PRINT "  HAVE ANY DATA TO INPUT."
6220   PRINT : PRINT "FOR THE PUSH-UP SCORES, IF YOU"
6240   PRINT "  USE THE MODIFIED PUSH-UP YOU MUST "
6260   PRINT "  TYPE A SPACE AND THEN 'MOD' AFTER"
6280   PRINT "  THE NUMBER."
6300   PRINT : PRINT "DO NOT USE THE SHIFT OR CONTROL KEYS"
6320   PRINT "  WHEN TYPING IN YOUR DATA."
6340   VTAB [22]: PRINT "HIT ANY KEY WHEN READY TO PROCEED": GET A$
6360   RETURN
```

Listing 6.2 Output program for fitness class.

```
10   REM      *  *  *  *  *  *  *  *  *  *
20   REM      *   OUTPUT PROGRAM FOR FITNESS CLASS
30   REM      *  *  *  *  *  *  *  *  *  *
100  HOME : VTAB [10]
110  DIM FP$[5],EX[4],P[8]
120  DIM NA$[2],AGE[2],IWT[2],BP$[2],SX$[2],PU[2],TU[2],ISAR[2],HR[2],SU
     [2]
130  DIM ASF[2,6],PU$[2],N$[30]
140  DIM DISU[5,2,2],NISU[5,2,7],O2[14],FM[21],FF[21]
150  DIM IMP[5,4],IGDE[5],CSC[2,5],DGDE[2,5,4]
160  DIM MO2[21],FO2[21],VM[26,14],VF[26,14]
170  HOME : VTAB [10]: INPUT "TESTING TIME 1 OR 2 ?? : ";TX
180  GOSUB 430: REM  READ NORMS FROM DATA STATEMENTS
190  GOSUB 2460: REM  SELECT CONTINUOUS REPORTS OR SELECT BY SUBJECT
200  Z9 = 0:R = R + 1
210  IF CZ = 1 THEN 280
220  HOME : INPUT "PRINT MORE FILES ?? ";Y$
230  IF Y$ < > "N" AND Y$ < > "Y" THEN 220
240  IF Y$ < > "Y" THEN 270
250  Q1 = 0:R = 0:RN = 2
260  GOTO 280
270  PRINT D$;"RUN HELLO"
280  GOSUB 720: REM  READ SUBJECT DATA FILE FROM DISK
290  GOSUB 2330: REM  CALC EST VO2 FROM STEP  TEST DATA
300  GOSUB 1140: REM  CALC % BODY FAT FROM SKINFOLDS
310  GOSUB 1320: REM  CALC VO2 PERCENTILE
320  GOSUB 1820: REM  CALC % FAT PERCENTILES
330  GOSUB 1990: REM  FIND AVERAGE % FAT FOR AGE AND SEX OF SUBJECT
340  GOSUB 2130: REM  CALC TARGET HEART RATE
350  GOSUB 1590: REM  CALC PERCENTILES FOR FITNESS TESTS
360  GOSUB 2730: REM  CALC IMPROVEMENT GRADE
370  GOSUB 2870: REM  CALC GRADE FOR FITNESS TESTS
380  GOSUB 3140: REM  DETERMINE BEST GRADE [IMPROVEMENT OR RAW SCORE]
390  GOSUB 3230: REM  CALC TOTAL GRADE [INCLUDE EXAMS]
400  GOSUB 7000: REM  PRINT REPORT FOR STUDENT
410  GOTO 200
420  END
430  FOR I = 1 TO 21: READ MO2[I]: NEXT I
440  FOR I = 1 TO 21: READ FO2[I]: NEXT I
450  FOR I = 1 TO 21: READ FM[I]: NEXT I
460  FOR I = 1 TO 21: READ FF[I]: NEXT I
470  FOR I = 1 TO 14: READ O2[I]: NEXT I
480  FOR A = 1 TO 5
490  FOR B = 1 TO 2
500  FOR C = 1 TO 7
510  READ NISU[A,B,C]
520  IF A < > 5 THEN 540
530  NISU[5,B,C] = NISU[5,B,C] / 12
540  NEXT C
550  NEXT B
560  NEXT A
570  GOSUB 2210
580  FOR A = 1 TO 5
590  FOR B = 1 TO 4
600  READ IMP[A,B]
610  NEXT B
620  NEXT A
630  FOR A = 1 TO 2
640  FOR B = 1 TO 5
650  FOR C = 1 TO 4
660  READ DGDE[A,B,C]
670  NEXT C
680  NEXT B
690  NEXT A
700  GOSUB 4000
710  RETURN
720  REM    INPUT ROUTINE:D$=CHR$[4]
```

(Cont.)

```
730   IF Q1 = 1 THEN 770
740   HOME : INPUT "COURSE AND SECTION NUMBER [16X-X]: ";CS$:FI$ = "F85" +
      CS$
750   Q1 = 1
760   PRINT :D$ = CHR$ [4]
770   IF CZ = 1 THEN 790
780   GOSUB 2500
790   PRINT D$;"OPEN ";FI$;",L400"
800   PRINT D$;"READ ";FI$;",R";R
810   FOR X1 = 1 TO TX
820   INPUT NA$[X1]
830   INPUT AGE[X1]
840   INPUT WT$:IWT[X1] = VAL [WT$]
850   INPUT SX$[X1]
860   INPUT BP$[X1]
870   FOR X3 = 1 TO 6
880   INPUT ASF$:ASF[X1,X3] = VAL [ASF$]
890   NEXT X3
900   FOR X2 = 1 TO 5
910   INPUT X$:DISU[X2,1,X1] = VAL [X$]
920   IF  LEN [X$] > 2 AND X2 = 3 THEN DISU[X2,1,X1] = VAL [ LEFT$ [X$,2
      ]] - 20
925   IF  LEN [X$] > 2 AND X2 = 3 THEN PU[X1] = VAL [ LEFT$ [X$,2]]
926   IF X2 = 3 AND PU[X1] = 99 THEN DISU[3,1,X1] = 999
930   IF X2 < 5 THEN 960
940   IF DISU[5,1,X1] > 3 AND DISU[5,1,X1] < 29 THEN 960
950   IF DISU[5,1,X1] > 30 THEN DISU[5,1,X1] = [ INT [DISU[5,1,X1] / 1760
      * 100]] / 100
960   IF X2 < > 2 THEN 1000
970   IF DISU[2,1,X1] = 999 THEN 1000
980   IF DISU[2,1,X1] > 60 THEN DISU[2,1,X1] = DISU[2,1,X1] / 4
990   IF DISU[2,1,X1] < 60 THEN DISU[2,1,X1] = DISU[2,1,X1] * 4
1000  NEXT X2
1010  NEXT X1
1020  FOR X4 = 1 TO 5
1030  INPUT FP$[X4]
1040  NEXT X4
1050  FOR X5 = 1 TO 4
1060  INPUT EX$:EX[X5] = VAL [EX$]
1070  NEXT X5
1080  SX$ = SX$[1]:AGE = AGE[1]
1090  WT = IWT[TX]
1100  SX = 2: IF SX$[1] = "M" THEN SX = 1
1110  NA$ = NA$[1]
1120   PRINT D$;"CLOSE ";FI$
1130   RETURN
1140  PCF = 0
1150   IF ASF[TX,1] = 999 THEN  RETURN
1160   IF SX$ = "F" THEN 1190
1170   F6 = ASF[TX,1] + ASF[TX,2] + ASF[TX,3] + ASF[TX,4] + ASF[TX,5] + AS
      F[TX,6]
1180  F4 = ASF[TX,1] + ASF[TX,2] + ASF[TX,3] + ASF[TX,5]
1190  F5 = ASF[TX,1] + ASF[TX,2] + ASF[TX,3] + ASF[TX,4] + ASF[TX,5]
1200  F3 = ASF[TX,1] + ASF[TX,3] + ASF[TX,5]
1210  PCF = 0
1220   IF S2 = 999 OR S8 = 999 OR S4 = 999 THEN  RETURN
1230  F6 = [.21661 * F6] - [.00029 * F6 ^ 2] + .13341 * AGE - 5.72888
1240  F4 = [.27784 * F4] - [.00053 * F4 ^ 2] + .12437 * AGE - 3.28791
1250  F5 = [.29731 * F5] - [.00053 * F5 ^ 2] + .03037 * AGE - .63054
1260  F3 = [.41563 * F3] - [.00112 * F3 ^ 2] + .03661 * AGE + 4.03653
1270   IF SX$ = "F" THEN PCF = F5
1280   IF SX$ = "F" AND ASF[TX,4] = 999 THEN PCF = F3
1290   IF SX$ = "M" THEN PCF = F6
1300   IF SX$ = "M" AND ASF[TX,4] = 999 THEN PCF = F4
1310   RETURN
1320   REM
1330   IF DISU[2,1,TX] = 999 THEN  RETURN
1340  Z1 = 1
1350   IF SX$ = "M" THEN 1430
```

(Cont.)

```
1360  FOR I = 1 TO 7
1370 D1F = (VO2 - FO2(I + Z1)) / (FO2(I - 1 + Z1) - FO2(I + Z1))
1380  IF VO2 >  = FO2(I + Z1) THEN 1400
1390  NEXT I
1400  GOSUB 1500
1410 OP = PE
1420  RETURN
1430  FOR I = 1 TO 7
1440 D1F = (VO2 - MO2(I + Z1)) / (MO2(I - 1 + Z1) - MO2(I + Z1))
1450  IF VO2 >  = MO2(I + Z1) THEN 1470
1460  NEXT I
1470  GOSUB 1500
1480 OP = PE
1490  RETURN
1500  REM
1510  P(0) = 0
1520  P(1) = 5:P(2) = 15:P(3) = 30:P(4) = 50:P(5) = 75:P(6) = 85:P(7) = 9
      5:P(8) = 100
1530  I = 8 - I
1540  PE = (P(I + 1) - P(I)) * D1F + P(I)
1550  IF PE > 100 THEN PE = 100
1560  PE =  INT (PE)
1570  IF PE < 0 THEN PE = 0
1580  RETURN
1590  FOR QQ = 1 TO TX
1600  FOR TT = 1 TO 5
1610  FOR I = 1 TO 7
1620  IF TT = 2 THEN 1690
1630  D1F = (DISU(TT,1,QQ) - NISU(TT,SX,I)) / (NISU(TT,SX,I - 1) - NISU(T
      T,SX,I))
1640  IF DISU(TT,1,QQ) < NISU(TT,SX,1) THEN 1670
1650  PE = 99
1660  GOTO 1780
1670  IF DISU(TT,1,QQ) >  = NISU(TT,SX,I) THEN 1750
1675  IF I = 7 THEN PE = 0: GOTO 1780
1680  GOTO 1770
1690  IF DISU(TT,1,QQ) > NISU(TT,SX,1) THEN 1720
1700  PE = 99
1710  GOTO 1780
1720  D1F = (NISU(TT,SX,I) - DISU(TT,1,QQ)) / (NISU(TT,SX,I) - NISU(TT,SX
      ,I - 1))
1730  IF DISU(TT,1,QQ) <  = NISU(TT,SX,I) THEN 1750
1735  IF I = 7 THEN PE = 0: GOTO 1780
1740  GOTO 1770
1750  GOSUB 1500
1760  GOTO 1780
1770  NEXT I
1780 DISU(TT,2,QQ) = PE
1790  NEXT TT
1800  NEXT QQ
1810  RETURN
1820  REM
1830  IF PCF = 0 THEN  RETURN
1840  IF SX$ = "M" THEN 1920
1850  FOR I = 1 TO 7
1860 D1F = (PCF - FF(I - 1 + Z1)) / (FF(I + Z1) - FF(I + Z1 - 1))
1870  IF PCF <  = FF(I + Z1) THEN 1890
1880  NEXT I
1890  GOSUB 1500
1900 FP = PE
1910  RETURN
1920  FOR I = 1 TO 7
1930 D1F = (PCF - FM(I - 1 + Z1)) / (FM(I + Z1) - FM(I - 1 + Z1))
1940  IF PCF <  = FM(I + Z1) THEN 1960
1950  NEXT I
1960  GOSUB 1500
1970 FP = PE
1980  RETURN
1990  REM
```

(Cont.)

```
2000  IF SX$ = "M" THEN 2070
2010  IF AGE < 18 THEN XPF = 21
2020  IF AGE > = 18 THEN XPF = 25
2030  IF AGE > 22 THEN XPF = 29
2040  IF AGE > 29 THEN XPF = 30
2050  IF AGE > 39 THEN XPF = 32
2060  RETURN
2070  IF AGE < 18 THEN XPF = 12
2080  IF AGE > = 18 THEN XPF = 13
2090  IF AGE > 22 THEN XPF = 14
2100  IF AGE > 29 THEN XPF = 16
2110  IF AGE > 39 THEN XPF = 21
2120  RETURN
2130  RHR = 70
2140  M4 = .60
2150  M5 = .75
2160  M6 = .85
2165  M8 = 220 - AGE
2170  MIN = RHR + M4 * [M8 - RHR]
2180  TAR = RHR + M5 * [M8 - RHR]
2190  MAX = RHR + M6 * [M8 - RHR]
2200  RETURN
2210  REM  READ STEP TEST TABLES
2220  FOR J = 1 TO 26
2230  FOR I = 0 TO 13
2240  READ VM[J,I]
2250  NEXT I
2260  NEXT J
2270  FOR J = 1 TO 23
2280  FOR I = 0 TO 12
2290  READ VF[J,I]
2300  NEXT I
2310  NEXT J
2320  RETURN
2330  REM  STEP TEST ROUTINE
2340  HR = DISU[2,1,TX]
2350  IF HR = 0 THEN  RETURN
2360  IF HR > 60 THEN HR = HR / 4
2370  WW = INT [WT / 10] - 11
2380  IF SX$ = "F" THEN WW = INT [WT / 10] - 7
2390  IF WW < 1 OR WW > 13 THEN  RETURN
2400  IF SX$ = "M" THEN HR = 19 - [HR - 19]
2410  IF SX$ = "F" THEN HR = 23 - [HR - 23]
2420  IF HR > 26 OR HR < 1 THEN  RETURN
2430  VO2 = VM[HR,WW]
2440  IF SX$ = "F" THEN VO2 = VF[HR,WW]
2450  RETURN
2460  HOME : INPUT "PRINT ALL <A> OR SELECT <S> FILES ? : ";Y$
2470  CZ = 0
2480  IF Y$ = "A" THEN CZ = 1
2490  RETURN
2500  D$ = CHR$ [4]
2510  HOME
2520  CT$ = "CT" + FI$
2530  PRINT D$;"OPEN ";CT$
2540  PRINT D$;"READ ";CT$
2550  INPUT CX
2560  PRINT D$;"CLOSE ";CT$
2570  PRINT D$;"OPEN ";FI$;",L400,D1"
2580  VTAB [1]
2590  FOR I = 1 TO CX
2600  PRINT D$;"READ ";FI$;",R";I
2610  INPUT N$[I]
2620  NEXT I
2630  PRINT D$;"CLOSE ";FI$
2640  FOR I = 1 TO CX
2650  PRINT I;". ";N$[I]
2660  IF I < > 20 THEN 2700
2670  PRINT
```

(Cont.)

```
2680   PRINT "HIT ANY KEY WHEN READY": GET Y$
2690   HOME : VTAB [5]
2700   NEXT I
2710   VTAB [20]: INPUT "SELECT FILE BY NUMBER : ";R
2720   RETURN
2730   REM   IMPROVEMENT ROUTINE
2740   FOR I = 1 TO 5
2750   CSC[1,I] = 0
2760   D1F = DISU[I,1,2] - DISU[I,1,1]
2770   IF I = 2 THEN D1F =  ABS [D1F]
2780   FOR J = 1 TO 4
2790   IF D1F > IMP[I,4] THEN 2820
2800   CSC[1,I] = 1
2810   GOTO 2850
2820   IF D1F < IMP[I,J] THEN 2840
2830   CSC[1,I] = [5 - J]: GOTO 2850
2840   NEXT J
2850   NEXT I
2860   RETURN
2870   REM   GRADING ROUTINE
2880   FOR I = 1 TO 5
2890   FOR J = 1 TO 4
2900   IF I = 2 THEN 3010
2910   IF DISU[I,1,2] > DGDE[SX,I,4] THEN 2940
2920   CSC[2,I] = 1
2930   GOTO 3120
2940   IF DISU[I,1,2] < DGDE[SX,I,1] THEN 2970
2950   CSC[2,I] = 4
2960   GOTO 3120
2970   IF DISU[I,1,2] < DGDE[SX,I,J] THEN 3110
2980   D1F = [DISU[I,1,2] - DGDE[SX,I,J]] / [DGDE[SX,I,J - 1] - DGDE[SX,I,
       J]]
2990   CSC[2,I] = [5 - J] + D1F
3000   GOTO 3120
3010   IF DISU[I,1,2] > DGDE[SX,2,1] THEN 3040
3020   CSC[2,I] = 4
3030   GOTO 3120
3040   IF DISU[I,1,2] < DGDE[SX,2,4] THEN 3070
3050   CSC[2,I] = 1
3060   GOTO 3120
3070   IF DISU[I,1,2] > DGDE[SX,I,J] THEN 3110
3080   D1F = [DGDE[SX,I,J] - DISU[I,1,2]] / [DGDE[SX,I,J] - DGDE[SX,I,J -
       1]]
3090   CSC[2,I] = [5 - J] + D1F
3100   GOTO 3120
3110   NEXT J
3120   NEXT I
3130   RETURN
3140   REM   BEST GRADE
3150   FOR I = 1 TO 5
3160   IF CSC[1,I] > CSC[2,I] THEN 3190
3170   BG[I] = CSC[2,I] *  VAL [FP$[I]]
3180   GOTO 3200
3190   BG[I] = CSC[1,I] *  VAL [FP$[I]]
3200   IF  VAL [FP$[I]] > 1 THEN BG[I] = BG[I] / 100
3210   NEXT I
3220   RETURN
3230   REM   GRADE CALCULATIONS
3240   G = 0
3250   FOR I = 1 TO 4
3260   G = G + BG[I]
3270   NEXT I
3280   IF EX[2] = 999 THEN EX[2] = 0
3290   IF EX[4] = 999 THEN EX[4] = 0
3300   G = G + [[EX[1] - 59] / 10] * [EX[2] / 100] + [[EX[3] - 59] / 10] *
       [EX[4] / 100]
3310   RETURN
4000   LA$[1] = "FLEXIBILITY":LA$[2] = "STEP TEST [HR/MIN]":LA$[3] = "PUSH
       -UPS":LA$[4] = "SIT-UPS":LA$[5] = "12 MIN RUN [MILES]"
```

(Cont.)

```
4010  RETURN
4020  FOR I = 1 TO 5
4030  FOR J = 1 TO 2
4040  FOR K = 1 TO 2
4050  DISU(I,J,K) = 0
4060  CSC(J,I) = 0
4070  NEXT K
4080  NEXT J
4090  NEXT I
4100  RETURN
4110  S1$ = "       ":A$ = " "
4120  X = LEN ( STR$ (DISU(I,1,1))):Y = LEN (S1$): IF X + Y > 10 THEN 4
      150
4130  S1$ = S1$ + A$
4140  GOTO 4120
4150  S2$ = "       "
4160  X = LEN ( STR$ (DISU(I,2,1))):Y = LEN (S2$): IF X + Y > 10 THEN 4
      190
4170  S2$ = S2$ + A$
4180  GOTO 4160
4190  S3$ = "       "
4200  X = LEN ( STR$ (DISU(I,1,2))):Y = LEN (S3$): IF X + Y > 10 THEN 4
      230
4210  S3$ = S3$ + A$
4220  GOTO 4200
4230  RETURN
7000  REM  OUTPUT SUBROUTINE
7005  D$ = CHR$ (4)
7010  PRINT D$;"PR#1"
7020  PRINT  TAB( 29);"IOWA STATE UNIVERSITY"
7030  PRINT  TAB( 21);"PE 163/165 PHYSICAL FITNESS/AEROBIC DANCE"
7040  PRINT
7050  PRINT  TAB( 10);"FITNESS ASSESSMENT FOR ";NA$;"    ";
7060  DT$ = "SEPTEMBER 1985"
7070  PRINT " DATA RECORDED ";DT$;"."
7080  PRINT
7090  PRINT  TAB( 10);"AGE : ";AGE;"    ";
7100  IF WT = 0 OR WT = 999 THEN 7120
7110  PRINT "WEIGHT : ";WT;" POUNDS "
7120  IF PCF = 0 THEN 7400
7130  PCF = INT (PCF * 10) / 10
7140  PRINT : PRINT  TAB( 10);"USING THE SKINFOLD MEASUREMENTS, YOUR PER
      CENT BODY FAT IS ";PCF;" %"
7150  IF F1 = 0 THEN 7180
7160  F1 = INT (F1 * 10) / 10
7170  PRINT  TAB( 10);"THE UNDER WATER WEIGHING DATA RESULTED IN A VALUE
      OF ";F1;" % BODY FAT."
7180  FP = INT (FP * 10) / 10
7190  PRINT  TAB( 10);"BASED UPON NATIONAL NORMS FOR YOUR AGE GROUP, YOU
      R PERCENTILE SCORE "
7200  PRINT  TAB( 15);"FOR THE PER CENT FAT DATA IS   ";FP;"."
7210  PRINT
7220  PRINT  TAB( 10);"THE AVERAGE PER CENT BODY FAT FOR YOUR AGE AND SE
      X IS ";XPF;" %."
7230  IF WT = 999 THEN 7420
7240  IW = (100 - PCF) * WT
7250  IF SX$ = "M" THEN JW = IW / .85
7260  LBW = .77
7270  IF AGE < 25 THEN LBW = .77
7280  IF SX$ = "F" THEN JW = IW / LBW
7290  FB = 100 - (100 * LBW)
7300  IF PCF < 15 AND SX$ = "M" THEN JW = WT
7310  IF PCF < FB AND SX$ = "F" THEN JW = WT
7320  JW = INT (JW * 10) / 10
7330  IF JW < 1000 THEN 7360
7340  JW = INT (JW / 100)
7350  IF PCF = 0 THEN 7420
7360  PRINT  TAB( 10);"BASED UPON THE PER CENT FAT CALCULATIONS, YOUR ID
      EAL"
```

(Cont.)

```
7370  PRINT  TAB[ 15];" BODY WEIGHT IS ";JW;" POUNDS."
7380  PRINT  TAB[ 10];"THIS RESULT WAS BASED ON IDEAL PER CENT FAT VALUE
      S "
7390  PRINT  TAB[ 15];"OF 15 AND ";FB;" FOR MEN AND WOMEN RESPECTIVELY."
7400  REM
7410  PRINT
7420  IF HR = O OR HR = 999 THEN 7590
7430  PRINT  TAB[ 10];"THE STEP TEST WAS USED TO ESTIMATE YOUR MAXIMUM"
7440  PRINT  TAB[ 15];" CAPACITY TO USE OXYGEN DURING EXERCISE.  THIS IS
      "
7450  PRINT  TAB[ 15]" RECOGNIZED AS THE BEST INDICATOR OF CARDIOVASCULA
      R FITNESS."
7460  PRINT  TAB[ 10];"THE SCORE IS THE MAXIMUM VOLUME [IN MILLILITERS]
      OF OXYGEN""
7470  PRINT  TAB[ 15];" YOUR BODY CAN USE PER KILOGRAM OF BODY WEIGHT PE
      R MINUTE."
7480  IF VO2 > 70 THEN 2370
7490  REM
7500  VO2 =  INT [VO2 * 10] / 10
7510  PRINT : PRINT  TAB[ 10];"YOUR SCORE WAS ";VO2;" ML/KG/MIN."
7520  PRINT  TAB[ 10];"BASED UPON NATIONAL NORMS FOR YOUR AGE GROUP, YOU
      R PERCENTILE SCORE"
7530  OP =  INT [OP * 10] / 10
7540  IF AGE = O THEN 7590
7550  PRINT  TAB[ 15];"FOR THE MAXIMUM OXYGEN CONSUMPTION TEST WAS   ";OP
      ;"."
7560  PRINT
7570  PRINT  TAB[ 10];"YOUR ESTIMATED MAXIMUM ATTAINABLE HEART RATE BASE
      D UPON YOUR AGE"
7580  PRINT  TAB[ 15];"IS ";220 - AGE;" BEATS/MINUTE."
7590  IF BP$[TX] = "999" THEN 7610
7600  PRINT  TAB[ 10];"YOUR BLOOD PRESSURE WAS ";BP$[TX]
7610  PRINT
7620  PRINT  TAB[ 10];"FOLLOWING ARE YOUR RAW SCORES AND PERCENTILE"
7630  PRINT  TAB[ 15];"SCORES FOR THE PUSH-UP, SIT-UP, AND 12 MINUTE"
7640  PRINT  TAB[ 15];"RUN FITNESS TESTS.  THE PERCENTILE SCORES WERE"
7650  PRINT  TAB[ 15];"CALCULATED FROM ISU STUDENT DATA.": PRINT
7660  PRINT  TAB[ 26];"T1 SCORE";"       ";"T1 %";"       ";"T2 SCORE";"
      ";"T2 %": PRINT
7665  FOR I = 1 TO 2:DISU[3,1,I] = PU[I]: NEXT I
7670  FOR I = 1 TO 4
7680  PRINT  TAB[ 8];LA$[I];
7690  GOSUB 4110
7700  PRINT  TAB[ 30];DISU[I,1,1];S1$;DISU[I,2,1];S2$;DISU[I,1,2];S3$;DI
      SU[I,2,2]
7710  NEXT I
7720  PRINT : PRINT  TAB[ 10];"* * * * * * * *  EXERCISE PRESCRIPTION
      * * * * * * * * * ": PRINT
7730  TAR =  INT [TAR]
7740  PRINT  TAB[ 10];"DURING YOUR EXERCISE ACTIVITY YOU NEED TO KEEP YO
      UR HEART"
7750  PRINT  TAB[ 15];" RATE AT APPROXIMATELY ";TAR;" BEATS PER MINUTE F
      OR"
7760  PRINT  TAB[ 15];" OPTIMUM EFFICIENCY IN IMPROVING CARDIOVASCULAR F
      ITNESS."
7770  MIN =  INT [MIN]:MAX =  INT [MAX]
7780  PRINT : PRINT  TAB[ 10];"THE MINIMUM EXERCISE HEART RATE NECESSARY
      TO IMPROVE"
7790  PRINT  TAB[ 15];" YOUR FITNESS IS ";MIN;", WHEREAS YOU SHOULD NOT
      EXCEED A "
7800  PRINT  TAB[ 15];" HEART RATE OF ";MAX;" DURING EXERCISE."
7810  PRINT : PRINT  TAB[ 10];"THE EXERCISE HEART RATE SHOULD BE MAINTAI
      NED FOR 20 "
7820  PRINT  TAB[ 15];"MINUTES FOR THE MAXIMUM TRAINING BENEFIT."
7830  XX = 4:A = O:B = O
7840  IF FP$[5] = "999" OR FP$[5] = "O" THEN XX = 4
7850  FOR I = 1 TO XX
7860  A = CSC[1,I] + A:B = CSC[2,I] + B: NEXT I
7870  G =  INT [G * 100] / 100
```

(Cont.)

```
7880   PRINT : PRINT G;"     ";[ INT [A / XX * 100]] / 100;"     ";[ INT [B /
       XX * 100]] / 100
7890   PRINT  CHR$ [12]
7900   PRINT D$;"PR#0"
7910   GOSUB 4020: REM   ZERO ARRAYS
7920   PRINT : RETURN
7930   DATA   54,49,46,36,32,28,24
7940   DATA   53,45,39,33,29,25,23
7950   DATA   43,38,34,30,27,24,20
7960   DATA   55,45,39,34,30,26,22
7970   DATA   49,43,37,33,29,26,22
7980   DATA   46,38,32,27,24,20,18
7990   DATA   6,9,14,18,22,25,30
8000   DATA   8,10,15,19,23,27,32
8010   DATA   9,11,16,21,24,29,34
8020   DATA   9,14,18,22,24,28,35
8030   DATA   10,16,20,23,26,31,37
8040   DATA   11,18,21,25,30,34,41
8050   DATA   .6,.9,1.2,1.5,1.8,2.1,2.4,2.8,3.2,3.5,3.8,4.2,4.6,5.0
8060   DATA   9,7.5,6.5,4,2,1,0,10,8.5,7.5,5,3,1.5,.5
8070   DATA   114,120,129,134,140,150,155,114,120,129,134,140,150,155
8080   DATA   62,54,51,42,32,19,13,31,23,20,12,8,5,3
8090   DATA     86,79,76,67,64,57,49,54,50,47,42,38,35,32
8100   DATA   24,22.8,22.2,20.9,19.1,16.8,15,22.8,21,20.4,18.5,16.7,15,14.
       4
8110   REM   **** MENS ****
8120   DATA   45,33,33,33,33,33,32,32,32,32,32,32,32,32,32
8130   DATA   44,34,34,34,34,33,33,33,33,33,33,33,33,33
8140   DATA   43,35,35,35,34,34,34,34,34,34,34,34,34,34
8150   DATA   42,36,35,35,35,35,35,35,35,35,35,35,34,34
8160   DATA   41,36,36,36,36,36,36,36,36,36,36,36,35,35
8170   DATA   40,37,37,37,37,37,37,37,37,36,36,36,36,36
8180   DATA   39,38,38,38,38,38,38,38,38,38,38,38,37,37
8190   DATA   38,39,39,39,39,39,39,39,39,39,39,39,38,38
8200   DATA   37,41,40,40,40,40,40,40,40,40,40,40,39,39
8210   DATA   36,42,42,41,41,41,41,41,41,41,41,41,40,40
8220   DATA   35,43,43,42,42,42,42,42,42,42,42,42,42,41
8230   DATA   34,44,44,43,43,43,43,43,43,43,43,43,43,43
8240   DATA   33,46,45,45,45,45,45,44,44,44,44,44,44,44
8250   DATA   32,47,47,46,46,46,46,46,46,46,46,46,46,46
8260   DATA   31,48,48,48,47,47,47,47,47,47,47,47,47,47
8270   DATA   30,50,49,49,49,48,48,48,48,48,48,48,48,48
8280   DATA   29,52,51,51,51,50,50,50,50,50,50,50,50,50
8290   DATA   28,53,53,53,53,52,52,52,52,52,52,51,51,51
8300   DATA   27,55,55,55,54,54,54,54,54,54,53,53,53,52
8310   DATA   26,57,57,56,56,56,56,56,56,56,55,55,54,54
8320   DATA   25,59,59,58,58,58,58,58,58,58,56,56,55,55
8330   DATA   24,60,60,60,60,60,60,60,59,59,58,58,57,00
8340   DATA   23,62,62,61,61,61,61,61,60,60,60,59,00,00
8350   DATA   22,64,64,63,63,63,63,62,62,61,61,00,00,00
8360   DATA   21,66,66,65,65,65,64,64,64,62,00,00,00,00
8370   DATA   20,68,68,67,67,67,66,66,65,00,00,00,00,00
8380   REM   **** WOMENS ****
8390   DATA   45,00,00,00,00,00,00,00,00,00,00,29,29,29
8400   DATA   44,00,00,00,00,00,00,00,30,30,30,30,30
8410   DATA   43,00,00,00,00,00,00,31,31,31,31,31,31
8420   DATA   42,00,00,32,32,32,32,32,32,32,32,32,32
8430   DATA   41,00,00,33,33,33,33,33,33,33,33,33,33
8440   DATA   40,00,00,34,34,34,34,34,34,34,34,34,34
8450   DATA   39,00,00,35,35,35,35,35,35,35,35,35,35
8460   DATA   38,00,00,36,36,36,36,36,36,36,36,36,36
8470   DATA   37,00,00,37,37,37,37,37,37,37,37,37,37
8480   DATA   36,00,37,38,38,38,38,38,38,38,38,38,38
8490   DATA   35,38,38,39,39,39,39,39,39,39,39,39,39
8500   DATA   34,39,39,40,40,40,40,40,40,40,40,40,40
8510   DATA   33,40,40,41,41,41,41,41,41,41,41,41,41
8520   DATA   32,41,41,42,42,42,42,42,42,42,42,42,42
8530   DATA   31,42,42,43,43,43,43,43,43,43,43,43,43
8540   DATA   30,43,43,44,44,44,44,44,44,44,44,44,44
```

(Cont.)

```
8550    DATA   29,44,44,45,45,45,45,45,45,45,45,45,45
8560    DATA   28,45,45,46,46,46,47,47,47,47,47,47,47
8570    DATA   27,46,46,47,48,48,49,49,49,49,49,00,00
8580    DATA   26,47,48,49,50,50,51,51,51,51,00,00,00
8590    DATA   25,49,50,51,52,52,53,53,00,00,00,00,00
8600    DATA   24,51,52,53,54,54,55,00,00,00,00,00,00
8610    DATA   23,53,54,55,56,56,57,00,00,00,00,00,00
8615    REM    IMPROVEMENT STANDARDS [ISU]
8620    DATA      3,2,1,0,15,10,5,1,15,11,9,5,11,8,4,3,.23,.18,.14,.10
8625    REM    NORMS FOR PERCENTILES [ISU]
8627    REM    **** MENS ****
8630    DATA      7,4,1,-2,124,143,157,162,54,43,32,23,80,70,60,55,2,1.8,1.6
        ,1.4
8635    REM    **** WOMENS ****
8640    DATA      8.75,5.75,2.75,.75,124,143,157,162,43,33,23,19,51,44,37,32
        ,1.8,1.6,1.4,1.25
```

Listing 6.3 Health related physical fitness text program.

```
100    REM  *  *  *  *  *  *  *  *  *  *  *  *  *  *  *  *
102    REM  *  *  HEALTH RELATED PHYSICAL FITNESS TEST PROGRAM
104    REM  *  *  *  *  *  *  *  *  *  *  *  *  *  *  *  *
120    DIM F$[13]
140    DIM ID$[40,13],RC[40]
160    VTAB [10]: HTAB [1]: INPUT "TODAY'S DATE [MO/DAY/YEAR] : ";DAY$
180    HOME : INPUT "FILE NAME FOR DATA : ";FF$
200    HOME
220 CF$ = "CT" + FF$
240    VTAB [1]: HTAB [6]: PRINT "HEALTH RELATED PHYSICAL FITNESS"
260    VTAB [2]: HTAB [18]: PRINT "TEST"
280    VTAB [6]: HTAB [5]: PRINT "1 - INPUT NEW STUDENT DATA"
300    VTAB [8]: HTAB [5]: PRINT "2 - CHANGE STUDENT DATA"
320    VTAB [10]: HTAB [5]: PRINT "3 - DISPLAY RESULTS"
340    VTAB [12]: HTAB [5]: PRINT "4 - HARD COPY OF RESULTS"
360    VTAB [14]: HTAB [5]: PRINT "5 - END"
380    VTAB [18]: HTAB [5]: PRINT "SELECT ONE : "
400    VTAB [18]: HTAB [20]: INPUT " ";A
420    IF A < 1 OR A > 5 THEN 400
440    ON A GOSUB 500,2320,3920,7300,480
460    HOME : GOTO 240
480    END
500    REM  INPUT ROUTINE
520    ONERR  GOTO 620
540 D$ = CHR$ [4]
560    PRINT D$;"OPEN ";CF$
580    PRINT D$;"READ ";CF$
600    INPUT R
620    PRINT D$;"CLOSE ";CF$
640    GOSUB 1940: REM  SCREEN SET-UP
660    GOSUB 1000: REM  GET DATA SUBROUTINE
680 R = R + 1: REM  INCREMENT FILE COUNTER
700    PRINT D$;"OPEN ";FF$;",L200": REM  WRITE DATA TO DISK FILE
720    PRINT D$;"WRITE ";FF$;",R";R
740    FOR I = 1 TO 13
760    PRINT F$[I]
780    NEXT I
800    PRINT D$;"CLOSE ";FF$
820    PRINT D$;"DELETE";CF$
840    PRINT D$;"OPEN";CF$
860    PRINT D$;"WRITE";CF$
880    PRINT R
900    PRINT D$;"CLOSE";CF$
920    HOME
940    VTAB [12]: HTAB [10]: INPUT "ANOTHER CHILD ?? ";Q$
960    IF Q$ = "Y" THEN 640
```

(Cont.)

```
980  GOTO 105: REM  RETURN TO MAIN MENU
1000  REM  INPUT ROUTINE
1020  POKE 216,0
1040 SET = 0
1060  VTAB [4]: HTAB [16]: INPUT " ";F$[1]
1080  IF SET = 0 THEN 1120
1100  GOTO 1780: REM  GET DATA
1120  VTAB [5]: HTAB [17]: INPUT " ";F$[2]
1140  IF SET = 0 THEN 1180
1160  GOTO 1780
1180  VTAB [6]: HTAB [26]: INPUT " ";F$[3]
1200  IF SET = 0 THEN 1240
1220  GOTO 1780
1240  VTAB [7]: HTAB [30]: INPUT " ";F$[4]
1260  IF SET = 0 THEN 1300
1280  GOTO 1780
1300  VTAB [8]: HTAB [15]: INPUT " ";F$[5]
1320  IF SET = 0 THEN 1360
1340  GOTO 1780
1360  REM
1380  VTAB [9]: HTAB [14]: INPUT " ";F$[12]: HTAB [16]: INPUT "WT : ";F$
      [13]
1400  IF SET = 0 THEN 1440
1420  GOTO 1780
1440  VTAB [11]: HTAB [36]: INPUT " ";F$[6]
1460  IF SET = 0 THEN 1500
1480  GOTO 1780
1500  VTAB [13]: HTAB [34]: INPUT " ";F$[7]
1520  IF SET = 0 THEN 1560
1540  GOTO 1780
1560  VTAB [15]: HTAB [24]: INPUT " ";F$[8]
1580  IF SET = 0 THEN 1620
1600  GOTO 1780
1620  VTAB [17]: HTAB [28]: INPUT " ";F$[9]
1640  IF SET = 0 THEN 1680
1660  GOTO 1780
1680  VTAB [18]: HTAB [34]: INPUT " ";F$[10]
1700  IF SET = 0 THEN 1740
1720  GOTO 1780
1740  VTAB [20]: HTAB [32]: INPUT " ";F$[11]
1760 SET = 0
1780  REM  DATA INPUT ROUTINE
1800  VTAB [22]: HTAB [17]: INPUT " ";Q$
1820  IF Q$ = "Y" THEN RETURN
1840  VTAB [23]: HTAB [28]: INPUT " ";N$:N = VAL [N$]
1860  IF N < 1 OR N > 12 THEN 1840
1880 SET = 1
1900  ON N GOTO 1060,1120,1180,1240,1300,1380,1440,1500,1560,1620,1680,1
      740
1920  GOTO 1780
1940  REM  SCREEN ROUTINE
1960  HOME
1980  VTAB [1]: HTAB [5]: PRINT "HEALTH RELATED PHYSICAL FITNESS"
2000  VTAB [2]: HTAB [18]: PRINT "TEST"
2020  VTAB [4]: HTAB [1]: PRINT "1 - LAST NAME : "
2040  VTAB [5]: HTAB [1]: PRINT "2 - FIRST NAME : "
2060  VTAB [6]: HTAB [5]: PRINT "3 - GROUP NUMBER : "
2080  VTAB [7]: HTAB [5]: PRINT "4 - AGE [MONTHS] : "
2100  VTAB [8]: HTAB [5]: PRINT "5 - SEX : "
2120  VTAB [9]: HTAB [5]: PRINT "6 - HT : ": VTAB [9]: HTAB [16]: PRINT
      "WT : "
2140  VTAB [11]: HTAB [10]: PRINT "7 - MILE RUN [MIN.SEC] : "
2160  VTAB [13]: HTAB [10]: PRINT "8 - 9 MIN RUN [YARDS] : "
2180  VTAB [15]: HTAB [10]: PRINT "9 - SITUPS : "
2200  VTAB [17]: HTAB [10]: PRINT "10 - TRICEPS SF : "
2220  VTAB [18]: HTAB [10]: PRINT "11 - SUBSCAPULAR SF : "
2240  VTAB [20]: HTAB [10]: PRINT "12 - SIT AND REACH : "
2260  VTAB [22]: HTAB [1]: PRINT "DATA CORRECT ?? "
2280  VTAB [23]: HTAB [1]: PRINT "CORRECT WHICH DATA POINT ?"
```

(Cont.)

```
2300  RETURN
2320  REM  CHANGE DATA ROUTINE
2340  SET = 0:R = 1:I = 1
2360  ONERR  GOTO 2620
2380  HOME : VTAB [10]: HTAB [10]: INPUT "WHICH GROUP ? ";G
2400  D$ -  CHR$ (4)
2420  R - 1:I - 1
2440  PRINT D$;"OPEN ";FF$;",L200"
2460  PRINT D$;"READ ";FF$;",R";R
2480  FOR J - 1 TO 13
2500  INPUT ID$[I,J]
2520  NEXT J
2540  IF ID$[I,3] <  > STR$ [G] THEN 2580
2560  RC[I] - R:I - I + 1:K - I
2580  R - R + 1
2600  GOTO 2460
2620  PRINT D$;"CLOSE ";FF$
2640  REM
2660  SET - 3: GOSUB 5000
2680  FOR I - 1 TO K - 1
2700  IF L$ <  > ID$[I,1] THEN 2960
2720  IF M$ <  > ID$[I,2] THEN 2960
2740  REM
2760  POKE 216,0
2780  GOSUB 1940
2800  GOSUB 3660
2820  GOSUB 3540
2840  PRINT D$;"OPEN ";FF$;",L200"
2860  PRINT D$;"WRITE ";FF$;",R";RC[I]
2880  FOR J - 1 TO 13
2900  PRINT ID$[I,J]
2920  NEXT J
2940  PRINT D$;"CLOSE ";FF$
2960  NEXT I
2980  HOME : VTAB [10]: HTAB [5]: INPUT "CHANGE ANOTHER ? ";Q$
3000  IF Q$ - "Y" THEN 2640
3020  GOTO 105
3040  RETURN
3060  VTAB [4]: HTAB [19]: INPUT " ";ID$[I,1]
3080  GOTO 3520
3100  VTAB [5]: HTAB [17]: INPUT " ";ID$[I,2]
3120  GOTO 3520
3140  VTAB [6]: HTAB [26]: INPUT " ";ID$[I,3]
3160  GOTO 3520
3180  VTAB [7]: HTAB [30]: INPUT " ";ID$[I,4]
3200  GOTO 3520
3220  VTAB [8]: HTAB [15]: INPUT " ";ID$[I,5]
3240  GOTO 3520
3260  VTAB [9]: HTAB [14]: INPUT " ";ID$[I,12]: VTAB [9]: HTAB [28]: INPUT
      "WT : ";ID$[I,13]
3280  GOTO 3520
3300  VTAB [11]: HTAB [36]: INPUT " ";ID$[I,6]
3320  GOTO 3520
3340  VTAB [13]: HTAB [34]: INPUT " ";ID$[I,7]
3360  GOTO 3520
3380  VTAB [15]: HTAB [24]: INPUT " ";ID$[I,8]
3400  GOTO 3520
3420  VTAB [17]: HTAB [28]: INPUT " ";ID$[I,9]
3440  GOTO 1780
3460  VTAB [18]: HTAB [34]: INPUT " ";ID$[I,10]
3480  GOTO 3520
3500  VTAB [20]: HTAB [32]: INPUT " ";ID$[I,11]
3520  REM
3540  VTAB [22]: HTAB [17]: INPUT " ";Q$
3560  IF Q$ - "Y" THEN  RETURN
3580  VTAB [23]: HTAB [28]: INPUT " ";N$:N - VAL [N$]
3600  IF N < 1 OR N > 12 THEN 3580
3620  ON N GOTO 3060,3100,3140,3180,3220,3260,3300,3340,3380,3420,3460,3
      500
```

(Cont.)

```
3640   GOTO 3520
3660   VTAB [4]: HTAB [16]: PRINT ID$[I,1]
3680   VTAB [5]: HTAB [17]: PRINT ID$[I,2]
3700   VTAB [6]: HTAB [26]: PRINT ID$[I,3]
3720   VTAB [7]: HTAB [30]: PRINT ID$[I,4]
3740   VTAB [8]: HTAB [15]: PRINT ID$[I,5]
3760   VTAB [9]: HTAB [14]: PRINT ID$[I,12]: VTAB [9]: HTAB [28]: PRINT I
       D$[I,13]
3780   VTAB [11]: HTAB [36]: PRINT ID$[I,6]
3800   VTAB [13]: HTAB [34]: PRINT ID$[I,7]
3820   VTAB [15]: HTAB [24]: PRINT ID$[I,8]
3840   VTAB [17]: HTAB [28]: PRINT ID$[I,9]
3860   VTAB [18]: HTAB [34]: PRINT ID$[I,10]
3880   VTAB [20]: HTAB [32]: PRINT ID$[I,11]
3900   RETURN
3902   REM  *   *   *   *   *   *   *   *   *   *   *   *   *   *   *

3903   REM  *   LINES 4040 TO 4640 READ IN 3 DATA FILES CONTAINING THE
3904   REM  *   TABLES OF PERCENTILES IN THE AAHPERD HEALTH RELATED
3905   REM  *     PHYSICAL FITNESS TEST MANUAL.   FIT3 CONTAINS THE
3906   REM  *   SIT-UPS AND SIT AND REACH SCORES.   FIT2 CONTAINS THE
3907   REM  *   SKINFOLD SCORES [SUM OF TRICEPS AND SUBSCAPULAR], AND
3908   REM  *   FIT1 CONTAINS THE MILE RUN NORMS.
3909   REM  *   ALL DATA ARE READ INTO ARRAY X[A,B,C].   THE FIRST POSITIO
       N
3910   REM  *   "A" IS THE PARTICULAR TEST: 1-MILE, 2-SKINFOLDS,
3911   REM  *   3-SIT-UPS, AND 4-SIT AND REACH.   THE SECOND POSITION "B"
3912   REM  *   INDICATES THE COLUMN OF THE TABLE, WHICH IS THE SUBJECTS
3913   REM  *   AGE.   THE THIRD POSITION INDICATES THE ROW OF THE TABLE,
3914   REM  *   WHICH IS THE TEST SCORE FOR THE SUBJECT.
3915   REM  *   THE TABLES FROM THE MANUAL WERE TYPED INTO TEXT FILES
3916   REM  *   TO BE READ BY THIS PROGRAM.
3919   REM  *   *   *   *   *   *   *   *   *   *   *   *   *   *   *

3920   REM  READ PERCENTILE TABLES
3940   POKE 216,0
3960   ONERR  GOTO 7340
3980 HC = 0
4000   DIM X[4,14,40],X6[6],P6[6]
4020 D$ =  CHR$ [4]
4040 F$ = "FIT3":I1 = 1
4060   PRINT D$;"OPEN ";F$
4080   PRINT D$;"READ ";F$
4100   FOR I = 3 TO 4
4120   FOR K = 1 TO 40
4140   FOR J = 1 TO 14
4160   INPUT X[I,J,K]
4180   IF X[I,J,K] = 0 THEN 4160
4200   NEXT J
4220   NEXT K
4240   NEXT I
4260   PRINT D$;"CLOSE ";F$
4280 F$ = "FIT1"
4300 A1 = 1:A2 = 14
4320   PRINT D$;"OPEN ";F$
4340   PRINT D$;"READ ";F$
4360   FOR J = 1 TO 40
4380   FOR I = A1 TO A2
4400   INPUT X[I1,I,J]
4420   NEXT I
4440   NEXT J
4460   PRINT D$;"CLOSE ";F$
4480   POKE 216,0
4500   IF F$ = "FIT2" THEN 4580
4520 A1 = 2:A2 = 14
4540 F$ = "FIT2":I1 = 2
4560   GOTO 4320
4580   FOR J = 1 TO 40
4600   X[2,1,J] = X[2,2,J]
```

(Cont.)

```
4620 X[2,2,J] - X[2,3,J]
4640 NEXT J
4660 HOME
4680 HOME : VTAB [5]: HTAB [5]: INPUT "DISPLAY DATA FOR WHICH GROUP ? "
     ;G
4700 R - 1:I - 1: ONERR  GOTO 4900
4720 PRINT D$;"OPEN ";FF$;",L200"
4740 PRINT D$;"READ ";FF$;",R";R
4760 FOR J - 1 TO 13: INPUT ID$[I,J]: NEXT J
4780 ID$[I,11] -  STR$ [[ VAL [ID$[I,11]] * 2.54] - 15]
4800 IF ID$[I,3] <  >  STR$ [G] THEN 4860
4820 I - I + 1
4840 NX - I - 1
4860 R - R + 1
4880  GOTO 4740
4900 PRINT D$;"CLOSE ";FF$
4920 POKE 216,0
4940 HOME : VTAB [5]: HTAB [5]: INPUT "PRINT ALL FOR GROUP ? ";Y$
4960 IF Y$ - "Y" THEN SET - 9
4980 IF SET - 9 THEN 5080
5000 HOME : VTAB [5]: HTAB [5]: PRINT "WHICH STUDENT ? "
5020 VTAB [15]: HTAB [10]: INPUT "LAST NAME : ";L$
5040 VTAB [18]: HTAB [10]: INPUT "FIRST NAME : ";M$
5060 IF SET = 3 THEN  RETURN
5080 HOME
5100 N - 1: IF SET - 9 THEN 5240
5120 FOR I - 1 TO 40
5140 IF ID$[I,1] <  > L$ THEN 5200
5160 IF ID$[I,2] <  > M$ THEN 5200
5180 N - I: GOTO 5240
5200 NEXT I
5220 HOME : VTAB [10]: HTAB [5]: PRINT "NAME NOT FOUND - TRY AGAIN": GOTO
     5020
5240 REM
5260 FOR I - 6 TO 11
5280 X6[I - 5] - VAL [ID$[N,I]]
5300 NEXT I
5320 MILE$ - ID$[N,6]
5340 X6[2] - X6[4] + X6[5]
5360 X6[4] - X6[6]
5380 X6[2] -  INT [X6[2]]:X6[3] -  INT [X6[3]]:X6[4] -  INT [X6[4]]
5400 AGE -  INT [ VAL [ID$[N,4]] / 12]
5420 IF AGE < 6 THEN AGE - 6
5440 CL - AGE - 3:IX - 0
5460 GOSUB 5680
5480 GOSUB 6460
5500 IF SET <  > 9 THEN 5580
5520 N - N + 1
5540 IF N >  - NX THEN 5620
5560 GOTO 5240
5580 HOME : VTAB [5]: HTAB [1]: PRINT "ANOTHER STUDENT FROM GROUP ";G;"
     ? ";: INPUT " ";Q$
5600 IF Q$ - "Y" THEN 4940
5620 VTAB [10]: HTAB [5]: INPUT "ANOTHER GROUP ? ";Q$
5640 IF Q$ - "Y" THEN 4680
5660 GOTO 105
5680 REM  PERCENTILE ROUTINE
5700 I1 - 1:I2 - I1 + 19
5720 IF ID$[N,5] - "F" THEN I1 - 21:I2 - I1 + 19
5740 FOR I - 3 TO 4
5760 FOR J - I1 TO I2
5780 IF X[I,CL,J - 1] - X[I,CL,J] THEN D1F - 0: GOTO 5820
5800 D1F - [X6[I] - X[I,CL,J]] / [X[I,CL,J - 1] - X[I,CL,J]]
5820 IF X6[I] >  - X[I,CL,J] THEN 5920
5840 NEXT J
5860 IF J < 1 THEN J - 1
5880 IF J > 40 THEN J - 40
5900 IF I1 - 1 AND J > 20 THEN J - 20
5920 GOSUB 6300
```

(Cont.)

```
5940  P6[I] = PE
5960  NEXT I
5980  FOR I = 1 TO 2
6000  FOR J = I1 TO I2
6020  IF X[I,CL,J] = X[I,CL,J - 1] THEN D1F = 0: GOTO 6060
6040  D1F = [X6[I] - X[I,CL,J - 1]] / [X[I,CL,J] - X[I,CL,J - 1]]
6060  IF X6[I] <  = X[I,CL,J] THEN 6160
6080  NEXT J
6100  IF J < 1 THEN J = 1
6120  IF J > 40 THEN J = 40
6140  IF I1 = 1 AND J > 20 THEN J = 20
6160  GOSUB 6300
6180  P6[I] = PE
6200  NEXT I
6220  FOR P = 1 TO 4:
6240  IF P6[P] <  = 0 THEN P6[P] = 99
6260  IF P6[P] >  = 100 THEN P6[P] = 99
6280  RETURN
6300  REM  PERCENTILE EXTRAPOLATION ROUTINE
6320  IF I = 3 OR I = 4 THEN D1F = D1F *  - 1
6340  PE = [X[I,1,J] - X[I,1,J - 1]] * D1F + X[I,1,J]
6360  IF I = 1 OR I = 2 THEN PE = PE + 5
6380  PE =  INT [PE]
6400  IF PE > 99 THEN PE = 99
6420  IF PE < 0 THEN PE = 2
6440  RETURN
6460  REM  DISPLAY ROUTINE
6480  HOME
6500  IF HC = 0 THEN 6640
6520  IF SET = 9 THEN 6540
6540  D$ =  CHR$ [4]
6560  PR# 1: REM  PRINTER SLOT NUMBER
6580  PRINT  CHR$ [27]"G"; CHR$ [12];
6600  PRINT  CHR$ [27]"S";"  ERNIE BANKS ELEMENTARY SCHOOL"
6620  PRINT  CHR$ [27]"4"
6640  PRINT : PRINT  CHR$ [27]"S";" HEALTH RELATED PHYSICAL FITNESS TEST
      "
6660  PRINT  CHR$ [27]"T";
6680  PRINT  CHR$ [27]"5";
6700  PRINT : PRINT "* * * * * * * * * * * * * * * * * * * * * * * * * *
      * * * * * * * * * *": PRINT
6720  PRINT "  NAME              SEX  AGE  HT    WT    DATE"
6740  PRINT "  ----                   ---  ---  --    --    ----"
6760  PRINT  CHR$ [27]"4";ID$[N,2]" ";ID$[N,1]; CHR$ [27]"5"; TAB[ 23];I
      D$[N,5]; TAB[ 27];AGE; TAB[ 32];ID$[N,12]; TAB[ 37];ID$[N,13];"    "
      ;DAY$
6780  PRINT
6800  PRINT  TAB[ 15];"EVENT"; TAB[ 39];"SCORE        PERCENTILE"
6820  PRINT  TAB[ 15]"-----"; TAB[ 39]"-----    ----------"
6840  PRINT
6860  L = 1:X6$ = MILES$
6880  IF  LEN [X6$] = 5 THEN L = 2
6900  X$ =  LEFT$ [X6$,L]:Y$ =  RIGHT$ [X6$,2]
6920  O$ = ":"
6940  Y1$ = X$ + O$ + Y$: IF ID$[N,6] = "-" THEN Y1$ = " "
6960  Z1$ =  STR$ [P6[1]]: IF Y1$ = " " THEN Z1$ = " "
6980  PRINT  TAB[ 15];"MILE RUN"; TAB[ 39 - L];Y1$;"        ";Z1$
7000  Y3$ =  STR$ [X6[3]]: IF ID$[N,8] = "-" THEN Y3$ = " "
7020  Z3$ =  STR$ [P6[3]]: IF Y3$ = " " THEN Z3$ = " "
7040  PRINT
7060  PRINT  TAB[ 15];"SIT-UPS"; TAB[ 40];Y3$;"        ";Z3$
7080  PRINT
7100  Y2$ =  STR$ [X6[2]]: IF ID$[N,9] = "-" THEN Y2$ = " "
7120  Z2$ =  STR$ [P6[2]]: IF Y2$ = " " THEN Z2$ = " "
7140  PRINT  TAB[ 15];"SKIN-FOLDS"; TAB[ 40];Y2$;"        ";Z2$
7160  PRINT
7180  Y4$ =  STR$ [X6[4]]: IF ID$[N,11] = "-" THEN Y4$ = " "
7200  Z4$ =  STR$ [P6[4]]: IF Y4$ = " " THEN Z4$ = " "
7220  PRINT  TAB[ 15];"SIT & REACH"; TAB[ 40];Y4$;"        ";Z4$
```

(Cont.)

```
7240  PRINT : PRINT "* * * * * * * * * * * * * * * * * * * * *
                     * * * * * * * * * * * *"
7260  PR# 0
7280  RETURN
7300  HC = 1: REM  SET DISPLAY FOR COPY ON PRINTER
7320  GOTO 4000
7340  PRINT  PEEK (222)
7360  END
```

Listing 6.4 Projectile motion program.

```
10    REM   * * * * * * * * * * * * * * *
20    REM
30    REM      PROJECTILE MOTION PROGRAM
40    REM
50    REM   * * * * * * * * * * * * * * *
100   HGR : HCOLOR= 5
150   REM      INPUT INDEPENDENT VARIABLES
200   VTAB 21: PRINT "ANGLE OF RELEASE - "
300   VTAB 22: PRINT "HEIGHT OF RELEASE - "
400   VTAB 23: PRINT "VELOCITY OF RELEASE -"
500   VTAB 21: HTAB 20: INPUT AR: REM  ANGLE OF RELEASE
600   VTAB 22: HTAB 21: INPUT HR: REM  HEIGHT OF RELEASE
700   VTAB 23: HTAB 23: INPUT VR: REM  VELOCITY
800   HPLOT 0,140 TO 279,140: REM  DRAW LINE FOR GROUND LEVEL
900   HPLOT 10,140 TO 10,140 - (HR / 3): REM  HEIGHT OF RELEASE POINT
1000  SP = 159 - HR / 3: REM  STARTING POINT FOR PROJECTILE PATH
1050  REM      CALCULATE HORIZONTAL AND VERTICAL VELOCITY COMPONENTS
1100  V = VR *  SIN (AR / 57.3)
1200  H = VR *  COS (AR / 57.3)
1300  HR = HR / 12: REM  CONVERT HEIGHT TO FEET
1390  REM      CALCULATE TIME IN FLIGHT (TT)
1400  TT = (VR *  SIN (AR / 57.3) +  SQR ((VR *  SIN (AR / 57.3)) ^ 2 + 2
         * 32 * HR)) / 32
1500  T = TT / 260: REM  FIND TIME INCREMENTS FOR CALCULATIONS
1600  NVP = SP: REM  STARTING VERT POSITION OF PROJECTILE
1700  NHP = 10: REM  STARTING HORIZ POSITION OF PROJECTILE
1750  REM      CALCULATE AND PLOT NEW POSITIONS OF PROJECTILE
1800  FOR I = 11 TO 500
1900  IF NVP > 140 THEN  GOTO 2700: REM  IF VERT OUT OF RANGE STOP
2000  IF NHP > 279 THEN  GOTO 270: REM  IF HORIZ OUT OF RANGE STOP
2100  HPLOT NHP,NVP: REM  PLACE DOT AT NEW PROJECTILE POSITION
2200  NVP = NVP - V * T: REM  CALCULATE NEXT VERTICAL POSITION
2300  NHP = NHP + T * H: REM  CALCULATE NEXT HORIZONTAL POSITION
2400  V = V - 32 * T: REM   CALCULATE NEW VERT VEL AFTER GRAVITY EFFECT
2500  NEXT I
2700  REM
2800  TT =  INT (TT * 100) / 100: REM  ROUND TIME TO HUNDREDTHS
2900  R =  INT (TT * H * 100) / 100: REM  CALCULATE HORIZONTAL RANGE
2950  REM      DISPLAY RESULTS
3000  VTAB 19: VTAB 2: HTAB 5: PRINT "TIME IN FLIGHT = ";TT: HTAB 28: VTAB
         2: PRINT "SECONDS": VTAB 19
3100  VTAB 22: VTAB 4: HTAB 10: PRINT "RANGE = ";R: HTAB 25: VTAB 4: PRINT
         "FEET": VTAB 22
3200  HOME
3210  VTAB (21): INPUT "CONTINUE ?? : ";Y$
3220  IF Y$ = "N" THEN  END
3230  IF Y$ = "Y" THEN 3260
3240  GOTO 3210
3260  VTAB (23): INPUT "PLOT ON SAME SCREEN ? : ";Y$
3270  IF Y$ = "N" THEN 100
3280  IF Y$ = "Y" THEN 200
3290  GOTO 3260
3300  END
```

CHAPTER 7

Managing Administrative Functions with Microcomputers

David K. Stotlar

Traditionally, the successful administration of sport programs has been based on the accomplishment of certain functions: planning, organizing, staffing, directing, controlling, and evaluating (VanderZwaag, 1984). These administrative functions have often been reorganized, reclassified, and otherwise rehashed, but they remain basically unchanged. If the duties of sport administrators have changed so little, why is the microcomputer necessary? Why do things have to change?

The answer to this question is basic: The microcomputer is fast becoming a necessity. The staggering growth and expansion of information that our society generates daily is obvious even to the average citizen. Our society now mass produces information as we mass produce cars. The major problem is that our thinking and attitudes are not in line with this reality. It has been estimated that administrators spend 80% of their time on information transactions (Naisbitt, 1984). This phenomenon has led to the development of a systematic method for administrators to process the overload of information that is received: the *management information system* (MIS).

Management Information Systems

The purpose of an MIS is to ''provide manager(s) with the necessary data for making intelligent decisions'' (Hodgetts, 1975, p. 395). The MIS does not make decisions but merely makes information available quickly and accurately in a form that managers can interpret. It should be noted that although not every MIS is computer based, the microcomputer and an MIS function well together. The advantages of microcomputers are that information can be retrieved much faster than through traditional methods and that computers are more accurate when calculations are involved.

Managers of sport organizations receive a variety of information from within their organization and from other organizations with which they must interact on an ongoing basis (Jackson, 1981). This information may involve budgeting, personnel, programs, students, clients, facilities, or other significant matters. It is imperative that when administrators are required to make decisions, they make informed decisions based on current information. All administrators can make decisions, but the success of a decision often depends on the quality of the information on which it is based.

Many of the administrative functions previously identified can be accomplished more accurately and more efficiently through the use of an MIS and a microcomputer. Thus, the task of the administrator is to ascertain the specific uses of the microcomputer that would facilitate the accomplishment of designated functions. Among those areas that lend themselves to computerization are office management, personnel management, facility/equipment management, student/client management, and fiscal management. In general, three options are available for the introduction of computers to the organization. An administrator can have a program written for the task at hand, a consultant firm can be secured to provide a system, or a prepackaged commercial program can be purchased and adapted for the task (see Appendix A for software directory), (Asbury, 1983). The remainder of this chapter focuses on specific applications of the microcomputer in the performance of these administrative tasks.

Office Management

One of the major administrative tasks in any sport or physical education program is managing the office. It is in this area that the flood of information can most easily be seen. How many letters are sent and received daily? How many telephone calls are made and received? Each of these functions can benefit from computerization.

Word Processing

Word processing presents an excellent example of how a computer can be used in place of a traditional typewriter. The word processor functions very much like the typewriter and in some instances is indistinguishable in appearance. The advantage of a word processor is that the information can be stored and retrieved electronically. This is particularly useful if the information is going to be used again, as in the case of form letters for prospective students, athletes, members, or clients. The word processor allows the user to personalize the form letters with specific names or insert a particular paragraph where needed. At the same time it eliminates reentry of identical material. Many word-processing programs can also create mailing lists and labels. Finally, some programs automatically merge mailing lists with form letters.

Another example of a word-processing application is revising written documents. Physical education administrators have used this technique for policy handbooks, curriculum guides, and academic catalog descriptions. Intramural directors have entered information on league policies, contest rules, and regulations. Other sports organizations have applied word processing to a variety of their text storage needs.

Creating and storing the information through the use of word processing is helpful, but one of the most useful tasks that can be performed is the retrieval and organization of the information. It should be pointed out that there are many word processors that do not fall under the banner of microcomputers. Many corporations, such as IBM and Wang, have created special hardware exclusively for word processing. This equipment is generally very good for the purpose of handling written information, and the finished product is usually printed by traditional typewriter methods or sent to letter-quality printers.

The advantage of a microcomputer over the dedicated word processor is that the hardware can be called upon to assist with other administrative tasks. A microcomputer with word-processing software is considerably more versatile. Specific word-processing software is available for almost every microcomputer. Some of the trade names of microcomputer word-processing packages include Super Text, Word Star, Microsoft Word, and MacWrite. A major drawback of using the microcomputer with word-processing software is that the dot matrix printers that accompany most microcomputers may not produce a print quality high enough to satisfy some users. However, printers are currently available that correct this deficiency, but their cost is somewhat higher than that of the dot matrix printer.

The versatility of the "microcomputer/software" package over the "word processor only" system is also evident when electronic mail is examined. There are those who believe that the present system of mail will soon be replaced by telephone lines and satellites. Microcomputers can send their information to other computers (micros, minis, or mainframes) through the use of a modem and existing telephone lines. Therefore, anyone with a computer and a modem can send information to anyone else with compatible equipment. This is often referred to as *networking* and can be accomplished across campus or across the world.

Filing System

Record keeping has been one of the traditional tasks of office personnel in any organization. Many filing cabinets could be replaced by the electronic files of the microcomputer. Software packages such as PFS:File, File Vision, Microsoft File, MegaFile, and Overvue are readily available to create and manage files. These programs perform functions identical to a normal filing system. These file programs or any program referred to as *database* can handle similar types of information storage and retrieval. Each filing program has unique strengths and weaknesses, but many of them will let you create custom forms for storing your information. Some programs will provide an established number of *fields*, or categories, for storage of the information. They allow for the input of information, which they will automatically arrange by topic, date, the alphabet, or any other factor that you like.

With this system, access to the information is quick, and updating the material is much simpler than with conventional files. Printouts can be requested by any combination of factors selected. However, as with any filing system, the key to success is the person who does the filing. If information is misfiled electronically, you cannot flip through the file drawer to find it.

Specific examples of computerized files in physical education include accident reports, professional correspondence, program costs, personnel records, student schedules and records, inventory, and curriculum documents. In athletics, files may include eligibility lists, season ticket holders, booster club members, contest management personnel, and schedules. Other sport organizations may have files such as client fee payment or intramural team rosters.

Personnel Management

All organizations are composed of people, and "personnel information is ideally suited to the storage and retrieval capabilities of the computer" (Dougherty & Bonanno, 1985, p. 114). The information normally contained in personnel files includes name, address, age, education, employment history, and evaluation (see Figure 7.1). It is precisely this type of information that is particularly well suited to file programs and the microcomputer because of the continual need to update and change entries. The administrator can include yearly evaluations and add other information to each person's file. The employee can combine this file with other information, which can then function as a résumé. This could also be of assistance when the administrator is called upon to furnish information about staff members to other organizations or the media.

```
┌──────────────────────────────────────────────────────────┐
│                                                            │
│   Last Name: Brooks              First Name: Andre         │
│   Street Address: 401 South Hillside                       │
│   City/Town: Kansas City      State: Mo.  Zip: 71601       │
│   Phone: 501-479-3119         Birthdate: 11-26-61          │
│                                                            │
│          Sex: M                                            │
│          Employment dates: 1981-Present                    │
│          Assignment: Teaching 80%                          │
│                      Research 20%                          │
│                                                            │
│          Evaluation:  Good Teaching Ratings                │
│                       Fair research productivity           │
│                                                            │
└──────────────────────────────────────────────────────────┘
```

Figure 7.1 Employee file that can be sorted or updated by any of the listed categories.

Sample fields and limitations may include Last Name, 15 characters; First Name, 10 characters; Street Address, 25 characters; City, 10 characters; Zip Code, 9 characters; Sex, 1 character. The program may allow for custom titles for field names, or they may have been preset. When considering either a preprogrammed filing package or one that will allow for custom fields for each file, the user must determine the exact information that will be needed for each individual. The computer can manage pieces of information only by field. Therefore, each piece of information that the administrator may wish to sort, list, or search for must have its own field, so it is important for the administrator to review carefully the ability of the program to handle files by fields.

Many of the programs have companion software that will allow the user to create and move information from one application to another. Thus, an athletic director could have a memo written on the word processor, have the file system select the addresses of all football coaches, and merge the mailing list with the memo. The result would be that while the printer produced the memos, the secretary would be free to handle other tasks. Finally, it should be noted that filing with a microcomputer cannot totally eliminate a traditional filing system because the user will still have a variety of forms and correspondence from people using traditional techniques.

Scheduling

One of the major tasks of any sport or physical education organization is scheduling. Administrators schedule staff, students, teachers, coaches, gyms, classrooms, weight rooms, swimming pools, and playing fields. Most central offices keep schedules for all of the employees. Information is often requested concerning a teacher's office hours or location at a specific time. This information can be processed by the computer quickly and modified weekly as meetings and appointments change (see Figure 7.2).

Employee: Grice, Corey

Schedule: September 23-27

	Monday	Tuesday	Wednesday	Thursday	Friday
8:00	P.E.270		P.E. 270		P.E. 270
9:00					
10:00		P.E. 155		P.E. 155	
11:00	office	P.E. 155	office	P.E. 155	office
12:00					
1:00					
2:00		coach/meet			
3:00	Football	Football	Football	Football	Football
4:00	Practice	Practice	Practice	Practice	Practice
5:00					

Figure 7.2   Individual faculty member schedule that can be changed daily to reflect appointments and can also be used to locate people at specified times.

The scheduling of hourly employees is also a task that can be facilitated by the microcomputer. Again, specific programs can be written for the task, or commercial programs can be used. Another interesting approach is the *cookbook* program. This occurs when one person or institution has developed the program but makes the program "list" available to others. Danziger (1984) has published such a program in *Athletic Business.* With these types of programs the names of the workers can be entered beside the times that they are scheduled to work. Individualized lists for each person can be generated along with daily or weekly blocks of time. Any changes that become necessary can be made quickly, and new schedules can be printed with relative ease. Information used repetitively can be duplicated for use from week to week with only minor changes as needed (see Figure 7.3).

When the possible combinations of facilities and people are compared to the number of hours in a day, it is easy to appreciate the scheduling difficulties often faced by the administrator. The two aspects

DATE: 9-18-86								
Employee	Telephone	7:00	8:00	9:00	10:00	11:00	12:00
Tom Jones	541-7893		Jones		Jones		
Bill Fowler	541-7845			Fowler			Fowler
Jack Wilson	535-8905	Wilson				Wilson	
Henry Mack	541-0265		Mack			Mack	Mack
Joe Sample	541-8573	Sample					
Bob Towns	541-8936			Towns	Towns		
Phil Nelson	541-9256		Nelson				Nelson
Rod Monk	535-9174	Monk					
J.T. Turner	535-0291			Turner			
Les Taylor	535-0291				Taylor	Taylor	

Figure 7.3 Weight room supervisors' schedule.

of this problem that make it suitable for computer application are its massiveness and repetitiveness.

The traditional method for scheduling a building has been to create a "big board" with each of the building's spaces identified and blocks listed for each available time slot. Reservations could then be written in for future reference. One of the major limitations of this method is that it is very limited in the amount of time that it can cover. Many athletic events demand scheduling years in advance, and the big board cannot handle them very easily. What most administrators do to handle the problem is construct a file that will be reviewed at a later date. Another problem is that often no record of the past schedule exists when events have come and gone.

The use of the microcomputer can avoid both of these problems and furnish added benefits as well. Most applications that are currently being used in this process are either programs that have been specially designed for a particular organization or ones that have been created from generic programs. The custom programs generally do a good job but are relatively expensive. Another problem is that they are often inflexible both within and between organizations. Therefore, if facilities change, the software must be reprogrammed.

The generic programs are most often spreadsheets from business software. These programs are specifically designed for accounting and data base management (as will be discussed later in this chapter), but they can be utilized for scheduling (see Figure 7.4). Spreadsheets are best described as "a very large, if only imaginary, piece of paper which has been divided by rows and columns into individual cells. Into each cell, the user may enter text, numbers, or formulas" (Danziger, 1985, p. 227).

The administrator can construct the same big board that was used before, but now the information can be recorded, saved, and projected many years into the future. Some commercial programs using the same format are beginning to appear and should make computer application easier.

	1	2	3	4	5	6	7	8
1				East	Gym			
2		Sunday	Monday	Tuesday	Wednesday	Thursday	Friday	Saturday
3	7:00		Fitness Lab	Fitness Lab	Fitness Lab	Fitness Lab	Fitness Lab	
4	8:00		P.E. 165	P.E. 264	P.E. 165	P.E. 264	P.E. 165	
5	9:00		P.E. 279	P.E. 264	P.E. 279	P.E. 264	P.E. 279	Recreation
6	10:00		P.E.148		P.E.148		P.E.148	Recreation
7	11:00	Recreation	P.E. 179		P.E. 179	Recreation	P.E. 179	Recreation
8	12:00	Recreation	Recreation	Recreation	Recreation	Recreation	Recreation	Recreation
9	1:00	Recreation	Recreation	Recreation	Recreation	P.E.Lab	Recreation	Recreation
10	2:00	Recreation				P.E.Lab		Recreation
11	3:00	Intramural	Men BB	Women BB	Men BB	Women BB	Men BB	Recreation
12	4:00	Intramural	Men BB	Women BB	Men BB	Women BB	Men BB	Recreation
13	5:00	Intramural	Men BB	Women BB	Men BB	Women BB	Men BB	Recreation
14	6:00	Intramural	Men BB	Women BB	Men BB	Women BB	Men BB	Recreation

Figure 7.4   "Big Board" for building is a spreadsheet with 64 columns and 256 rows.

The power of the microcomputer can be seen in the manner in which it manages the information from the big board. The computer can be used to search, find, and print specific information. Examples might be finding all reservations made by the intramural program or finding and printing all reservations made for a certain playing field in the month of May. Some of the programs have a feature that will also print a reservation card for the person making the request (Maas, 1984).

A larger variety of programs have been produced for the scheduling of athletic tournaments. Companies such as Market Computing and Sports Log have programs that will handle all of the tasks associated with the conduct of a tournament. This includes team registration, seeding, and tournament bracket generation. The round robin tournaments are printed with team or player names instead of the old format where numbers (1 vs. 28) appeared. For those competitions that require ranking of players, these programs automatically rank and assign flights, lanes, or heats (see Figures 7.5 and 7.6).

Facility and Equipment Management

Scheduling is not the only task that the microcomputer can complete regarding facilities. The microcomputer can be used to keep accurate records of maintenance and repair. The development of a computerized maintenance system (CMS) can give the administrator valuable information concerning specific equipment and/or facilities. This system provides information on "(1) equipment status, (2) maintenance due, (3) maintenance history, (4) maintenance budget, and (5) performance and services history" (Horine, 1985, p. 329).

The process for establishing a CMS involves a team approach. Trade workers, supervisors, and facility engineers all need to have input

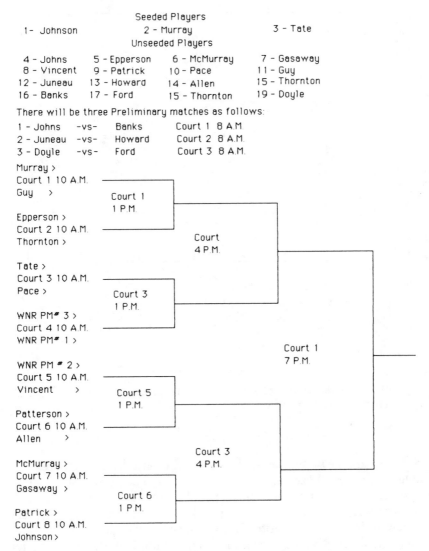

Seeded Players

1- Johnson   2 - Murray   3 - Tate

Unseeded Players

4 - Johns	5 - Epperson	6 - McMurray	7 - Gasaway
8 - Vincent	9 - Patrick	10 - Pace	11 - Guy
12 - Juneau	13 - Howard	14 - Allen	15 - Thornton
16 - Banks	17 - Ford	15 - Thornton	19 - Doyle

There will be three Preliminary matches as follows:

1 - Johns   -vs-   Banks   Court 1 8 A.M.
2 - Juneau -vs-   Howard   Court 2 8 A.M.
3 - Doyle   -vs-   Ford   Court 3 8 A.M.

Murray >
Court 1 10 A.M.
Guy   >
        Court 1
        1 P.M.

Epperson >
Court 2 10 A.M.
Thornton >
                    Court
                    4 P.M.

Tate >
Court 3 10 A.M.
Pace >
        Court 3
        1 P.M.

WNR PM⁺ 3 >
Court 4 10 A.M.
WNR PM⁺ 1 >
                              Court 1
                              7 P.M.

WNR PM ⁺ 2 >
Court 5 10 A.M.
Vincent   >
        Court 5
        1 P.M.

Patterson >
Court 6 10 A.M.
Allen   >
                    Court 3
                    4 P.M.

McMurray >
Court 7 10 A.M.
Gasaway >
        Court 6
        1 P.M.

Patrick >
Court 8 10 A.M.
Johnson >

Figure 7.5 Sample printout of program for scheduling an athletic tournament.

into the system. Common elements in computerized facility operations include maintenance tasks for each facility, determination of time needed for each task, personnel required for each task, time required to complete the task, time interval for required maintenance, and generation of work orders (Asbury, 1983).

Climate and lighting control are functions that have traditionally been reserved for minicomputers or mainframes. However, with the

```
                         400 Meter Dash
                           2:00 P.M.
                            Heat 1


      Lane               Times            Team

       1. Lee             55.0            Striders
       2. Poe             54.8            Prairie Track Club
       3. Brown           53.3            Unattached
       4. Edwards         54.6            Sacramento
       5. Robinson        54.82           D.C. Lions
       6. Hampton         55.47           P.B. Track Club



                            Heat 2


      Lane               Times            Team

       1. Settles         55.31           Striders
       2. Flicklin        54.75           L.A. Track Club
       3. Whitener        53.0            D.C. Lions
       4. Garner          53.5            Prairie Track Club
       5. Merlo           54.9            P.B. Track Club
       6. Anderson        55.57           Sacramento
```

Figure 7.6 Sample printout of a sports computer program that automatically assigns lanes and heats based on times.

recent upgrades in memory to 512K (and/or hard drives) that are available for micros, these functions can be carried out by a "stand alone system" in the department. One problem that can occur in this area is that each institution will probably have to have an individualized program designed and written for the specific tasks at hand. Although this may presently be beyond the financial limits of the organization or the skills of the current staff, an increased demand of this application will conceivably yield prepackaged programs.

Equipment inventory and equipment ordering are areas that can also be accomplished through the use of a microcomputer. The primary capabilities of the program should include the ability to monitor current inventory status, locate inventory items, control reordering and lead time, produce inventory lists and reports, and provide for forecasting and planning (Falk, 1983). Separate files can be created for each sport. Each piece of equipment and its location can be documented and recorded in the file. For example, when equipment is issued to

```
Last Name: Brooks            First Name: Andre
Street Address: 401 South Hillside
City/Town: Kansas City       State: Mo.  Zip: 71601
Phone: 501-479-3119


Equipment Issued: 8-15-86
Helmet  6-86   Size  7 1/2
Shoulder pads  14-83  Size 44
Practice jersey ☑        Practice pants ☑
Game jersey   43         Game pants ☑
Shoes:  Size   10
```

Figure 7.7 Sample printout of computer program used for equipment inventory and ordering.

an individual athlete or student, that information would then be placed in the individual's file (see Figure 7.7)

A data base program could then organize the information by team, player, student, location, or equipment type. This would be useful in answering several questions that are not uncommon: "Where are all of the stopwatches?" or "To whom does this jersey belong?" Of greater importance to the administrator, the system would also facilitate the analysis of composite inventories.

Financial Management

The efficient financial operation of any organization is imperative. However, this aspect of organizational management is often the major source of difficulty for sport and physical education administrators because few administrators have received sound preparation in fiscal management. Therefore, it may be the area that could benefit most from the application of computers.

A variety of functions related to financial management can be accomplished through the use of the microcomputer: accounts receivable, accounts payable, general ledger, payroll, and forecasting. Precaution must be taken for educational institutions because many of the functions, such as payroll, are not required (or permitted) to be done at the department level. Therefore, it is important to assess the specific needs of the organization regarding the fiscal management capabilities of the microcomputer.

Two basic types of programs are available for financial management, accounting packages and spreadsheets. Accounting packages are usually designed for business operations and have formats that are relatively inflexible. The accounts receivable segment usually performs the following functions: preparation of invoices, maintenance of customer accounts, and production of sales and other reports. In sports organizations, this function is often limited to ticket sales or membership payments. The accounts payable segment of the program would generally enjoy a wider application through the organization of all vendors with whom business is transacted. The features that often appear in this function are purchase order control, invoice processing, check writing and control, cash requirement forecasting, and vendor information analysis (Falk, 1983). In the educational setting, these features may surpass the needs and desires of the administrator, but they may be fully compatible with the needs of sports organizations operating in the commercial sector.

Spreadsheet programs allow the user to enter text, numbers, or formulas into the cells present on an electronic worksheet. VisiCalc is one of the most popular spreadsheet programs, and others are also available through such companies as Microsoft and Lotus. With these programs the administrator can make headings, categories, entries, and titles that are specific to the organization. One of the advantages of the ability to design custom documents is that it avoids some of the problems encountered with professional accounting terminology. Mathematical formulas can then be entered to accomplish the same task as the accounting program.

These formulas refer to specific numbers that have been entered into the cells and direct the program to compute numerical analyses. These calculations can be performed much faster with a spreadsheet program than they can with the more traditional paper, pen, or calculator. The computer's ability to erase a cell allows for easy corrections. Similarly, reusing a cell can assist revisions and yield results not only more rapidly but also more neatly than traditional means (Danziger, 1985).

Figure 7.8 shows sections from a spreadsheet used for an athletic department budget. Each sport has been assigned a segment of the spreadsheet where specific items can be entered and totaled. This segment is linked by a formula and then summarized into general headings. In turn, this segment is linked to a sport summary section of the entire athletic budget. The formulas make it possible to change one entry in the individual item section for a selected sport, and the change will be calculated and carried throughout the entire budget in a few seconds.

Forecasting has been mentioned previously as an advantage of computerization. Exactly what is forecasting, and why is it necessary? Forecasting is the ability of managers to see how the future will be affected

	1	2	3	4	5	6	7
1	TENNIS (Men & Women)				BUDGET SUMMARY		
2	Current Income		$0.00		Sport	Income	Expenses
3					Football	$1152000.00	$847200.00
4	Current Expenses				Basketball (Men)	$334000.00	$352600.00
5	Salaries	1 Head @ $30,000	$40000.00		Baseball	$0.00	$82800.00
6		1 Asst @ $10,000			Swimming (M & W)	$0.00	$62850.00
7	Recruiting Travel		$720.00		Tennis (M & W)	$0.00	$48670.00
8	Game Management	(staff, courts)	$250.00		Golf (M & W)	$0.00	$28100.00
9	Telephone		$200.00		Track / C.C. (Men)	$2500.00	$98800.00
10	Printing	(xerox, schedules)	$100.00		Track/C.C.Women	$0.00	$78600.00
11	Equip./Supplies		$2500.00		Gymnastics (Men)	$2500.00	$59100.00
12	Photog/Films		$100.00		Gymnastics Women	$0.00	$46900.00
13	Team Travel	10 away matches	$4800.00		Volleyball	$11000.00	$81850.00
14		Total Expenses	$48670.00		Softball	$0.00	$69200.00
15		Balance	($48670.00)		Basketball(Women)	$3500.00	$90500.00
16							
17					Capital Improv.		$157500.00
18					Administrtative	$1526100.00	$1138700.00
19							
20					TOTAL	$3031600.00	$3243370.00
21					BALANCE	($211770.00)	

Figure 7.8 Athletic budget on an electronic spreadsheet.

by present decisions. This can be very beneficial to an administrator because hypothetical figures can be entered into a program for such items as salaries, ticket prices, or membership fees. The program will then perform automatic calculations that will detail the financial consequences of those decisions.

Considerable attention has been devoted thus far to the various tasks and programs for the accomplishment of those tasks. One more type of program must be addressed: the *integrated software package*. This program combines word processing, graphics, spreadsheets, data base, and telecommunication. This enables the user to purchase one piece of software that will do just about everything. Some important matters, however, must be considered. First, most of these programs require at least 128K of memory to operate, and other needs of the organization may not be as demanding. Secondly, if needs dictate all of the features equally, then integrated software may be appropriate. However, if demands are primarily for one aspect of the package, such as word processing, the word-processing progam that best meets the needs of the organization should be purchased. These programs have been compared to the Swiss army knife: It provides a tool for every job but does not do any job exceptionally well (Gutman, 1985).

Time Management

One of the assets of an organization that cannot be increased is time, and administrators are particularly vulnerable to excessive time demands. By now it is apparent that the microcomputer can be a valuable tool in assisting administrators to derive the maximum benefit from the time available by increasing the efficiency of administrative functions. But what about personal time management? Several programs are available for this purpose, and most function like an electronic desk calendar. The user can enter and select such tasks as meetings, telephone calls, or appointments, which are then presented on a daily agenda. Each task can also be given a priority rating from urgent to nonessential. These items are then continually presented to the administrator until completed, sort of a computerized "to do" list (Falk, 1983).

On a much larger scale, some time management functions involve enormous projects and span several years. Project planning has existed for many years and has received considerable study. The Project Evaluation and Review Technique (PERT) was first developed in 1958 by the U.S. Navy for tracking the progress of the construction of military weapons (Jackson, 1981). Similar methods of critical path analysis for construction planning have developed since that initial framework was established. IBM's PERT program was the first and most successful attempt to computerize this process, but the complexity of the program was such that it could be handled only by large computers. Increases in the capabilities of computers and advances in programming have recently made the process compatible with microcomputers. Two specific programs are VisiSchedule and MacProject. These programs offer the following features:

> A calendar representation of start and stop dates, slack time, holidays, and deadlines for up to 300 tasks may be displayed and automatically printed out. Many different computer generated reports can be produced covering project milestones, cost estimates, staffing levels, slack time, earliest start dates, late finish, deadlines and prerequisites of all or some of the project tasks. The interactive time chart and the reports allow a user to investigate the tradeoffs among staffing, dollars, and time. A critical path capability indicates which group of tasks must directly affect the overall length of the schedule. If any task along the critical path slips, the overall project does, too (Falk, 1983, p. 73).

The project can be displayed in graphic form (see Figure 7.9) or by text and can be arranged in a variety of ways: by date, critical path, or task classification.

The value of this program can easily be seen in the planning and construction of facilities in sport, but are there other, more frequent applications? How many major sporting events, tournaments, or sports camps occur within an organization each year? Each of these projects could be handled by programs such as these, and the probability of last minute panic or forgotten details could be reduced. Each step or task in the planning process could be identified, placed in sequence,

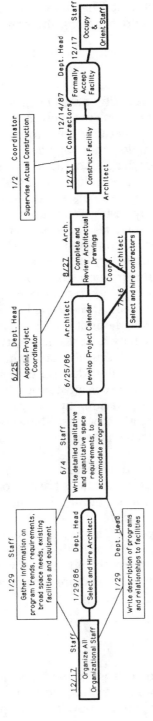

Figure 7.9 Sample printout of time management program for construction planning.

and assigned a time allotment. The program could then calculate the finish date and milestone dates along the critical path.

Data Security

Two distinct types of security problems accompany the use of microcomputers. The first problem involves the software utilized to perform the various tasks. Because the information on the software program and the information that has been entered by the staff is stored on a disk, the characteristics of that disk are important. Almost all microcomputers use magnetic floppy disks. Although these disks are relatively durable, they can be erased through exposure to any magnetic object. This totally destroys any information—program and/or files—on the disk. Disks have also been known to "crash" on their own. For some unknown reason the disk will simply fail. Therefore, one of the most important aspects of data security is making a back-up of all programs and information stored on disks. This may seem like a tremendous amount of work, but the penalty for failing to make a duplicate is that someone must reenter all of the information that was lost. This would seriously limit the time-saving aspect of computerization. Not only is failing to "back up" software costly in down-time for personnel, but replacing the program is expensive. Most computers have features that allow the user to make duplicates of files with relative ease, a function that most offices routinely perform at the end of each day's work. Backing up software is sometimes more difficult because of protection schemes. Many companies, however, supply backups, and commercial programs are also available to perform this task.

The second problem regarding security involves access to restricted information. Most sports organizations have information that is confidential in nature. It is important that this information be reserved for viewing only by appropriate people. This is often accomplished through the password system. The user must enter a predetermined password to gain access to the files.This process is also quite useful when any unauthorized change could cause severe problems for the organization. Areas that typically require such protection are personal and financial records.

Office Computerization

Having discovered the broad range of functions that can benefit from computerization, the job of integrating the computer has just begun. The question "Where do I start?" now becomes paramount. Several authorities have suggested that the first application selected for computerization should be a relatively simple one. It should also be one that was not being accomplished efficiently by traditional methods (Asbury, 1983; Danziger, 1985). The rationale for this approach is that the organization can move into the computer age and experience some success. If the application chosen for computerization was a task that was already functioning well, the benefits would be more difficult to discern. It should also be pointed out that the computer cannot be expected to be efficiently solving problems as soon as it comes out of the box. It takes about 40 hours for a person to become fully acquainted with the operation of any hardware system and about 20 hours to become familiar with a specific software package (Danziger, 1985). Therefore, it has been suggested that computers and the tasks for which they are needed be selected gradually (Falk, 1983). This is not to say that an administrator should ignore possible future applications when purchasing a computer, but rather that the introduction of tasks be at a pace that the organization and its personnel can handle.

Two mistakes that are often made in the use of computers in organizations can be avoided with foresight. First, both the computer and the software should be purchased with specific requirements and needs in mind. Secondly, the people who will be using the computer should be directly involved in the testing and purchase of the computer (Danziger, 1985). On many occasions, a well-intentioned administrator purchases a computer to assist staff only to discover that the computer will not perform the functions that the staff needs it to perform.

The electronic office can become a reality. However, the success of the transition will depend upon the people who staff it. The computer will not immediately make a poor accountant competent or an inefficient secretary a good one. It is a tool that can be used by skilled employees and administrators to assist in the performance of certain tasks.

References

Asbury, G. (1983). Bringing your operations into the computer age. *Athletic Business*, **6**, 20-22.

Danziger, G. (1984). Computers can simplify work force scheduling in public use facilities. *Athletic Business*, **8**, 44-49.

Danziger, G. (1985). Computer applications in sport. In G. Lewis & H. Appenzeller (Eds.), *Successful sport management* (p. 227). Charlottesville, VA: Michie.

Dougherty, N.J., & Bonanno, D. (1985). *Management principles in sport and leisure services*. Minneapolis: Burgess.

Falk, H. (1983). *Handbook of computer applications for the small or medium-sized business.* Radnor, PA: Chilton Book.

Gutman, D. (1985, August 7). Swiss army knife software. *Ames Daily Tribune*, p. A2.

Hodgetts, R.M. (1975). *Management: Theory, process and practice.* Philadelphia: W.B. Saunders.

Horine, L. (1985). *Administration of physical education and sport programs.* New York: Saunders College Publishing.

Jackson, J.J. (1981). *Sport administration: Learning designs for administrators of sport, physical education, and recreation.* Springfield, IL: Charles C. Thomas.

Maas, G.M. (1984). Selected considerations regarding microcomputer hardware and software in intramural sports applications. *NIRSA Journal*, **9**, 37-53.

Naisbitt, J. (1984). *Megatrends.* New York: Warner Books.

VanderZwaag, H.J. (1984). *Sport management in schools and colleges.* New York: John Wiley & Sons.

CHAPTER 8

Microcomputer Systems for Motor Learning and Control

Richard Engelhorn

Microcomputers are finding their way into applications in every field, including physical education and, more specifically, motor learning and control. Teachers, coaches, and researchers are finding new ways to use the microcomputer to enhance the quality and efficiency of their work. Those individuals interested in the learning and performance of motor skills are now using microcomputers to enhance teaching, to study aspects of sports skills performance, and to investigate neuromuscular mechanisms underlying the control of complex goal-directed movements. The examples and descriptions provided in this and the following chapter attempt to cover a broad spectrum of potential applications in motor learning and control but should not be assumed to be complete. It is also impossible to provide examples of software that are immediately useful to readers because the differences in computers and peripherals dictate critical aspects of the programming of the projects to be described. It is instead the intention of these chapters to provide ideas and some structure related to the use of the microcomputer in various motor-learning and control situations.

The computer is a relatively new addition to the motor-learning laboratory. Most labs, including those leading the way in the quality and direction of research, were not using a computer for more than off-line statistical analysis as late as 1978. Even those labs investigating electrophysiological variables and motor skill learning were relying heavily on analog techniques for initial data reduction and a computer for statistical analyses of these data. Applications of computers in physical education as well as in motor learning and control have generally followed their use in other disciplines. However, the current availability of relatively inexpensive microcomputer systems will soon result in many laboratories going on-line for both teaching and research activities in motor learning and control.

Scope of Microcomputer Usage

The applications for the microcomputer in motor learning and control are as varied as the area itself. Currently research and teaching in this area range from that related to teacher behavior and skill learning to neurophysiological mechanisms in the control of skilled movement. The experimental designs and instrumentation employed also vary considerably. As an introduction to the applications of microcomputers in motor learning and control, it is useful to review the recent development and growth of this area of study, particularly as it relates to the different research directions and methodologies being used.

Traditionally, there have been two divisions within motor learning: motor behavior and motor control. More recently these subareas have merged somewhat, for teachers and researchers now understand the necessity to investigate all of the factors that impact on motor skill acquisition and performance. The motor behaviorists have typically investigated questions related to information processing, memory, attention, and individual differences as they affect motor skill learning and performance. The effect of various factors on a movement outcome, as measured by a performance score, has been the primary focus of motor behavior research.

The motor control investigators have been more active in exploring the process through which skilled movements are performed. Motor control research has focused on neuromuscular mechanisms responsible for skill acquisition and performance and has included reflex contributions to movement, motor programming, sensory feedback dependence, muscular contraction patterns, and kinematic analyses of movement (displacement, velocity, and acceleration patterns). The motor-learning and control researcher today is likely to pay close attention to both motor control processes and the various behavioral factors that affect the outcome of a motor response.

Versatility in the Laboratory

Investigations into the behavioral factors affecting human movement and the neuromuscular control processes underlying movement performance have manipulated a wide range of independent variables and observed an equally diverse set of dependent measures. Apparatus and instrumentation to record the various performance assessments— from stabilometers and pursuit rotors to electrophysiological amplifiers—have also varied widely. It is in the instrumentation and measurement area that the microcomputer has its greatest impact. The microcomputer, when equipped as a flexible system rather than as one designed for a single task, is quite capable of replacing or enhancing the function of much of the hardware associated with a motor-learning laboratory. In addition, the computer can collect data, control external devices, and present immediate analyses of the data in tabular or graphic form. With the right peripheral devices and software, the computer can provide measurements of the dependent variables often used by the motor-learning teacher and researcher. From the behavioral area the microcomputer can provide direct assessments of reaction and movement time, coincidence anticipation error, movement distance or position error (one- or two-dimensional), and other performance measures. Also efficiently recorded and stored in a microcomputer are the motor control variables: movement kinematic patterns, force production patterns, electromyographic (EMG) or electroencephalographic (EEG) activity, and reflex time components. The following sections will elaborate on the computer's role in the collection of the previously mentioned variables and the various control functions capable of being performed during an experiment.

Examples of Microcomputer Use

In order to appreciate the possible uses for a microcomputer in the motor-learning laboratory, the role and functions performed by a microcomputer in measuring several of the more common dependent variables will be described. The relative usefulness and efficiency of the microcomputer in each task may vary from efficiently performing an essential function to being only moderately convenient.

- *Reaction and movement times.*   The microcomputer is quite useful for assessing simple and choice reaction and movement times. Several analog or digital timers may be replaced by a microcomputer, and in addition to the timing function, the data collected are stored for subsequent analysis. A detailed example of a microcomputer in this application is described in the applications chapter.
- *Time-on-target scores.*   Performance scores from such devices as a pursuit rotor or stabilometer can also be easily measured using a microcomputer. The advantage in this situation is again in the relatively automatic data collection and storage, control over the experimental procedures, and immediate analysis and feedback capabilities.
- *Movement distance and location.*   Sampling movement patterns in order to determine distance or relative location is the function in

which the microcomputer makes its greatest contribution. Several examples of this function of the microcomputer are provided in the following chapters.

- *Coincidence-anticipation timing error.*   Depending upon the situation, the microcomputer in conjunction with other devices is capable of measuring coincidence-anticipation timing error and controlling other aspects of an experiment. The relative contribution a computer can make in this situation depends entirely on the type of task used. The computer could easily provide a visual stimulus and subject-controlled cursor to create a coincidence task on the computer's visual display.

- *Neuromuscular/neurophysiological variables.*   The computer is able to greatly facilitate the collection of reflex time components and EMG or EEG data. Without the microcomputer in this situation, the task of collecting and processing data of this type becomes extremely cumbersome and time consuming. Several examples of the microcomputer in this function are provided in the applications chapter.

There are other variables of interest to the motor-learning teacher/ researcher; however, the variables discussed provide a general perspective on the computer as a precision-measuring instrument. The microcomputer makes an even greater contribution in experimental control and data storage functions. Subsequent sections will discuss the computer hardware and software requirements for the motor-learning and control laboratory as well as provide several examples of programs currently being used for both student labs and research. The microcomputer provides the teacher or researcher with a data collection and control system that can be easily modified to vary its function and purpose as well as provide the capacity for rapid data analysis and display of experimental results. By using the computer in student laboratory situations, students gain insight into the manner in which experimental research projects are conducted. Students are also able to understand more about microcomputers and the computer's role in motor learning as well as in other areas of physical education and sport.

Microcomputer Functions

If a computer system is to be maximally useful and flexible for the teacher and researcher in motor learning and control, the computer must be able to perform several essential functions. First of all, the system must be able to interact with a subject and the environment. This function is accomplished through the computer's data collection and data or information output capabilities. Data collection activities include timing (both reaction and movement), monitoring one- and two-dimensional movement positions, sampling voltages from transducers (force, angular rotation, acceleration), or bioelectric phenomena, electromyographic (EMG) or electroencephalographic (EEG) activity. The data output functions include controlling devices external to the computer, such as lights, sound effects, visual displays, electric motors, and others. A computer system with a combination of data collection and data output capabilities and related external devices allows both the teacher and researcher to control the experimental station and conduct sophisticated experiments in motor learning and control.

The ability to store large quantities of data, perform data reduction and analysis, and display results of these operations are also essential functions of the microcomputer in the motor-learning environment. Subsequent sections will illustrate the hardware and software requirements of an efficient and adaptable microcomputer system for motor-learning and control applications.

In applications using bioelectric or kinematic data, it is necessary to collect and store large quantities of data from each trial in the computer's memory and then load these data onto a disk for long-term storage. In certain types of research, especially in the motor control area, it would not be unusual to collect many thousands of data points per trial. In order for the microcomputer to be maximally useful in motor-learning applications, at least 48K of memory plus two disk drives are needed for program and data storage. All of the applications described in this and the following chapter have made use of an Apple II+ microcomputer with 48K of memory and two floppy disk drives.

To make efficient use of the microcomputer for data analysis and display, software must allow for ease of data handling, flexibility in type of analysis, and, of greatest importance, high execution speed. These and other software considerations will be discussed in a later section of this chapter.

Hardware

The peripheral components for a motor-learning and control application are similar to components for any system with a need for a wide range of potential applications. Figure 8.1 illustrates a system with most of the commonly used peripheral devices and their relationship to the computer. The following descriptions will illustrate the factors to consider regarding each peripheral device and the role of these components in the motor-learning lab and classroom.

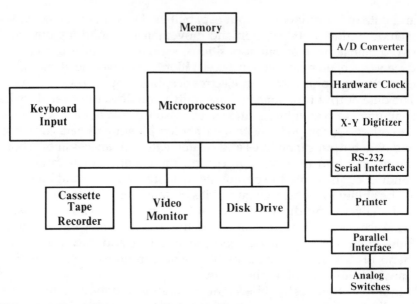

Figure 8.1 Example components of a laboratory microcomputer system for motor-learning applications.

Data Collection

The A/D converter is the heart of any laboratory microcomputer system. Recall from the previous discussion in chapter 2 that the A/D converter samples incoming voltages at finite time intervals and converts the analog voltage values into digital numbers capable of being stored in the computer memory. For the motor-learning lab where bioelectric data are to be recorded, the sampling rate is the single most important feature of an efficient A/D converter. For all but bioelectric data, sampling rates of less than 500 samples per second are adequate. However, for high-frequency signals like the electromyogram, sampling rates of 1,000 cycles per second (i.e., hertz) are often required, especially if frequency analyses are contemplated.

The potential sampling rate of an A/D system is directly affected by two other important factors, the number of channels (simultaneous voltage inputs) that can be sampled and the number of bits or resolution of the A/D converter. Sampling rate must be considered for the total number of voltage inputs and not just that of a single channel. Most systems should have an A/D converter capable of sampling four to eight channels at 1,000 samples per second. The number of bits of resolution of the A/D converter is usually 8, 10, or 12. The 8-bit

A/D converter provides the fastest conversion rate but the least accuracy. The 8-bit A/D converter also allows for the storage of twice as many conversions in the computer's memory as the 10- or 12-bit converters. A single byte (i.e., 8 bits) in the memory of a typical microcomputer can hold one number from an 8-bit converter; however, two bytes are required for each conversion from a 10- or 12-bit A/D converter.

The accuracy factor may be important in considering an A/D converter, especially if high-frequency bioelectric signals, such as the electromyogram, are sampled. An 8-bit converter is capable of converting incoming voltages into numbers ranging from 0 to 255. In binary arithmetic 0000 0000 is 0 in decimal and 1111 1111 is 255 in decimal. A 10-bit converter has a range of 0 to 1,024 and a 12-bit provides a 0 to 4,096 range. To calculate the resolution or accuracy of the system, divide the total voltage input range (usually from $+2.5$ or $+5$ to -2.5 or -5, respectively) by the highest conversion value. For the 8-bit A/D converter (assuming a range of 5 V), this is 5/255, or a 0.02 V minimum increment between converted values. A 10-bit A/D converter provides a minimum increment of 0.005 V (5/1024), and a 12-bit A/D allows for a 0.001 V increment (5/4096). For high-frequency A/D sampling, the 8-bit A/D converter may distort the incoming signal due to its resolution. For most other A/D applications the 8-bit may be desirable due to the lower memory storage requirements.

The motor-learning laboratory computer must also have a timing capability. The computer's internal clock cannot efficiently carry out the many timing functions required for the teacher and researcher. To provide an efficient and accurate timing function, a hardware clock is required. Most of the available hardware clocks provide multiple simultaneous timers that operate independently of the computer itself. This independence allows BASIC and/or machine language programs to perform various functions, using one or more timers, without having to take time to monitor the computer's clock continuously. In high-speed data acquisition using an A/D converter, the independent hardware clock is essential to facilitate rapid program execution.

Most hardware clocks provide a range of clock rates so that the resolution can range from ten-thousandths of a second to minutes. Reaction and movement times are easily sampled by a microcomputer equipped with a hardware clock. In the laboratory and research applications to be described, a hardware clock is used extensively to perform various timing functions related to motor learning and control.

Although infrequently used in motor learning, an X-Y digitizer is a useful device if two-dimensional movements are to be studied. A *digitizer* is an instrument that is capable of converting points on a two-dimensional surface into the x and y coordinates of a point in relation to some point of reference. A digitizer is most used by biomechanists to convert points on successive film frames into points that can be used to determine patterns of movement of body segments. Computer-controlled X-Y digitizers are most frequently used in biomechanics labs for cinematographical analysis. The motor-learning researcher interested in more than one-dimensional linear or angular movement can make efficient use of an X-Y digitizer to study the learning and performance of movements in two dimensions, such as curvilinear motion and movements requiring more than one joint action (e.g, elbow and shoulder joint integration). An X-Y digitizer could also be used in conjunction with the video display of the microcomputer to create two-dimensional mazes with an infinite number of maze patterns.

Depending upon the digitizer and the laboratory situation, the computer may be used to sample the movement of the cursor continuously, upon the initiation of the subject, or at specific time increments. Essentially the X-Y digitizer functions as a two-channel A/D converter by providing two simultaneous numbers. One number relates to a relative x-axis position and the other to a relative y-axis position. The accuracy and sophistication of X-Y digitizers varies considerably. Currently, prices range from $350 to $2,500, with accuracy and sophistication improving with cost. However, for the motor-learning laboratory, the low-cost digitizers are generally adequate. However, if extensive analysis of high-speed films is contemplated, then a higher quality device is required.

Peripheral Devices for Other Applications

All of the other peripheral devices illustrated in Figure 8.1 are generally applicable to many situations, including the motor-learning and control laboratory. The need for these devices by the teacher and researcher in motor learning depends entirely on the intended applications of the computer system. If hard copy outputs of programs or results are required, then a printer is needed. If other types of graphic output are desired, a digital plotter is the peripheral device of choice. Both of these devices add considerably to computer capabilities and facilitate program creation, data presentation, and other general functions. Other devices, such as serial or parallel interfaces, modems, or a D/A converter, may also be useful or necessary in certain applications. An analog or buffered switch is needed if electrical appliances or motors are to be controlled by the microcomputer. More will be presented on the use of some of these devices in the applications chapter to follow.

Software Options

Once the hardware aspect of a system is complete, it is important to make the proper choice of computer languages and software to support fully the intended applications. The computer language important for the teacher may not be the language most suited for the laboratory and researcher. The teacher using the computer for CAI requires capabilities that include strong visual and interactive display techniques. Typically these techniques are not dependent on time and, therefore, can make use of languages like BASIC, which, although slow, are easy to use. The researcher or teacher using the computer for experiments, experimental simulations, or data and statistical analyses finds the execution speed of languages to be a potential problem. Without a language capable of running at high speeds, procedures such as bioelectric data collection are not possible.

An important consideration for data collection is the software requirement of the A/D system. To collect four to eight channels of data at 500 or 1,000 samples per second, a machine language routine is necessary for controlling the A/D and data storage in memory. Many commercially available A/D systems are furnished with a machine language subroutine to control the A/D converter. These routines can be called from a high-level language program written in BASIC, Fortran, or Pascal. Listing 8.1 is an example of a machine language routine used to control a 10-bit A/D converter and the subsequent storage of the predetermined number of conversions in memory. In this example six channels are being sampled at a predetermined sampling frequency, with the sampling rate controlled by a hardware clock.

BASIC, although a slow executing language, can be compiled and run as machine language 10 to 20 times faster than the standard interpretive version. Other languages like Fortran and Pascal, both of which are compiler based, are ideal for research due to their execution speed and straightforward data-handling capabilities. For most purposes, compiler-BASIC is a suitable language for a wide range of applications in the laboratory environment. However, when graphics are of primary importance, Pascal may be a better choice. BASIC, Fortran, and Pascal are all relatively easy to learn and use. However, the research programmer must also rely on assembler or machine language programming when execution speed of a program is a limiting factor in a particular application. To maintain the greatest flexibility and power, the motor-learning researcher and teacher needs to use programs written in a high-level language, such as BASIC, Fortran, or Pascal, that calls fast-executing machine language subroutines. Examples of both BASIC and assembler language programming are provided in the applications chapter to follow.

Listing 8.1 Assembler language program that controls the A/D converter.

```
:LIST

  1 *
  2 *                 A/D      CONVERSION SUBROUTINE
  3 *
  4              ORG  $4000
  5              JSR  $FF4A    ;SAVE ALL REGISTERS AND
  6              JSR  $FF3A    ;SOUND BELL TO SIGNAL SUBJECT TO BEGIN TRIAL
  7              LDA  #$10
  8              STA  $08      ;STORE LOWER BYTE OF DATA STARTING ADDRESS
  9              LDA  #$41
 10              STA  $09      ;STORE UPPER BYTE OF DATA STARTING ADDRESS
 11              LDA  #$F0
 12              STA  $40F0    ;LOWER BYTE OF END OF DATA
 13              LDA  #$6F
 14              STA  $40F1    ;UPPER BYTE OF END OF DATA
 15              LDX  #$00
 16              JSR  $C200    ;INITIALIZE HARDWARE CLOCK
 17              LDA  #$92
 18              STA  $C0A0    ;SET RATE AND FUNCTION PARAMETERS
 19 ;                                  AND START CLOCK
 20 LOOP1:       LDA  $C0A1    ;LOAD CLOCK STATUS
 21              STA  $07      ; STORE CLOCK STATUS
 22              LDA  $C0A4
 23              LDA  $C0A5    ;PREPARE CLOCK FOR NEXT READ
 24              LDA  $07      ;LOAD CLOCK STATUS
 25              CMP  $06      ;HAS REQUIRED TIME PERIOD ELAPSED
 26              BEQ  LOOP2:   ;IF YES, THEN PROCEED
 27              BPL  LOOP3:   ; IF PAST TIME INTERVAL THEN GIVE ERROR MESSAGE
 28              LDA  #$02
 29              STA  $06      ;PREPARE FOR NEXT CLOCK PULSE
 30              JMP  LOOP1:   ;IF INTERVAL NOT COMPLETE, CHECK AGAIN
 31 ;
 32 LOOP2:       LDA  $40F1    ;LOAD THE NUMBER OF CONVERSIONS COMPLETED
 33              CMP  $09      ;COMPARE WITH THE TOTAL DESIRED
 34              BNE  LOOP4:   ;IF MORE DATA TO GET, THEN CONTINUE
 35              JSR  $FF3F    ;IF COMPLETE RESTORE REGISTERS AND RETURN
 36              RTS
 37 *
 38 *            SAMPLING            AND                 STORAGE ROUTINE
 39 *
 40 *
 41 LOOP4:       STY  $C0F1 ;SET MULTIPLEXOR ADDRESS
 42              DEY
 43              STY  $C0F1    ;SAMPLE CHANNEL
 44              INC  $FF
 45              INC  $FF      ;PREPARE TO SAMPLE NEXT CONSECUTIVE CHANNEL
 46 LOOP5:       LDA  $C0F2    ;READ A/D READY PIN AND TWO MOST SIGNIFICANT BITS
 47              ROL  A
 48              BCS  LOOP5:   ; IF NOT READY, CHECK AGAIN
 49              ROR  A
 50              AND  #$03
 51              STA  [$08,X]  ;STORE TWO MOST SIGNIFICANT BITS
 52              LDY  $08
 53              INY  ; INCREMENT               STORAGE LOCATION POINTER
 54              STY  $08
 55              BNE  LOOP6:   ; IF LOW BYTE OF DATA ADDRESS IS ZERO,
 56 ;                                  INCREMENT THE HIGH BYTE OF THE ADDRESS
 57              INY
 58              STY  $09
 59 ;
 60 LOOP6:       LDA  $C0F4    ;LOAD LOWER 8 DATA BITS AND STORE
 61              STA  [$08,X]
 62              LDY  $08
 63              INY
 64              STY  $08      ;INCREMENT AND STORE ADDRESS FOR NEXT
 65 ;                                  CONVERSION
 66              BNE  LOOP7:
 67              LDY  $09
 68              INY
 69              STY  $09
 70 ;
 71 LOOP7:       DEC  $FE      ;DECREMENT CHANNEL COUNTER
 72              BNE  LOOP4:   ;IF MORE CHANNELS, THEN GET DATA
```

(Cont.)

```
73            LDA   #$01
74            STA   $FF        ;RESET FOR NEXT SAMPLE TO START AT CHANNEL 1
75            STA   $06        ;PREPARE CLOCK FLAG
76            LDA   $FD        ;LOAD NUMBER OF CHANNELS
77            STA   $FE        ;STORE IN CHANNEL COUNTER BYTE
78            JMP   LOOP1:     ;TAKE ANOTHER SAMPLE FROM ALL CHANNELS
79 *
80 *
81 *          ERROR     HANDLING ROUTINE
82 *
83 *
84 LOOP3:     LDA   #$F3       ;SET ERROR FLAG
85            STA   $FC
86            RTS
```

CHAPTER 9

Microcomputer Applications in Motor Learning and Control

Richard Engelhorn

The microcomputer has a multitude of uses in a motor-learning and control laboratory environment. Some were mentioned in the previous chapter, and many others are possible for the creative individual with a well-equipped microcomputer system. In the following examples, several different types of experimental situations are presented in an attempt to provide a general overview of the computer acquisition of several types of dependent variables and data, as well as different computer hardware requirements. Each example provides the purpose of the experiment, the hardware required, the relative advantages of using the microcomputer, the program flowchart and its logic, procedures for data analysis, and specific programming examples.

Complete programs are not provided because the programming for certain aspects of each experiment would be dependent on hardware, especially as it concerns the A/D converter and hardware clock. The program segments included, however, should illustrate certain programming techniques and provide the novice programmer with realistic examples of functional software. All of the programs are written in BASIC and are normally used after being compiled. This increases the execution speed dramatically and makes the BASIC language far more useful to the teacher and researcher in motor learning.

Simple and Choice Reaction Time

The microcomputer with the necessary timing capabilities can be efficiently used to provide both simple and choice reaction timing (RT) functions. *Simple reaction time* is a measure of the time required by an individual to respond to an unanticipated event. This time includes the sensory detection of the event, the processing of the sensory information, and finally the generation of the muscular response. For *choice reaction time* measurements, two or more unanticipated events are possible with each having a unique response. Choice RT scores reflect an information-processing or decision-making time in addition to those components included in the simple RT. This experiment is used to illustrate the duration and range of the typical simple RT and to illustrate the increased time requirements when choices or decisions must be made between stimulus event detection and motor response generation.

The minimal hardware requirements are illustrated in Figure 9.1. The essential features are the timers and the input/output ports that allow the micro to provide a starting stimulus or signal to the subject and to detect the changes in state (off or on) of the necessary switches. In this experiment neither disk nor memory storage capacities are limiting factors. The only hardware limitation that may affect the acquisition of accurate reaction times is the clock itself and the resolution it can provide. A resolution of 1 millisecond (ms) is more than adequate for most purposes.

Figure 9.2 illustrates the various time periods that must be either precisely controlled or measured during the experiment. The computer advantage in this experiment relates primarily to the precision at which the computer can control the foreperiod and the intertrial interval and measure and save the RT score from each trial. In the simple RT experiment, the computer replaces a digital or analog clock, which, although accurate, requires that a reading be made and recorded after each trial. The micro also replaces the timer used to calculate the foreperiod and intertrial interval and eliminates human error relat-

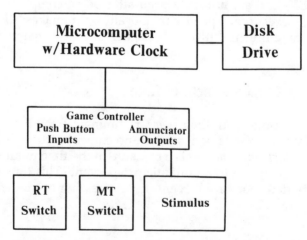

Figure 9.1 Hardware devices for reaction time/movement time application.

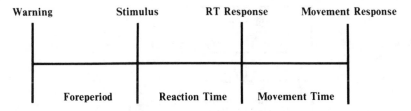

Figure 9.2 The stimuli to be provided and the time periods to be measured by the microcomputer for reaction and movement time experiments.

ed to the presentation of these intervals to the subject. The resulting RT data from this experiment are relatively free from contamination by errors or biases resulting from the presentation times of the warning and start signals, as well as errors in reading a clock and recording the data.

The program flow for the simple RT experiment is illustrated in Figure 9.3. Students work in groups of three to four with each taking turns as the experimenter and as the subject. After the subject's age and sex are input, along with the number of trials and the date, the micro takes command of the testing.

The subject is instructed to depress a switch and wait for the warning signal and then the stimulus to react. These signals could be auditory or visual and are controlled by the computer. The flowchart illustrates the sequence of functions the computer performs after the presentation of the stimulus to respond. After the response the RT is stored in the computer's memory until the session is complete, at which time the RTs are all transferred to a disk for long-term storage. The teacher may want to have the computer calculate individual and class averages after the completion of a laboratory. Listing 9.1 located at the end of the chapter provides an example of the programs, both BASIC and assembler, that are used in the RT experiment.

In many instances a *movement time* (MT) following an RT is of importance. By adding another switch to the RT hardware, it is very easy to measure both RT and MT. The programming is very similar to the RT program except for the addition of a loop to monitor the MT switch and store the MT result. Figure 9.4 illustrates the flowchart for an experiment of this type. The computer monitors the RT switch first, and then after the subject reacts, the MT switch is monitored until the subject moves and depresses that switch.

The RT program (see Listing 9.1) may also be modified to produce a choice RT situation. Instead of producing a single repeating stimulus requiring only one response, the program presents one of three possible stimuli. The subject reacts to the stimulus by depressing one of

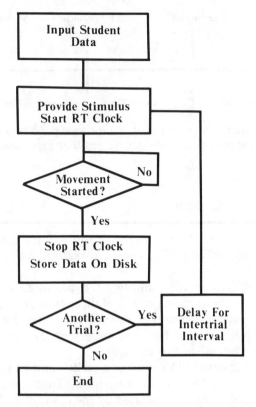

Figure 9.3 Flowchart for a typical reaction time experiment.

three switches. The microcomputer monitors the three switch inputs and detects and records the choice RT of the subject. The flowchart for this experiment is the same as that for the simple RT experiment except for the addition of routines to randomize the presentation order of the three stimuli.

These three examples illustrate the capabilities of a microcomputer for use in RT (simple and choice) and MT experiments. For the teacher, coach, or researcher interested in studying RT or MT and/or illustrating concepts related to RT or MT and motor learning and performance, the microcomputer equipped with a hardware clock is a versatile and accurate laboratory instrument.

Memory

Memory and short-term motor memory were active research areas for many years, and their relationship to motor skill learning and perfor-

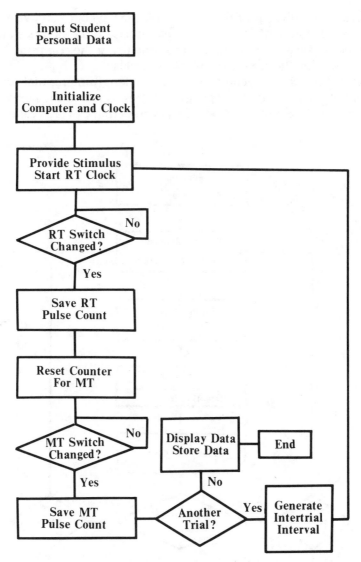

Figure 9.4 Flowchart for reaction times and movement times experiment.

mance is an important area of study for the physical education student. Two computer applications illustrating memory, both for
character strings and movements, are described. The character string
program manipulates either the interval between presentation and
recall of a character string or the number of characters in the string.
Students investigate the effect of both factors on their recall ability
during a self-paced motor-learning laboratory session. No peripheral

devices are required for this experiment; the keyboard and visual display are all that is necessary. Because precise time intervals are not required in this experiment, a subroutine using the computer's own clock provides the necessary recall intervals.

Figure 9.5 is the flowchart for the string length manipulation component of the program. The purpose of this aspect of the lab is to determine the maximum number of characters that can be recalled after

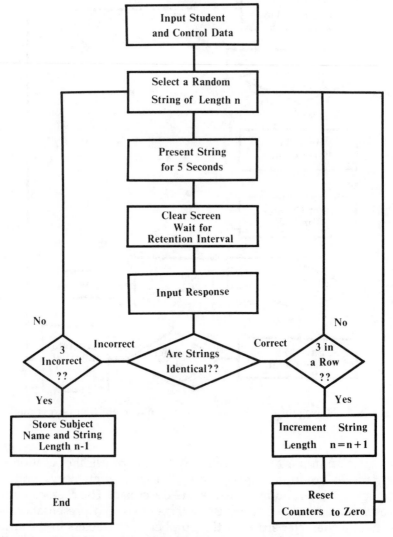

Figure 9.5 Flowchart for determining the maximum number of characters recalled after a short time interval experiment.

a constant time interval. If a student correctly recalls three different random strings of a certain length in a row, the computer increases the string length by one. Three incorrect responses at any one character string length ends the program with the student's last level being taken as the maximum string length recall capacity. Listing 9.2 at the end of the chapter provides the BASIC program for this experiment. The computer, in this case, provides an interesting and challenging activity for the student and illustrates important concepts regarding memory and recall.

Much research has been completed regarding short-term motor memory and the factors that affect the recall of simple movements. This computer-controlled experiment duplicates a rather complex study of the effect of the retention interval on movement recall. Two students work together on this project, both taking their turn as subject and experimenter.

Listing 9.3 at the chapter's end provides the program for this experiment, and Figure 9.6 illustrates an example of the hardware organization for this experiment. In this situation it is an angular movement of the elbow joint that is monitored with a potentiometer linked to the shaft of a movement apparatus. Subjects perform horizontal elbow flexion or extension movements with their forearm resting on the movement apparatus. This experiment could also be performed using an X-Y digitizer for a one- or two-dimensional movement task.

The programming flowchart is depicted in Figure 9.7 and illustrates the various functions performed by the microcomputer. Once the student data are input, the computer controls all aspects of the movement until the required number of trials are completed. Different auditory signals inform the subject regarding the tasks to be performed

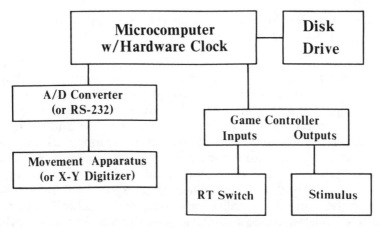

Figure 9.6 Hardware components for a short-term motor memory experiment.

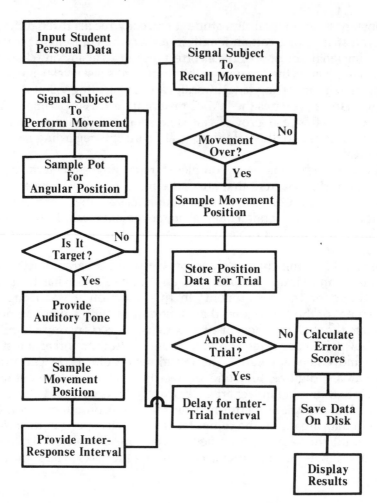

Figure 9.7   Flowchart for a short-term motor memory experiment.

during each trial, such as beginning the first movement, stopping at the movement end point, returning to the starting position, and performing, after a programmed time delay, the movement recall. The computer samples and stores movement end points and calculates, displays, and saves the movement error scores. During the initial input of subject data, the student acting as the experimenter may select several options related to retention interval lengths, movement distances, and number of trials. Through structured but independent work on the computer, small groups of students manipulate various parameters related to motor memory. After the computer has provided analyses of all the subjects' data, students are able to evaluate and understand important concepts related to memory and motor skill learning and performance.

Attention Demands During Movement

Another experiment for the student lab is one illustrating attention demands during movement performance. During a goal-directed motor response with one limb, a secondary task, such as a simple RT, is performed with the other hand. If a part of the movement requires a high attention level, then the RT should be long. Conversely, if a segment of the movement requires relatively little attention during performance, the secondary task RT performed by the other limb should be shorter and closer to a normal RT. The primary task in this experiment is a 60° elbow flexion positioning movement performed in a time of either 300 or 1,500 milliseconds. The movement time difference allows the student to study attention demands during a movement relying primarily on motor programming mechanisms (300 milliseconds) and a movement in which peripheral feedback from the response is extensively used for control (1,500 milliseconds).

Figure 9.8 outlines the program flow for this experiment. After the relevant parameters have been input about the subject and the experiment, the computer takes control and measures the subject's RT as in the first experiment described in this chapter. This RT serves as a baseline for the RTs to be collected during the movement performance. The computer then prepares for the secondary task portion of the experiment by reading a data file to determine the segment of the movement in which the RT stimulus will be provided. A signal to begin the movement is then given, and at the predetermined point during or prior to the movement, the RT stimulus will be presented.

The data collection for this experiment can be accomplished in two ways. First, an A/D converter can continuously sample the movement position and the status of the RT switch during a trial and calculate the movement errors and RT from these records. A second technique is that illustrated in the flowchart (see Figure 9.8). The computer monitors the status of the RT switch and of an electronic movement time switch that signals the subject has reached the target point. As these switches change from off to on, the program stops and reads the appropriate clock. The data are then stored, and the next trial is presented. Either technique can be used, but if a record of the movement pattern is desired, then the continuous sampling method must be used.

For the student laboratory, the method shown in Figure 9.8 is used so that students may obtain immediate feedback from the experiment

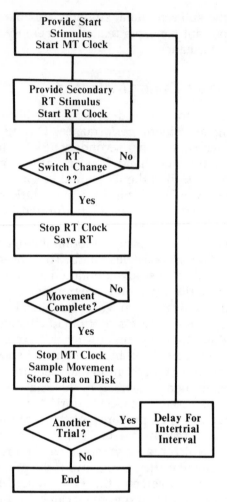

Figure 9.8 Flowchart for attention demands during movement experiment.

and the trials can be presented with shorter intertrial intervals. Students enjoy the challenge of this experiment and develop a better conception of the attention demands placed upon them by a motor response. Once again, after all students have completed the task, analyses are printed for each student.

Motor Control Applications

The sophistication provided by the micro in data collection, control, and data handling and storage functions significantly enhances the quality and efficiency of the motor control research process. Because of the interest in underlying neuromuscular control mechanisms, motor control research applications may include a more extensive use of the A/D converter for sampling EMG and kinematic patterns. In the first experiment described, several channels of EMG activity, an angular displacement record, and an input from an accelerometer are sampled at 500 or 1,000 samples per second.

The purpose of this experiment is to investigate learning-related changes in the EMG and kinematic patterns. Therefore, it was necessary to collect large quantities of EMG and kinematic data and store these data on disk for later analysis. Of primary interest in this investigation were the relative amounts of EMG activity from the muscles sampled as observed prior to and following a skill practice session. The hardware configuration used in this research is shown in Figure 9.9. The game controller input/output port is used to control the presentation of the starting stimulus, the rezeroing after each trial of a movement time clock providing feedback to the subject, and the monitoring of the status of the RT switch. As mentioned previously, a parallel interface can also be used in place of the game controller port. A linear potentiometer attached to the movement apparatus provided the angular displacement record. An accelerometer located at the end of the movement arm signaled the pattern of acceleration from the movement, and input from two bioamplifiers provided the EMG activity records. The hardware clock, which controls the A/D sampling rate, is an essential feature of the system and allows for a high sampling rate, 1,000 samples per second across four channels.

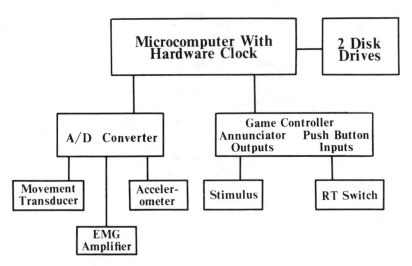

Figure 9.9   Hardware components of a motor control research application system.

The programming for this experiment is both in BASIC and assembler language. The assembler portion is illustrated in Listing 8.1 in the previous chapter. Due to the long program length, only select segments are provided at the end of this chapter in Listing 9.4. Figure 9.10 illustrates the flowchart for the program. Once the subject data and control information are input, the computer takes control and col-

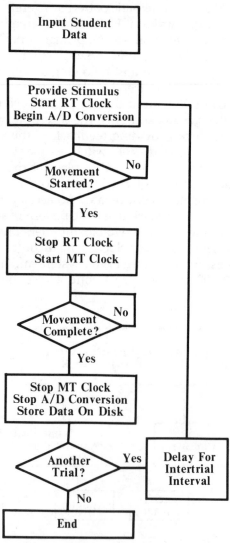

Figure 9.10 Example motor control research flowchart.

lects the desired number of trials of data. If an error should occur, the program transfers control to the experimenter in an effort to continue without leaving the program.

After the data are in memory from a trial, they must be transferred to disk for later analysis. Due to the large quantity of data collected and the extensive data reduction and analysis required, the most efficient analysis can usually be performed on a large mainframe computer system. Data can be easily transferred via an acoustic modem and the phone lines, although a substantial time investment may be required. However, the much faster execution speed and the availability of a wide range of statistical packages on the large mainframe systems make the transfer time worthwhile.

The final example of a microcomputer application in motor learning and control closely resembles the data collection aspect of the last experiment; however, there is one additional feature of the data collection phase and an on-line interactive data analysis program. This experiment also collects EMG and kinematic data, but the data are analyzed for time components of the EMG signal and kinematic patterns rather than relative amounts of activity or shapes of the waveforms.

The extra feature of the data collection phase is the generation of a disturbance or perturbation to the ongoing movement. By so doing, the investigator is able to study the error correction mechanisms used following the error induced by the mechanical disturbance. The addition of the perturbation adds some complexity to the data collection process and places a greater demand on the execution speed of the A/D collection process. After each sample is taken, a segment of the program must evaluate some aspect of the kinematic data, such as position, velocity, or acceleration, to decide when to perturb the movement. The perturbation may be in the form of a rapidly decelerating or accelerating force generated by an electric motor or braking device.

The hardware configuration (see Figure 9.11) is like that of the previous experiment except for the addition of the mechanical perturbation controlled by the computer through the game controller or parallel interface. An analog or buffered switch is necessary between the mechanical device and the computer to protect the computer from the large voltages used by the motor or brake. Such switches are readily available and are the same as those that allow a computer to turn electrical appliances around the home on and off.

The flowchart for this program, illustrated in Figure 9.12, differs from the previous experiment's flowchart only by the addition of the loop used to make the decision to perturb the movement. After the

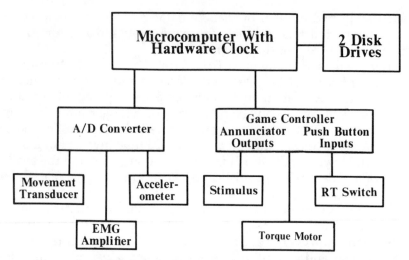

Figure 9.11 Hardware devices for controlling an external motor or braking device.

data collection is complete, however, the data analysis for this experiment is quite different. If time parameters related to the EMG waveform are of interest in evaluating the error correction response, it is necessary to inspect each waveform manually and measure the latencies of the various events. The microcomputer can significantly facilitate this process by displaying each waveform on the video display for evaluation. The researcher, using a joystick, positions a cursor at the points of interest and depresses a key that corresponds to the various components being measured. The program reads the position of the joystick, horizontal for time and vertical for the amplitude of the signal, and stores and/or prints these values. By so doing, the researcher can quickly and accurately measure the time latencies of interest. Figure 9.13 illustrates an example of an EMG activity record from a perturbed movement and the parameters that may be of interest. This same technique could be used to evaluate motor and premotor reaction times or time parameters related to other data, such as an acceleration pattern.

Other situations in motor control exist where the computer, as a laboratory instrument, is absolutely essential. These two examples of research applications illustrate the efficiency of data collection, con-

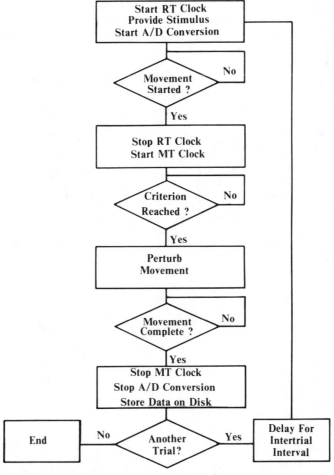

Figure 9.12 Flowchart for an experiment perturbing an ongoing movement to elicit a reflex error correction response.

trol, and storage functions as well as one example where a tedious data analysis process can be greatly facilitated by using the microcomputer. For motor-learning and control researchers, the microcomputer can perform tasks that both enhance the quality of the research and facilitate the entire experimental process.

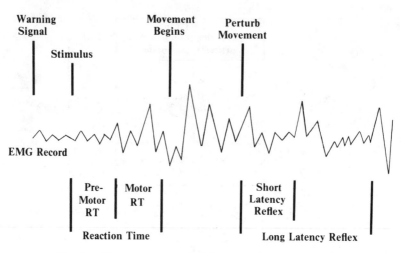

Figure 9.13   Sample EMG recording and the critical time periods for a reflex error correction study.

Listing 9.1 BASIC language program controlling the reaction time experiment.

```
10  REM  * * * * * * * * * * * * * * * * * * * * * * * * * * * * * * * *
12  REM
14  REM        REACTION TIME [RT] PROGRAM
16  REM
18  REM  * * * * * * * * * * * * * * * * * * * * * * * * * * * * * * * *
30  DIM RT[30]:I - 0: REM  SET UP ARRAY FOR STORAGE OF RT'S
35  D$ - CHR$ [4]: REM  DISK CONTROL CHARACTER
40  INPUT "SUBJECT CODE - ";SUBJ$
400 REM  * * * * * * * * * * * * * * * * * * * * * * * * * * * * * * * *
402 REM
404 REM        PROVIDE STIMULUS AND RECORD REACTION TIME
406 REM
408 REM  * * * * * * * * * * * * * * * * * * * * * * * * * * * * * * * *
412 I - I + 1: REM  TRIAL COUNTER
414 PRINT "TYPE CTRL G TO START TRIAL"
416 GET A$: REM  GET A CHARACTER FROM KEYBOARD
417 REM  * * * * IF CHARACTER NOT CONTROL G WAIT FOR ANOTHER
418 IF  ASC [A$] > < 07 THEN  GOTO 414
420 PRINT CHR$ [7]: REM  RING BELL TO SIGNAL SUBJECT TO BEGIN
450 REM    CALL CLOCK READ SUBROUTINE
480 REM  * * * * THE SUBROUTINE PRESENTS A VISUAL STIMULUS ON THE VIDEO

490 REM  * * * * DISPLAY AND THEN WAITS FOR THE SUBJECT TO RESPOND.
500 REM  * * * * AFTER THE RESPONSE THE COMPUTER STORES THE CLOCK COUNT

510 REM  * * * * OF THE REACTION TIME IN MEMORY.
520 CALL 28928: REM  ASSEMBLER SUBROUTINE
521 TEXT : REM  RESTORE SCREEN TO NORMAL
530 W - PEEK [255]: REM  CHECK FOR CLOCK ERROR
540 IF W > < 243 THEN  GOTO 560: REM  IF NO ERROR CONTINUE
550 PRINT " ERROR "
552 I - I - 1: REM  IF ERROR, REPEAT TRIAL, DECREMENT TRIAL COUNTER
554 GOTO 412
557 REM  * * * IF NO ERROR READ MEMORY FOR CLOCK COUNT AND SAVE
558 REM  * * * * READ MEMORY LOCATIONS FOR BINARY CODED RT TIME
560 I1 - PEEK [250]:I2 - PEEK [251]
570 REM  CALCULATE DECIMAL VALUE FROM BINARY CODED NUMBER
580 RT - I2 * 256 + I1
600 RT[I] - RT: REM  SAVE RT IN AN ARRAY
605 REM  * * * * PRINT TRIAL RESULT
610 PRINT : PRINT "TRIAL - ";I;"  REACTION TIME - ";RT
620 IF I < 30 THEN  GOTO 412: REM  IF LESS THAN 30 TRIALS THEN CONTINUE

622 REM  * * * * IF 30 TRIALS COMPLETED THEN SAVE DATA
625 REM  * * * * * * * * * * * * * * * * * * * * * * * * * * * * * * *
    *
626 REM
627 REM        SAVE RT DATA TO DISK
628 REM
629 REM  * * * * * * * * * * * * * * * * * * * * * * * * * * * * * * *
    *
630 PRINT D$;"OPEN SUBJ$"
635 PRINT D$;"WRITE SUBJ$"
640 FOR Q - 1 TO 30
660 PRINT RT[Q]
670 NEXT Q
680 PRINT D$;"CLOSE SUBJ$"
690 END
```

Listing 9.2 Character string memory program in BASIC.

```
7   REM     * * * * * * * * * * * * * * * * * * * * * * * * * * * * * *
8   REM
9   REM          CHARACTER STRING LENGTH MEMORY PROGRAM
10  REM
11  REM     * * * * * * * * * * * * * * * * * * * * * * * * * * * * * *
12  PRINT D$;"BLOAD TIMER": REM    L              OAD ASSEMBLER SUBROUTINE
    FOR              TIMING
15  DIM CRRT[10]: REM   SET UP ARRAY
18  IT - 1: REM   SET START TRIAL TO 1
20  INPUT "LENGTH OF STARTING STRING - ";N%
30  INPUT "RETENTION INTERVAL - ";I%: REM   INPUT RI IN SECONDS
37  REM   * * * GENERATE RANDOM CHARACTER STRING ONE CHARACTER AT A TIM
    E
40  C$ - ""
45  C% - [ RND [5] * 100] / 4: REM    GET RANDOM NUMBER BETWEEN 1 AND 25
50  C% - C% + 65: REM   CREATE ASCII CHARACTER
60  C$ -   CHR$ [C%]
70  T$ - T$ + C$: REM   ADD CHAR TO STRING
80  X% - X% + 1: REM   INCREMENT STRING LENGTH COUNTER
90  IF X% < N% GOTO 40: REM   IF LESS THAN DESIRED LENGTH, ADD ONE
95  IT - IT + 1: REM   TRIAL COUNTER
100 HOME : REM   CLEAR THE SCREEN
110 VTAB [10]: HTAB [16]: REM   POSITION CHARACTER STRING IN CENTER OF S
    CREEN
120 PRINT T$: REM   DISPLAY CHARACTER STRING FOR 5 SECONDS
128 REM   * * * * DELAY FOR FIVE SECONDS
130 FOR I - 1 TO 50: CALL 16384: NEXT I
140 HOME : REM   CLEAR SCREEN
145 FOR I - 1 TO 10: PRINT : NEXT I
150 GOSUB 400: REM   PROVIDE RETENTION INTERVAL
160 INPUT "TYPE YOUR RESPONSE - ";R$
162 REM   * * * AFTER SUBJECT RESPONDS, PRINT CORRECT RESPONSE
165 PRINT "THE CORRECT RESPONSE IS - ";T$
167 REM   * * * IF STRINGS ARE DIFFERENT LENGTH, RESPONSE IS WRONG
170 IF  LEN [T$] <  >  LEN [R$] GOTO 300
175 REM   * * * * COMPARE STRINGS CHAR BY CHAR
180 FOR I - 1 TO N%
190 IF  MID$ [T$,N%,1] <  >  MID$ [R$,N%,1] GOTO 300
200 NEXT I
205 REM   * * * * 'CORRECT' ROUTINE
210 PRINT : PRINT : PRINT "CORRECT"
220 A$ -  CHR$ [7]: FOR I - 1 TO 10: PRINT A$: NEXT I
230 CRRT[IT] - 1: REM   IF CORRECT RESPONSE PUT 1 IN ARRAY
240 IF IT < 3 THEN 250
241 REM   * * * * IF 3 IN ROW CORRECT, INCREASE STRING LENGTH
242 IF CRRT[IT - 2] - 1 AND CRRT[IT - 1] - 1 AND CRRT[IT] - 1 THEN 246
244 GOTO 250
246 N% - N% + 1: REM   INCREASE STRING LENGTH BY ONE
248 WR - 0: REM   RESET WRONG TO ZERO FOR NEW STRING LENGTH
249 IT - 0: REM   RESET TRIAL COUNTER FOR NEW STRING LENGTH
250 T$ - "":X% - 0
280 GOTO 40
290 REM   * * * * 'WRONG' ROUTINE
295 REM   * * * * SOUND BUZZER IF RESPONSE INCORRECT
300 PRINT : PRINT : PRINT "********** ERROR **********"
305 FOR I - 1 TO 100:X -  PEEK [ - 16336]: NEXT I
310 CRRT[IT] - 0: REM   IF RESPONSE INCORRECT PUT 0 IN ARRAY
315 WR - WR + 1: REM   COUNT WRONG RESPONSES
320 IF WR - 3 THEN 480: REM   IF THREE WRONG RESPONSES THEN STOP
325 T$ - "":X% - 0: REM   RESET VARIABLES
330 GOTO 40
390 REM   * * * * RETENTION INTERVAL ROUTINE
400 FOR I - 1 TO I%
410 CALL 16384: REM   THIS ASSEMBLER ROUTINE PROVIDES A ONE SECOND DELAY

420 NEXT I
430 RETURN
480 HOME : VTAB [10]: HTAB [5]: PRINT "YOUR MEMORY LENGTH IS ";N% - 1;"
    CHARACTERS."
500 PRINT : PRINT " TO RESTART THE PROGRAM TYPE 'RUN'": END
```

Listing 9.3   BASIC language program controlling the short-term motor memory experiment.

```
4    REM     * * * * * * * * * * * * * * * * * * * * * * * * * * * * * *
5    REM
6    REM          SHORT TERM MOTOR MEMORY EXPERIMENT PROGRAM
7    REM
8    REM     * * * * * * * * * * * * * * * * * * * * * * * * * * * * * *
9    PRINT D$;"BLOAD STMM": REM   LOAD ASSEMBLER A/D CONVERTER PROGRAM
10   DIM RES[30,2],MP[30],RI[30]: REM  SET UP ARRAYS
12   HOME : INPUT "WHAT IS SUBJECT'S NAME : ";N$
20   IT = 1: REM  SET TRIAL COUNTER TO 1
21   REM   * * * * READ RETENTION INTERVAL TIMES IN TENTHS OF SECONDS
22   FOR I = 1 TO 30: READ RI[I]: NEXT I
24   DATA    50,50,250,150,150,250,50,150,50,150
25   DATA   250,150,50,150,50,250,50,250,150,250
26   DATA    50,250,250,150,50,250,150,150,250,50
29   REM   * * * * READ MOVEMENT DISTANCES IN DEGREES ANGULAR ROTATION
30   FOR I = 1 TO 30: READ MP[I]: NEXT I
40   DATA   30,45,20,60,80,75,50,35,30,10
50   DATA   20,70,55,45,75,80,40,60,20,65
55   DATA   75,80,35,45,60,55,60,40,75,30
58   HOME : VTAB [5]: HTAB [16]: PRINT "TRIAL # ";IT
60   VTAB [10]: HTAB [5]: PRINT "MOVE UNTIL THE TONE IS HEARD": PRINT  CHRS
     [7]
100  PRINT
105  REM   * * * * SAMPLE ANGULAR POSITION OF FOREARM
110  CALL 16400: REM  ASSEMBLER A/D CONVERTER SUBROUTINE
115  X =  PEEK [254] * 256 +  PEEK [255]: REM  CONVERT BINARY TO DECIMAL
116  REM   * * * * IF NOT AT TARGET TAKE ANOTHER POSITION READING
118  IF X < MP[IT] THEN 110
119  REM   * * * * IF AT TARGET RING BELL ONCE
120  PRINT CHR$ [7]: PRINT  CHR$ [7]
121  REM   * * * * SAMPLE POSITION AND STORE ACTUAL STOPPING POINT
122  CALL 16400:L = 256 *  PEEK [254] +  PEEK [255]:RES[IT,1] = L
123  REM   * * * * PROVIDE A SHORT DELAY AND THEN SIGNAL SUBJECT TO RETUR
     N
124  FOR I = 1 TO 1000: NEXT I: PRINT  CHR$ [7]
126  RI = RI[IT]: REM  GET RETENTION INTERVAL FOR THIS TRIAL
128  REM   * * * * PROVIDE THE REQUIRED RETENTION INTERVAL
130  FOR I = 1 TO RI: CALL 16384: NEXT I
140  HOME : REM  CLEAR SCREEN
150  REM   * * * * SIGNAL SUBJECT TO BEGIN THE REPRODUCTION MOVEMENT
160  VTAB [15]: HTAB [1]: PRINT "RECALL THE PREVIOUS MOVEMENT": PRINT  CHR$
     [7]: PRINT  CHR$ [7]: PRINT  CHR$ [7]
170  PRINT : PRINT "HIT SPACE BAR WHEN SUBJECT STOPS MOVING": PRINT
175  REM   * * * * AFTER SUBJECT STOPS SAMPLE THE MOVEMENT POSITION
180  GET A$
185  REM    * * * * CONVERT BINARY POSITION DATA INTO DECIMAL NUMBER
190  CALL 16400:R = 256 *  PEEK [254] +  PEEK [255]:RES[IT,2] = R
210  IT = IT + 1: REM  INCREMENT TRIAL COUNTER
215  HOME : REM  CLEAR SCREEN
216  VTAB [5]: HTAB [5]: PRINT "TRIAL # ";IT - 1;" RESULTS"
217  VTAB [10]: HTAB [10]: PRINT "TARGET = ";L / 2;" DEGREES"
218  VTAB [12]: HTAB [10]: PRINT "RECALL = ";R / 2;" DEGREES"
219  VTAB [16]: HTAB [10]: PRINT "MOVEMENT ERROR = ";L / 2 - R / 2;" DEG
     REES"
220  IF IT < 30 THEN 300: REM  IF ALL TRIALS COMPLETE THEN STORE DATA
225  REM   * * * * IF MORE TRIALS NEEDED GO BACK AND REPEAT PROCEDURES
228  REM   * * * * DISK WRITING ROUTINE
229  REM   * * * *
230  PRINT D$;"APPEND MOTOR MEMORY RESULTS"
240  PRINT D$;"WRITE MOTOR MEMORY RESULTS"
245  PRINT N$
250  FOR I = 1 TO 30: PRINT RES[I,1]: PRINT RES[I,2]: NEXT I
260  PRINT D$;"CLOSE MOTOR MEMORY RESULTS"
270  END
290  REM   * * * * PROVIDE DELAY FOR INTERTRIAL INTERVAL
300  FOR I = 1 TO 100: CALL 16384: NEXT I: GOTO 58
```

Listing 9.4 Motor control research data acquisition program written in the BASIC language.

```
100   REM   A/D AND CONTROL PROGRAM
170   D$ - CHR$ [4]: REM   DISK COMMAND CHARACTER
180   IF D% > 1 THEN 200
190   PRINT D$;"BLOAD GETEMG,A$4000": REM   LOAD A/D SUBROUTINE INTO MEMOR
      Y
200   GOSUB 560: REM    INPUT SUBJECT AND EXPERIMENT DATA
210   GOSUB 730: REM   CALCULATE AND STORE END OF DATA LOCATION
220   GOSUB 860: REM   STORE SUBJECT DATA IN MEMORY
230   GOSUB 920: REM   SET CLOCK PARAMETERS [CONVERSION PULSES/SECOND]
240   GOSUB 1030: REM   MOVEMENT APPARATUS CALIBRATION ROUTINE
250   GOSUB 1270: REM   DATA COLLECTION SUBROUTINE
290   INPUT "SAVE THIS TRIAL ? : ";A$
300   IF A$ - "Y" THEN 320
310   GOTO 380
360   GOSUB 1820: REM   DISK STORAGE ROUTINE
370   ITRIAL - ITRIAL + 1: REM   INCREMENT TRIAL COUNTER
380   IF NTRIAL > - ITRIAL THEN 250: REM   ENOUGH TRIALS ??
390   END
555   REM   * * * * * * * * * * * * * * * * * * * * * * * * * * * * *
560   REM
570   REM   SUBJECT DATA SUBROUTINE
575   REM
600   INPUT "SUBJECT CODE : ";SUBJ
610   INPUT "NUMBER OF TRIALS : ";NTRIAL
620   INPUT "AGE OF SUBJECT IN MONTHS : ";AGE
650   INPUT "STARTING TRIAL : ";ITRIAL
670   INPUT "VELOCITY OF MOVEMENT : ";VEL
680   INPUT "DISPLAY DATA ? : ";DP$
690   INPUT "SAMPLE HOW MANY MSEC : ";MSEC
700   INPUT "NUMBER OF INPUT CHANNELS : ";CHAN
710   INPUT "INTERVAL BETWEEN SAMPLES [SEC] : ";P1
720   RETURN
1022  REM   * * * * * * * * * * * * * * * * * * * * * * * * * * * * *
1030  REM   MOVEMENT CALIBRATION
1035  REM
1040  PRINT : PRINT "POSITION ARM AT START - HIT ANY KEY "
1050  PRINT : GET A$
1060  CALL 16576: REM   READ A/D CONVERTER FOR POSITION OF LEVER
1070  Z1 - PEEK [250]:22 - PEEK [251]: REM   READ MEMORY
1090  ZS - Z1 * 256 + 22: REM   CONVERT BINARY TO DECIMAL
1120  PRINT "START AT - ";ZS
1130  PRINT : PRINT "POSITION ARM AT TARGET POINT ": PRINT
1140  PRINT "HIT ANY KEY": GET A$
1150  CALL 16576: REM   READ A/D CONVERTER FOR POSITION
1160  Z3 - PEEK [250]:24 - PEEK [251]
1180  ZF - Z3 * 256 + 24: REM   CONVERT BINARY TO DECIMAL
1210  PRINT "TARGET POINT - ";ZF
1240  INPUT "RECALIBRATE ???? : ";A$
1250  IF A$ - "Y" THEN 1040
1260  RETURN
1262  REM   * * * * * * * * * * * * * * * * * * * * * * * * * * * * *
1265  REM
1270  REM   DATA COLLECTION ROUTINE
1275  REM
1280  PRINT : PRINT : PRINT " * * * * * TRIAL - ";ITRIAL;" * * * * *"
1290  POKE 16644,ITRIAL: REM   STORE TRIAL IN MEMORY
1320  PRINT "TYPE CTRL G TO BEGIN ": GET A$
1330  POKE 06,01: REM   SET CLOCK TO ZERO
1340  IF   ASC [A$] < > 07 THEN 1320: REM   IF A$ NOT CTRL G THEN WAIT FO
      R ANOTHER CHAR
1370  PRINT : PRINT "* * * * * START * * * * *"
1380  REM   RESET AND ZERO EXTERNAL CLOCK
1390  FOR I - 49242 TO 49245: PRINT   PEEK [I]: NEXT I
1400  CALL 16384: REM   BEGIN A/D SAMPLING FOR TRIAL
1410  CK - PEEK [16563]: REM   READ ERROR FLAG
1420  IF CK < > 243 THEN   RETURN : REM   IF NOT ERROR, CONTINUE
1425  REM   * * * * IF ERROR OCCURS IN CLOCK RATE, RESET SAMPLING RATE
```

(Cont.)

```
1430  PRINT : PRINT " * * * * * DATA OVERRUN * * * * * "
1440  GOSUB 690: REM  SAMPLING RATE SET TOO HIGH, RESET LOWER RATE
1450  RETURN
1813  REM  * * * * * * * * * * * * * * * * * * * * * * * * * * * * * * *
1814  REM
1820  REM    DISK STORAGE ROUTINE
1822  REM
1830  XTRIAL = XTRIAL + 1: REM  DISK FILE LABELING COUNTER
1850  S3$ =   STR$ [XTRIAL]: REM  SET UP DISK FILE NAME
1860  S2$ =   STR$ [SUBJ]
1870  S0$ = " "
1880  S1$ = "FILE"
1890  SS$ = S1$ + S0$ + S2$ + S0$ + S3$
1900  IF XTRIAL > 10 THEN  GOTO 1950: REM  PUT TRIALS 11-20 ON DISK 2
1910  REM  * * * TRIALS 1-10 ON DISK 1
1920  PRINT D$;"BSAVE ";SS$;",A$4100,L12016,D1"
1940  RETURN
1950  PRINT D$;"BSAVE ";SS$;",A$4100,L12016,D2"
1970  RETURN
1971  REM  * * * * * * * * * * * * * * * * * * * * * * * * * * * * * * *
1972  REM
1974  REM  ERROR HANDLING ROUTINE
1976  REM
1980  INPUT "TRY TO WRITE AGAIN ?? : ";A$
1990  IF A$ < > "Y" THEN  GOTO 2020
2000  GOSUB 1900: REM  WRITE TO DISK AGAIN
2010  GOTO 1270: REM  RESUME DATA COLLECTION
2020  GOTO 200: REM  START OVER
```

CHAPTER 10

Microcomputer Control of Graded Exercise Testing

Joseph E. Donnelly

The microcomputer has rapidly become a standard instrument associated with exercise physiology and sports testing. Once viewed solely as a vehicle for rapid data reduction, the microcomputer is now often the very heart of the increasingly sophisticated testing and analysis systems available throughout universities and private enterprises. Because it is quite mobile, the microcomputer can be readily adapted to various environments. This mobility frequently allows for testing in the actual competitive environment instead of in a sterile laboratory.

Data collection in physiological and sports testing often requires compiling enormous amounts and varieties of information simultaneously or in a very short period of time. No longer are tests and test results a simplistic endeavor. As society and especially technology become more complex, we have come to expect our information-gathering and reporting systems to reflect this complexity. For example, no longer are track races started by a pistol and timed with a stopwatch. Today, the starter's pistol may be interfaced with the timing clock, and the finish of the race is detected by photocell or other electronic means. In exercise physiology the step test, once accepted as a good measure of cardiovascular fitness, has been replaced by motor-driven treadmills, gas analyzers, and electrocardiographs.

Although the increasing ability to gather information is generally considered desirable, the utility of the information depends on quality control. The usefulness of the testing procedure, no matter how sensitive or precise, depends on the ability to control, reduce, organize, and summarize the results. All the data in the world is useless unless it is accurate and is presented in a manageable and relevant way. Fortunately, the microcomputer represents a tool capable of managing the testing environment and decreasing the complexity of the situation to the user's advantage.

Dedicated Black Box Systems

The early attempts to automate testing in physiology and sports were evidenced by a proliferation of black box systems. In this section, the term *black box* refers to dedicated instruments or systems that are designed to perform one task and cannot be altered. For example, in physiology it is quite common to use a motor-driven treadmill as an ergometer for performing fitness tests. A treadmill controller, sometimes available and purchased separately from the treadmill itself, is designed to control the speed and grade of the treadmill and is not capable of performing any other task. In short, a black box is dedicated to one task exclusively and cannot be altered.

The dedicated system is like the so-called role player on a sports team. The role player performs a limited function and does so quite well. Unfortunately, when the role changes, the player's contribution toward the final product is diminished due to the limited scope of abilities and poor adaptability to new tasks. So goes the black box system, one day providing a limited but useful function, the next day obsolete and on the shelf collecting dust.

The dedicated system may be explored in terms of financial impact also. Educational institutions at all levels are experiencing hard times and must make optimum use of financial resources. Testing instruments share a common set of problems relative to their operation. Control of the instrument is necessary in all situations, and most often the information that is generated must be treated or refined. If a dedicated system is developed for five separate instruments, the consumer suffers five times the cost and ends up with five inflexible systems. That is also five systems to check and maintain instead of one main system. It will generally save considerable dollars if the five hypothetical systems are interfaced with a microcomputer instead of creating five separate dedicated systems. Additionally, consider the decreasing cost of microcomputers. The entire microcomputer system may be purchased for a cost lower than the dedicated system. True, it needs to be programmed; however, with the emphasis on computer use in public schools, programmers are increasingly available.

Use of Programmable Systems

In contrast to the black box or dedicated instrument is the concept of the *multi-use programmable system*. Programmable systems offer advantages over dedicated systems in the areas of cost and versatility. The cost of microcomputers continues to decline due to the influence of competition and technological breakthroughs. An Apple II+

microcomputer purchased for $2,400 in 1982 may be purchased currently for about $1,400. The programmable system is versatile both internally and externally; that is, the microcomputer can be adjusted to reflect changes within a system and can be adapted to accept different or additional information from outside a system (new systems).

Perhaps an example would dramatize the advantages of the progammable system. Stress testing (graded exercise testing) has become a standard procedure to determine cardiovascular fitness. Generally, an electrocardiograph is used to monitor heart rate and rhythm. Electrocardiographs are available that will turn on and off at predetermined intervals according to the treadmill protocol you are using. What if you want intervals, however, that are different from the preprogrammed intervals? If you are using a bicycle ergometer, how will you be able to adapt the different time intervals to those usually found with treadmills? Moreover, if you wish to use the electrocardiograph independent of any ergometer, how will you adjust the time intervals for switching? Of course, the answer is that you will not be able to. Even though this stress-testing example uses sophisticated equipment, this dedicated system is not versatile. A programmable system, on the other hand, allows for (a) choice of time intervals for switching on the electrocardiograph, (b) various lengths of time for the electrocardiograph to remain on once switched, and (c) spontaneous creation of an infinite number of protocols. It should be clear that a programmable system would provide for internal versatility as new situations occur within the system.

External versatility may be illustrated by continuing the previous example. Perhaps after switching the electrocardiograph on and off, you decide it would be nice to avoid the task of subjective calculations of heart rate and would like heart rates recorded automatically for you. Instead of purchasing another dedicated system in the form of a cardiotachometer, you can program your microcomputer to accept the additional system and probably realize a considerable financial savings.

Cardiovascular Fitness Testing

Physical educators, coaches, physicians, and others have long had an interest in quantifying cardiovascular fitness. Coaches may be interested in fitness as it relates to athletic performance, and physical educators may be concerned about fitness as it relates to health. Regardless of the reason, a reliable, valid, and objective test is necessary if quantification is to be accomplished. Early tests, such as bench stepping or running on a track, have given way to sophisticated tests and testing instruments. Currently, the *graded exercise test* (GXT) using a motor-driven treadmill and supporting physiological devices is utilized extensively in laboratories and clinics. The GXT is used to present increasing stress to the cardiovascular system until some criteria are met and the test is terminated. It is called a ''graded test'' because it contains increments of increasing difficulty and is graded to match the subject's abilities to perform work successfully. Although the GXT can take many forms, the usual situation demands a motor-driven treadmill, electrocardiograph, and sphygmomanometer. Data are collected as the subject performs by walking, running, or a combination of both. The minimum information collected would include heart rates, blood pressures, and treadmill speeds and grades. Many situations demand much more complex and voluminous data acquisition. The results of the GXT are organized, summarized, and placed in report form for helping to establish the subject's current physical condition and developing the exercise prescription.

Problems With the Manually Operated GXT

The GXT appears to be a straightforward procedure; however, it is more complicated than it may appear. Problems facing all of those who administer the GXT include equipment, personnel, data acquisition, data reduction, and time. In addition to these common problems, the sheer quantity of the GXTs administered can represent a major headache to an active testing center.

Equipment

I would suggest it is the rule, rather than the exception, that testing centers are pieced together with equipment obtained at different times by different directors and with less than ideal funding. In an attempt to conserve funds, instruments are purchased that require considerable user training, expertise, and manipulation rather than more expensive automated instruments. In graded exercise testing, the most important instruments are the motor-driven treadmill and electrocardiograph. The treadmill will have an easily accessible control panel with switches for speed and elevation. Operation of these switches is easy; however, assuring operation at the correct time is not particularly easy when the typical exercise technician is distracted by other simultaneous duties. It should be mentioned that an automatic control panel may be available, although such items generally cost as much or more than a microcomputer and represent dedicated systems.

The electrocardiograph (ECG) is used to obtain accurate heart rates and to provide a means of monitoring the electrochemical activity of the heart as progressive workloads are administered during the fitness test. Depending on the ECG used, one or several switches must be manipulated at various time intervals to obtain the information. If the protocol for obtaining the heart rate is not adhered to, the reliability of the test suffers. Automated ECGs to produce the required data are available, but they are expensive and perform only one job.

Personnel

Two to four trained persons are required to operate a standard fitness test. Personnel are difficult to obtain, train, and fund. It may be suggested that with each additional person, the probability of subjective investigator error increases. With teamlike coordination, each person must understand his or her responsibilities in relation to those of the others. As the number of personnel increases, a coordinated effort becomes more difficult. Arranging testing times with multiple individual schedules is yet another struggle. It is apparent that testing logistics would be easier if fewer personnel are required.

Data Acquisition

Human error constantly threatens the acquisition of "good data." The testing area is a busy place, and it is easy to overlook responsibilities or to perform responsibilities at times other than as specified by the protocol. This problem becomes particularly evident when exercise technicians are assigned multiple duties that demand data acquistion in close time intervals or when close attention to the subject is necessary. It is not uncommon for a single technician to attempt to take blood pressure, obtain a heart rate, and adjust speed and grade of the treadmill all in a 30-second period.

In addition to data acquisition, subjective judgments are made when data are recorded. For example, if heart rates are recorded using several quick methods (ruler, 6 seconds, etc.), considerable variation in interpretation results among individuals. Objective data can be obtained by using the microcomputer for flexible system control.

Data Reduction

Fitness testing produces a great amount of data that needs to be organized and summarized. Information relative to speed and grade of the treadmill, total exercise time, heart rate, blood pressure, oxygen consumption, calories, and perceived exertion are examples. Generally, an individualized exercise program is based on these and other data. Although data reduction is not a difficult process, it requires considerable treatment of numbers and calculations. This process is time consuming, monotonous, and prone to simple mistakes. It is a job for which the microcomputer is ideally suited.

Time

Little needs to be said about the value of time. In business, the standard expression is "time is money." In exercise testing, depending on the situation, this may or may not be applicable. In the educational setting the fees may be minimal, whereas in the clinical setting the fees for testing may be considerable. Regardless of the immediate financial impact, most individuals would like to avoid excessive time spent on data acquisition and data reduction and use that time for more creative, important work.

Solution for the GXT

The microcomputer represents a very attractive solution to most of the problems previously discussed. The use of the microcomputer represents a certain philosophical approach to solving multiple problems. The microcomputer represents one instrument performing many jobs instead of many dedicated instruments performing one job. With the microcomputer the job descriptions may range infinitely, whereas the dedicated system is not trainable for new tasks.

An example of how the fitness testing environment may be controlled by microcomputer is presented in the following section. The system is one used in the Human Performance Laboratory at Kearney State College. It represents a reasonable attempt to solve the problems encountered in fitness testing and has many of the features common to other fitness testing centers.

Hardware

The microcomputer-controlled system shown in Figure 10.1 consists of the following: (a) 48K microcomputer, (b) single floppy disk drive, (c) printer, (d) monitor, (e) language card/word processor, (f) A/D board, (g) relay and controller, (h) motor-driven treadmill, (i) electrocardiograph, and (j) pulse conditioner.

A 48K microcomputer is recommended to allow for adequate memory space for the software that controls the system. Not all microcomputers accept peripheral inputs, and some that do accept inputs more easily than others. Software can be stored on a single floppy disk; however, a dual disk system may be employed also. The advantage of the dual drive is that programs controlling the testing environment may be placed on one disk and subject information and

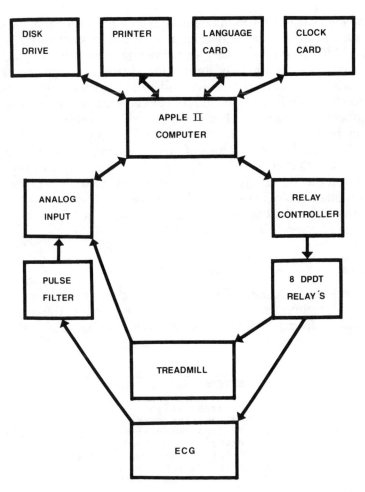

Figure 10.1   Microcomputer-controlled fitness testing.

results may be placed on the other disk. This separation of information will allow the results of more subjects to be stored on a disk before it is filled and avoids filling the disk of controlling programs with results from subjects. The disadvantage of the dual drive system is the cost of the second disk drive. Because a drive may cost about $500 and a disk can be bought and duplicated for about $3.50, the single disk drive is used in the system described in this chapter. A dot matrix printer is adequate for the formulation of fitness reports, thus avoiding the expense of the letter quality printer. A monitor can be purchased, or an old television set will do nicely. A language card is necessary if the programs are written in a higher language than BASIC.

These are available through any microcomputer dealer and are simple to insert into the internal workings of the microcomputer.

The A/D board has been explained in previous chapters and represents the capability of interfacing peripheral instruments with the microcomputer. The relays and relay controller are switching devices to open and close circuits between the microcomputer and peripheral instruments. For graded exercise testing the treadmill should be a minimum capability of 0.5 to 7.5 mph and 0 to 25% grade. The electrocardiograph can be of any type, from a single-channel to a multiple-channel model, because the ECG will simply be turned on and off. If the electrocardiograph does not have a built-in cardiotachometer, one should be purchased or created. In the present example, a homemade pulse conditioner is used to allow the ECG to pass heart rate information to the microcomputer.

Software

The software associated with the microcomputer-controlled GXT will vary with testing sites. The current system presents the user with a main menu from which to choose. As shown in Figure 10.2, the selec-

```
              STRESS TEST SYSTEM

        1.  Fitness Tables
        2.  Patient Information
        3.  Self-Designed Protocol
        4.  Heart Rate Control
        5.  Electrocardiograph Control
        6.  Print Patient Records
        7.  Print Stress Tests

        SELECTION  (              )
```

Figure 10.2 Stress test system main menu.

tions include fitness tables, patient information, self-designed protocol, heart rate control, electrocardiograph control, and two print modes.

Patient information, self-designed protocol, fitness tables, and patient records pertain directly to the GXT and will be discussed. The remaining files, which are not directly related to the GXT, control the individual exercise session of a subject and are beyond the topic of this chapter.

```
                    PATIENT INFORMATION

          (A)   Add a patient
          (C)   Change Patient Information
          (D)   Delete a patient
          (Q)   Query a patient

          SELECTION   (              )
```

Figure 10.3 Patient information menu.

Demographic Information

To initiate a GXT, certain information is needed for each subject. By selecting the patient information file, the user is presented with the choices shown in Figure 10.3.

For example, to enter a subject to be tested, the letter "A" is selected and the screen presents a set of pertinent demographic questions (see Figure 10.4). These questions have been programmed; however, other questions based on personal preference and needs of the fitness center could be used.

It should be noted that any information used in subsequent files (programs) is automatically transferred when the subject's identification number is entered. This process avoids duplication and saves time. Once the demographic information is entered, the user has an opportunity to change the information before the file is closed, the information stored, and the main menu is again displayed.

```
                    PATIENT INFORMATION

Patient ID                  ( 65)
Name                        ( John Doe)
Address                     ( 402 Oak Dr.)
City & State                ( Kearney, NE)
Birthdate                   ( 11/19/49)
Sex                         ( M )
Last Visit                  ( 8/6/81)
First Visit                 ( 6/5/79 )
Telephone                   ( 308 234-5006 )
Social Security Number      ( 157-32-4665 )
Office Telephone            ( 236-4181 )
Occupation                  ( Mechanic)
Employer                    ( Stan's Auto Repair)
Medications                 ( None)
```

Figure 10.4 Demographic information found in patient information file.

```
          SELF-DESIGNED PROTOCOL

    1.   Begin Self-Designed Test
    2.   Print Exercise Report
    3.   Store Test Results

    SELECTION  (               )
```

Figure 10.5 Self-designed protocol menu.

Selection and/or Creation of a GXT Protocol

Selection of number 3, "self-designed protocol," from the main menu begins the graded exercise test with the screen display as shown in Figure 10.5.

Logically, the user is asked if it is necessary to create a protocol or if a previously created protocol should be requested by name. Unlike standard treadmill controllers that have a limited number of "canned" protocols, the user is free to create an infinite number of protocols, name them, and store them for future use. If a protocol must be created, the duration of exercise stages, speed, and grade of elevation is specified by the user in any combination within the limits of the treadmill (see Figure 10.6).

Using the Patient Information Data Base

Once the protocol has been created, or if an established protocol is named, the screen asks for the subject's identification number (see

```
               SELF-DESIGNED PROTOCOL

    1.   Begin Self-Designed Test
    2.   Print Exercise Report
    3.   Store Test Results

    SELECTION   (1)
    TEST NAME   ( SMITH GXT)
                SMITH GXT NOT FOUND
    CREATE A PROTOCOL  ( Y or N )              ( Y )

    NUMBER OF STAGES
STAGE #    GRADE      SPEED       DURATION
  ( 1 )    ( 0 )      ( 3.0 )       ( 5 )
  ( 2 )    ( 3 )      ( 3.4 )       ( 3 )
  ( 3 )    ( 6 )      ( 3.8 )       ( 3 )
  ( 4 )    ( 3 )      ( 3.4 )       ( 3 )
  ( 5 )    ( 0 )      ( 3.0 )       ( 5 )
```

Figure 10.6 Development of new GXT protocol.

JOHN DOE	ID # 65
TESTING DATE	(02/28/84)
PATIENT AGE	(34)
TEST ADMINISTRATOR	(JD/LP)
SITTING BP	(124/86)
SITTING HR	(76)
PREDICTED MAX HR	(186)
PREDICTED 90% HR	(167)
PREDICTED 70% HR	(130)
PATIENT WT (LB)	(150)
TEST TIME	(1:00)
STRIP LENGTH (sec.)	(6)
BEGINNING STAGE #	(1)

Figure 10.7   Preliminary GXT information.

Figure 10.7). When the number is entered, the microcomputer searches the appropriate patient information file and transfers all pertinent information. The subject's name, age, and sex appear on the screen. When the resting heart rate and blood pressure are entered, the predicted maximum heart rate is calculated and placed on the screen along with 90% and 70% of the maximum. The predicted heart rates remain on the screen throughout the test so a comparison may be made between exercise heart rates and those that are predicted.

Selecting GXT Options and Obtaining the Heart Rate

The electrocardiograph is turned on during the last 10 s of every exercise stage. The user may specify the length of time the ECG is to remain on. The present system allows a selection between 1 and 12 s. Additionally, the user may switch the ECG on at any time by pressing the space bar. This allows a hard copy of the subject's ECG to be available for inspection.

The user has the option to begin the exercise test at any of the specified stages and need not start at the beginning. For example, if you have a well-conditioned subject, you may wish to speed up the testing procedure by starting the test at the fifth stage instead of the first stage. This option is presented by asking the user to enter the beginning stage (see Figure 10.7).

The programmed GXT is initiated by pressing the ESC key, which sets initial speed and grade according to the beginning stage previously specified. The clock is programmed to display both the total elapsed time and the current stage time. Treadmill speed and grade are displayed and total mileage is calculated and displayed (see Figure 10.8).

CURRENT GXT INFORMATION	
TIME ELAPSED	(5:15)
TIME STAGE	(0:15)
STAGE NUMBER	(2)
CURRENT GRADE	(3.0)
CURRENT SPEED	(3.4)
HEART RATE	(116)
DISTANCE (MILES)	(.28)

Figure 10.8 Current GXT information.

Heart rates are calculated during the last 10 seconds of every exercise stage and displayed on the monitor screen. The subject must be either directly connected to the ECG or send a signal of the activity of the heart via telemetry to a receiver. The receiver sends this information to the ECG, which in turn sends the information to an oscilloscope. To obtain heart rates that may be interpreted by computer software, it was necessary to create a custom pulse conditioner, which serves as an intermediary between the ECG and computer. The pulse conditioner is hard wired to the ECG and to the A/D board of the microcomputer. As shown in Figure 10.9, the pulse conditioner accepts an electrical voltage, filters it, ensures it is of sufficient magnitude, and sends it in a more usable form to the microcomputer. The software then counts the impulses and checks the clock to see how much time has elapsed. A simple mathematical calculation then provides the number of beats per minute, which is displayed on the screen and stored for future use in the exercise reports.

Control of the Treadmill

The speed and elevation of the treadmill is controlled by the microcomputer according to the selected protocol. The treadmill control panel is directly wired to the A/D converter of the microcomputer. Essen-

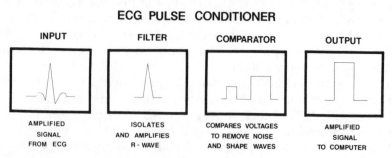

Figure 10.9 Custom pulse conditioner.

tially, the computer replaces the need to press switches manually at the treadmill control panel. The voltage found in the analog meters of the treadmill control panel will correspond to the speed and elevation of the treadmill. The voltage found in the analog meters passes through the A/D converter and is assigned a digital number. According to the protocol, the microcomputer "reads" the numbers at predetermined times and checks the software to see if the number is correct. If the number is not correct, the appropriate relay will be opened and the treadmill will adjust speed and/or elevation as if the user were pressing a switch on the treadmill control panel.

Termination of the GXT and Recovery

Upon completion of the GXT a period of recovery is usually observed to monitor the subject as heart rate, blood pressure, and respiration return toward resting values. In the present system this is initiated by pressing the ESC key. Upon initiating recovery, the treadmill is stopped and the microcomputer will reset the elevation to zero. The current elapsed time and current stage time are also reset to zero. Heart rates are still obtained during the last 10 seconds of each recovery stage. At the end of recovery the screen displays the heart rates as they were obtained stage by stage and provides a space to enter blood pressures.

All pertinent information from the GXT is saved and transferred to the summary report. At the end of the recovery period, the user is asked to enter the perceived exertion rating of the subject. The screen then presents questions relative to the performance of the subject, including reasons for terminating the test, comments relative to the ECG, and several lines of space for any additional information (see Figure 10.10).

Once all information is entered, the screen presents the self-designed protocol menu. The user may then print the summary report or store it, or both. It should be noted at this point that the only procedures that require the attention of the exercise technician who administers the GXT are checking blood pressure and monitoring the oscilloscope. An automatically inflated sphygmomanometer could be used to make the GXT totally automated; however, the automatic systems tend to be costly and unreliable. Because the administrator serves only one manipulative function during GXT, he or she should have the time necessary to monitor both the oscilloscope and the patient, procedures often overlooked.

Data Reduction and Report Summary

Once the GXT is completed, the time-consuming, monotonous task of reducing the data, summarizing the results, and formulating the

GXT COMMENTS	
RATED PERCEIVED EXERTION	(18)
REASON FOR STOPPING TEST	(general fatigue, especially in legs)
RESTING (STANDING) ECG	(normal)
POST HYPERVENT, ECG	(normal)
EXERCISE ECG	(normal)
POST EXERCIXE ECG	(normal)
CONCLUSIONS	(begin low risk adult fitness program)

Figure 10.10 Rated perceived exertion, ECG, and conclusions from the GXT.

exercise prescription awaits. If the process is microcomputer controlled, it will be accomplished (in the present example) by pressing key number 2 of the "self-designed protocol." The necessary data will be transferred from patient information and self-designed protocol files, reduced, organized, and delivered on the printer in approximately 75 seconds.

The data from the GXT itself are shown in Figure 10.11. The GXT data are categorized as preliminary information, actual test data, and recovery data. The format in which the test data and recovery data are presented will vary with the protocol specified by the user.

The graded exercise record shown in Figure 10.12 represents a summary of the GXT. Demographic information has been transferred from the patient information file, and data from the test itself are subjected to calculations and summarized. The calculations programmed into the exercise record are at the discretion of the user and may be changed as needed. For example, notice that a fitness level of "good" is presented in Figure 10.12.

The fitness levels utilized in this program are based on the familiar tables of Astrand (1960). Recall that one of the selections from the original main menu is "fitness tables." These tables may be altered to reflect the preference of the user as shown in Figure 10.13.

The written information, such as the reason for stopping, standing ECG, and so on, are simply transferred from the GXT. The current program presents the user with three lines of space available for general comments such as injuries, cautions, exercise preferences, or any pertinent notes. Refer to Figure 10.10 to see how these items are presented.

Comments on Microcomputer-Controlled GXT

The GXT is an example of a physiological fitness testing procedure that can be automated through the use of the microcomputer. The

```
*********************************************************************
                        ***GRADED STRESS TEST***
*********************************************************************
```

Fred Kempf   Patient ID#: 50

Test Administrator: JD

Test Name: Balke

Test Date: 01/17/84   Test Time: 2:00

Age: 48   Weight(Lbs): 167   Sitting BP: 128/84

Sitting HR: 80   Pred Max HR: 172   Pred 90%: 154   Pred 70%: 120

Current Medications: None

ECG Strip Length: 6 seconds

TEST DATA

```
*********************************************************************
```

Stage Number	Duration	Elapsed Time	Speed MPH	Elevation % Grade	Heart Rate	Blood Pressure
1	2:00	2:00	3.0	0.0	110	144/80
2	2:00	4:00	3.0	2.5	110	152/88
3	2:00	6:00	3.0	5.0	120	152/88
4	2:00	8:00	3.0	7.5	136	158/80
5	2:00	10:00	3.0	10.0	142	162/80
6	2:00	12:00	3.0	12.5	162	166/80
7	2:00	14:00	3.0	15.0	175	166/86
8	2:00	16:00	3.0	17.5	184	172/80
9	2:00	18.00	3.0	20.0	0	172/80
10	2:00	20:00	3.0	22.5	0	0

RECOVERY DATA

```
*********************************************************************
```

Stage	Duration	Elapsed Time	Heart Rate	Blood Pressure
1	1:00	1:00	97	150/90
2	2:00	3:00	122	158/98
3	2:00	5:00	118	128/94
4	2:00	7:00	122	124/86

Figure 10.11 Printed format of preliminary information, test data, and recovery data of the GXT.

cost of the system is only slightly more expensive than if a treadmill, controller, and cardiotachometer are purchased separately. However, the versatility and capability cannot be compared. If we had purchased the above items separately to control the GXT, no capability would exist for handling patient information, designing an infinite amount

```
**********************************************************

                 GRADED EXERCISE RECORD

**********************************************************

Fred Kempf              Patient ID #:   50

Test Administrator:  JD

Test Name:  Balke

Test Date:  01/17/84     Test Time:  2:00

Age:  48  Weight (Kg):  75    Sitting BP:  128/84

Sitting HR: 80    Pred Max HR: 172  Pred 90%: 154  Pred 70%: 120

Attained Stage: 9  Attained Speed: 3.0   Attained Grade:   20

Elapsed Time:  16:41      Attained Maximum Heart Rate:   184

Attained Maximum RPP:  316.48   RPE:  16

Atained VO2:  2.79 L/min   36.77 ml/kg/min

Energy Expenditures:  13.94 Kcal    Mets:  10.51

Functional Class (AHA):  I  Fitness Level:   good

Reason for Stopping:      general fatigue

Resting (standing) ECG:   normal

Post Hypervent. ECG:      normal

Exercise ECG:             normal

Post Exercise ECG:        normal

Conclusions:              begin low risk Adult Fitness Program

Comments:
```

Figure 10.12 Printed summary of test data, energy expenditure, fitness level, and comments from the GXT.

of protocols, and formulating the exercise record and prescription. You must also remember that the GXT system is only *one* of the functions the microcomputer will perform. When not controlling GXTs, the microcomputer can control other systems, perform statistical procedures, act as a word processor, or be used for entertainment. As the

FITNESS TABLES

```
1.    Enter # of age groups
2.    Enter # of fitness levels
3.    Edit fitness amounts

SELECTION  ( 3 )
```

FEMALE

AGE	CLASS	POOR	FAIR	AVE	GOOD	HIGH
20	I	( )	( )	( )	( )	( )
30	II	( )	( )	( )	( )	( )
40	III	( )	( )	( )	( )	( )
50	IV	( )	( )	( )	( )	( )
60	V	( )	( )	( )	( )	( )

Figure 10.13 Example of programmable fitness tables.

needs of the user change, the microcomputer can change correspondingly with peripheral devices and software. In short, the microcomputer represents a considerable advantage in cost, versatility, and data gathering over individual dedicated systems.

Reference

Astrand, I. (1960). Aerobic work capacity in men and women with special reference to age. *Acta Physiologica Scandinavia,* **49**(Suppl. 169), 45-60.

CHAPTER 11

Microcomputer Applications in Exercise Physiology

Joseph E. Donnelly

Exercise physiology is inundated with technological advances. Manual systems are out; automated systems are in. Records are entered into huge data bases for instant recall at a subsequent date and for comparisons to previously existing data. Dedicated systems control huge electronic scoreboards that are capable of displaying anything from statistics to the instant replay. Races are started with a pistol interfaced to a timer and force plates in the starting blocks to detect false starts. The average physical educator interested in exercise physiology and sports may be overwhelmed and intimidated by the sophistication and expense of these systems and wonder what can be accomplished via a microcomputer on a more down-to-earth level.

In order to stimulate ideas and create interest, several applications will be presented. The topics represent situations commonly encountered by professionals in athletics, fitness testing, and laboratory research. If the concept of the application can be appreciated, each individual can modify the system to fit his or her situation more completely. For example, a microcomputer-controlled timing device used in football for the 40-yard run may be adapted for use to time speed around the base path in softball.

Determination of Oxygen Consumption

It is generally accepted that maximum oxygen consumption is the single best indicator of cardiovascular fitness. The previous section illustrated the control of exercise testing as it may exist in conjunction with an adult fitness program or medical clinic. In these situations oxygen consumption is frequently calculated from the test results and represents a reasonable estimate of the actual oxygen consumption. Researchers, however, rely on a more precise measurement of oxygen consumption and generally employ a methodology known as

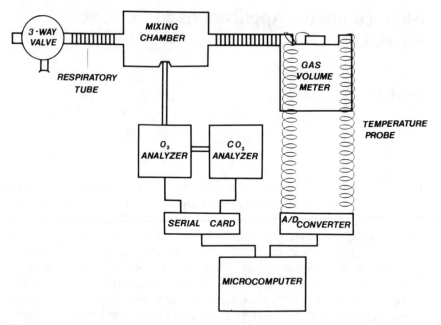

Figure 11.1 Components in a typical open circuit system.

the *open circuit* procedure. Although open circuit systems differ, there seem to be some universal components. Figure 11.1 represents a schematic of typical components in our open circuit system; however, many variations are possible.

The major objectives of using the microcomputer are

- To read the gas analyzers and calculate percentages of the relevant gases.
- To read the volume meter for flow rates.

Auxiliary functions may include monitoring gas temperature and barometric pressure; however, this may represent a waste of space on the peripheral input board because these items may be easily entered via the keyboard by the user.

The system to be illustrated uses a 48K microcomputer, one A/D input, a serial card, a timer/calendar, a monitor, and a printer. The *serial card* is used with gas analyzers that are equipped with computer outputs. The output accepts a standard male plug and sends the results of the gas analysis to the serial card in the form of 0s and 1s. The microcomputer is programmed to read the serial card and assigns a value to the various combinations of 0s and 1s. These items are generally considered as standard equipment with the exception of the timer/calendar, serial card, and the A/D input. The additional cost of these items is approximately $650.

Figure 11.2 shows the screen presented to the user for preliminary input. The identification number of the subject is entered for future reference in obtaining test results that are stored when the test is com-

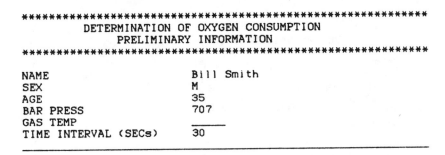

Figure 11.2 Preliminary input data for determination of oxygen consumption.

pleted. The age and sex of the subject are used for subsequent calculation of fitness levels. This procedure was explained previously with the illustration of the graded exercise test. In the current example, oxygen consumption is actually determined instead of estimated from treadmill speed and grade. Weight in pounds is used to calculate oxygen consumption expressed as ml/kg/min. Pounds are obtained from a standard balance scale and converted to kilograms by the program for subsequent calculations. Barometric pressure is obtained on any standard barometer and input by the user. It is assumed that the barometric pressure does not change significantly during the exercise test. Depending on the gas collection system, temperature of the expired air may change as the test progresses. The current system utilizes a thermometer probe from an electronic thermometer inserted into the gas meter. It is read by the microcomputer at intervals corresponding to the gas analysis or the depression of the space bar. The last input before beginning the test is the time interval for gas analysis. In this example, gas is analyzed continuously; however, the calculations are updated according to the user's discretion. Typically, the update process may occur during the last 30 seconds of an exercise stage or at continuous 30-second intervals.

During the exercise test the microcomputer receives information through the A/D input from the temperature probe. A serial card allows communication between the gas analyzers and the microcomputer. The information through both the A/D input and the serial card must be integrated and interpreted by software.

The output from the gas analysis may be designed to meet the needs of the user. Figure 11.3 represents an output that may be useful in a variety of situations. This output appears each time an analysis update is performed.

```
*******************************************************************
              DETERMINATION OF OXYGEN CONSUMPTION
*******************************************************************
        STPD FACTOR =            .775
        VE STPD =              166.27
        MEASURED % CO2=           3.2
        TRUE CO2 =               3.16
        MEASURED % OXYGEN =      17.6
        TRUE CO2=                 3.3

        RQ =                      .93
        V O2 (L/MIN) =           3.93
        V O2 (ML/KG/MIN) =      57.90
        V CO2 L/MIN =            3.6
        VE O2 L/100 ML           3.8
        VE CO2 L/100 ML          4.0
CORRECTED FOR SEX AND AGE, YOUR MAXIMAL OXYGEN UPTAKE IS
CONSIDERED HIGH
```

Figure 11.3 Output for determination of oxygen consumption.

The top six items represent calculations necessary to determine oxygen consumption. The bottom six items represent summary data often used to add meaning to the results. For instance, respiratory quotient (RQ) may be monitored by those administering the test to help determine if the subject is exercising near maximal capacity. Generally, RQ starts at about 0.75 and increases to 0.95+ as the subject approaches maximal work capacity. This allows for a somewhat objective approach for the determination that a test was indeed maximal. The other data may be used in various ways depending on the user's needs and objectives. Upon completion of the test, a printed report may be generated and the results stored for future reference by identification number.

Fitness Prescription

The rise of fitness testing has given corresponding rise to the concept of individualized fitness prescriptions. The administration of group activities where each individual performs the same routine without regard for individual fitness levels is no longer accepted. Individualized programs help assure safety, enjoyment, compliance, and success for the individual who seeks an enhanced level of fitness. The example provided is typical of an adult fitness situation; however, modifying activities, intensities, durations, and frequencies would make it applicable to athletic training as well.

In adult fitness, the exercise prescription generally focuses on aerobic fitness, muscular strength and endurance, and flexibility. Body composition and diet are frequently part of the fitness prescription and will be discussed separately. Aerobic exercise involves selecting an appropriate duration, frequency, intensity, and mode of activities. Figure 11.4 is an example of a fitness table where duration, frequency, and intensity have been assigned values dependent on the individual's measured fitness level.

FITNESS CLASSIFICATION				
LOW	FAIR	AVERAGE	GOOD	HIGH
Duration 10" x 2	15" + 5"	15" x 2	30" + 5"	45"
Frequency 3	3	4	4	5
Intensity 60	65	70	75	80

INTENSITY REPRESENTS % USED IN KARVONEN FORMULA. DURATION IS MINUTES PER EXERCISE SESSION. FREQUENCY IS EXERCISE SESSIONS PER WEEK._

Figure 11.4 Intensity, frequency, and duration of aerobic activity based on fitness level.

As the fitness level increases, the fitness components also increase. Therefore, a relatively fit individual will have to exercise at a higher heart rate, for a longer period of time, and at a greater frequency than an individual who is less fit. Because assigning values to the various fitness components is somewhat arbitrary, they may be altered. Selection of the mode of exercise can be accomplished by individual counseling or by computer grading of an activity questionnaire and matching individual choices with those that are preprogrammed as acceptable.

Using the computer to select the exercise prescription must be done with caution due to the tremendous variability of confounding physical limitations, the variety and/or lack of equipment, and the inability of the computer to translate precisely the exact meaning of the prescription. The professional must always assume responsibility for determining that the exercise prescription is appropriate.

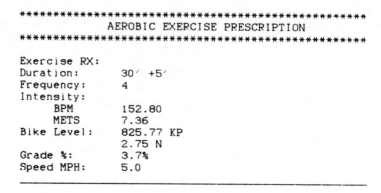

Figure 11.5   Example of exercise prescription based on fitness classification.

Figure 11.5 represents an example of a computer-generated aerobic exercise prescription based on fitness classification. The intensity is expressed a variety of ways (e.g., bpm, METS), and examples are given to the individual for appropriate use of the treadmill and bicycle ergometer to satisfy the prescription.

Prescription of weight training for the muscular strength component may be accomplished in a similar fashion. Figure 11.6 shows normal values adopted for an adult population. The table has been entered into the computer, and the user enters the one repetition maximum (1RM) scores from the individual who is tested. A ratio is calculated from 1RM and body weight and may be used for posttest comparison, motivation, and the calculation of a strength fitness classification.

An example of a strength prescription is shown in Figure 11.7. The fitness instructor may select an appropriate percentage of 1RM to achieve the purpose of weight training and satisfy individual needs. In the current example, 60% of 1RM has been chosen for the initial intensity and projections have been made for 50 and 70% of 1RM. As the individual progresses through training, 70% will be used. Repetitions and sets are chosen from the strength fitness category. As the category moves from "poor" to "excellent," the number of repetitions and sets increases.

Flexibility may be assessed in a variety of ways and degrees of sophistication. Three areas often tested are the shoulder, spinal column, and low back region. Flexibility tests are described in almost all fitness textbooks, and the fitness professional may choose those

NAME: JOHN DOE
WT (LB)   150

STRENGTH SCORES

ITEM	RAW SCORE	RATIO
BENCH PRESS	150	1.00
LATERAL PULL-DOWN	160	1.07
KNEE FLEXION	70	0.47
KNEE EXTENSION	80	0.53

STRENGTH CLASSIFICATION

MEN

BENCH PRESS	LATERAL PULL-DOWN	LEG EXTENSION	LEG CURL	POINTS
1.20	1.10	0.70	0.60	10
1.10	1.05	0.65	0.55	9
1.00	1.00	0.60	0.50	8
0.90	0.95	0.55	0.45	7
0.80	0.90	0.50	0.40	6
0.70	0.85	0.45	0.35	5
0.60	0.80	0.40	0.30	4
0.50	0.75	0.35	0.25	3

WOMEN

BENCH PRESS	LATERAL PULL-DOWN	LEG EXTENSION	LEG CURL	POINTS
0.70	0.75	0.60	0.55	10
0.65	0.70	0.55	0.50	9
0.60	0.65	0.50	0.45	8
0.55	0.60	0.45	0.40	7
0.50	0.55	0.40	0.35	6
0.45	0.50	0.35	0.30	5
0.35	0.45	0.30	0.25	4
0.30	0.40	0.25	0.20	3

TOTAL POINTS	STRENGTH FITNESS CLASSIFICATION
33 To 40	Excellent
25 to 32	Good
17 to 24	Average
9 to 16	Fair
0 to 8	Poor

Figure 11.6 Strength fitness classification from 1RM and body weight.

Strength Training Program

Item	Sets	REPS	Weights	50%	60%	70%
Bench Press	3	6-8		75	90	105
LAT Pull Down	3	6-8		80	96	112
Knee Flexion	3	6-8		35	42	49
Knee Extension	3	6-8		40	48	56

Figure 11.7   Strength-training program based on strength fitness classification.

that are appropriate. Figure 11.8 shows how the user is presented with simple questions to enter test scores. A table of normal values is presented. This table is programmable so it may be changed if different values and tests are used. A list of 11 flexibility activities are stored in the microcomputer. If an individual scores in the low category, appropriate flexibility exercises are chosen by the microcomputer. These exercises may be used to supplement a general stretching program to give areas of concern some extra work.

Fitness prescriptions are not unusually difficult to figure by hand; however, if many prescriptions have to be calculated, it becomes time consuming and rather boring. With commercially available software that prescribes fitness programs, the fitness professional can accomplish the task quickly. It is up to the user to decide if these programs are adequate, affordable, and applicable to the situation at hand.

Body Composition

Body composition is of interest to a wide variety of health/fitness professionals. The public has always been obsessed with the cosmetics of obesity exemplified by the saying "You can never be too rich or too thin." Health/fitness professionals and coaches are concerned with body composition because of the relationship to health/fitness and athletic success. Measurement of body composition may be accomplished by a variety of methods. Perhaps the most common methods include the use of skinfold calipers, circumference measures, or hydrostatic weighing. Those familiar with these procedures admit that the necessary mathematical calculations are not difficult but are rather laborious, time consuming, and error prone.

```
************************************************************
                 Flexibility Assessment
************************************************************
```

                Name: John Doe   Sex: M

Item	Enter Score	Classification
Sit and Reach	[-2]	Below Ave
Shoulder Lift	[22]	Ave
Trunk Extension	[19]	Ave

```
************************************************************
                 Flexibility Exercise
************************************************************
```

Item	Effect
*Knees to chest	Hamstrings
Heel to buttocks	Quads
*Rocker	Spine
*Plow	Spine
Spine extension	Spine, abdomen
*Butterfly	Adductors
Twist	Spine
Shoulder stretch	Shoulder
Heel cord stretch	Gastroc
*Hurdler	Hamstring
Reverse Hurdler	Quads

 *   Supplemental exercises

Figure 11.8 Supplemental stretching exercises based on flexibility category.

To alleviate this problem, a few of the skinfold and circumference body composition equations have nomograms that reduce or eliminate the need for complex calculations. Unfortunately, there are a vast number of equations and relatively few nomograms. Additionally, nomograms are not applicable to hydrostatic weighing, which is a more accurate method and which is becoming increasingly popular as a research and clinical method.

It is useful to have body composition software that allows entry of demographic information, provides selection of body composition methods, is programmable, and provides for storage and retrieval. The software program that follows is designed for use in health enhancement programs offered through medical clinics. The program can be modified to suit the needs or ideas of different medical clinics.

The user is presented with the menu shown in Figure 11.9. If records are to be retained on the individual patient, the appropriate selection is number 1, "patient information," which is a simple file allowing entry of identification number and name. The user may enter an individual's patient information and proceed to another file to enter body composition data or may enter a list of patients for subsequent testing. When body composition data are available for entry, number 2 on the body fat system menu is the correct response. Figure 11.10 illustrates which choices are available for data entry. In this example "hydrostatic weighing," number 3, is selected.

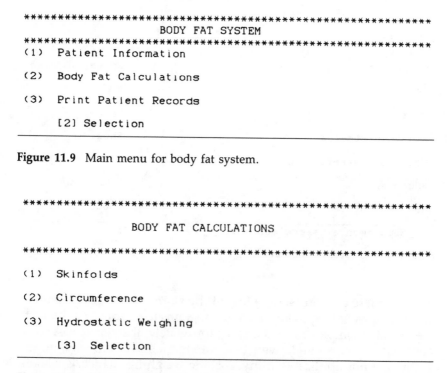

```
*********************************************************************
                          BODY FAT SYSTEM
*********************************************************************
(1)    Patient Information

(2)    Body Fat Calculations

(3)    Print Patient Records

       [2] Selection
```

Figure 11.9 Main menu for body fat system.

```
*********************************************************************
                       BODY FAT CALCULATIONS

*********************************************************************

(1)    Skinfolds

(2)    Circumference

(3)    Hydrostatic Weighing

       [3] Selection
```

Figure 11.10 Menu for body fat calculations.

```
******************************************************************
Body    Composition         by         Hydrostatic   Weighing
******************************************************************
(1) ID# = 0160 Joe Bird

(2) Method used                                    RV-Determined

(3) Sex                                                     Male

(4) Body Wt (LBS.)                                        150.0

(5) Gas Temp. (C)                                         28.0

(6) Bar Press (mmHG)                                     707.0

(7) Water Temp (C)                                        36.0

(8) Vital Capacity (ML/ATPS)                            5400.0

(9) Residual Volume (ML/ATPS)    1240      1250         1245.0

(10) Tare Wt (Gm)                                       5450.0

(11) Underwater Wt (GM) 8725.0  8750.0   8725.0        8733.3
```

Figure 11.11 Input data for hydrostatic weighing at residual volume.

The screen presented to the user asks for simple responses and is based on normal data collection and reduction procedures, although procedures will vary somewhat among testing facilities (see Figure 11.11).

The user enters the identification number that corresponds with the data of the individual, and the name of the individual is retrieved from the patient information file. The user selects the method of hydrostatic weighing from those available. This software program calculates body composition using four different lung volume procedures. Three of these procedures—residual lung volume (RLV), total lung capacity (TLC), and functional residual capacity (FRC)—are well known; hydrostatic weighing at total lung capacity nonsubmerged (TLC-NS), however, is an experimental method currently under development (Donnelly & Sintek, 1986).

The traditional RV procedure is selected in this example. A choice is available regarding the method for determining residual volume. If residual volume is estimated, it will be calculated from vital capacity ATPS (ambient temperature, pressure, saturated) and corrected to BTPS (body temperature, pressure, saturated) for subsequent use. If residual volume is actually determined, it is entered at line number

9. Space is provided to enter two residual volumes, which are averaged and corrected to BTPS. The user responds to the questions, thereby supplying the necessary raw data for calculation of body composition. The results are shown in Figure 11.12. All conversions of raw data necessary to complete body density are made by the software. An option is available to generate predicted body fat and corresponding body weight should the individual wish to reduce.

The results may be printed, stored, or both and may be retrieved by identification number at a future date. Any number of tests may be stored under the identification number of an individual so comparisons can be made in subsequent testing. Although not shown here, this body composition program also generates a report explaining the results in regards to normal values for age and sex. The circumference and skinfold programs are not illustrated in this example; however, they function similarly to hydrostatic weighing.

```
****************************************************************
Body   Composition   by   Hydrostatic   Weighing
****************************************************************
BTPS                                    1.0591

VC(BTPS)                                5719.2

RV(BTPS)                                1372.6

TLC(BTPS)                               7091.8

Water Density                           0.9937

Body Wt (GM)                            68181.8

Body Density                            1.0664

% Body Fat                              14.34

% LBM                                   85.65

Fat Wt (LB)                             21.5

Lean Body Wt (LB)                       128.5

            13.0% Body Fat =            147.7 LB

            12.0% Body Fat =            146.0 LB

            11.0 Boby Fat  =            144.4 LB

            10.0 Body Fat  =            142.8 LB
```

Figure 11.12 Output data for hydrostatic weighing at residual volume.

This system requires 48K memory, a single disk drive, a printer, and a monitor. The equipment is generally present on existing microcomputer systems; therefore, only the software needs to be purchased or developed. The time savings, the accuracy, and the flexibility of the program make the microcomputer an attractive device if much body composition testing is expected in the facility.

Dietary Analysis

Quantification of the composition of foods is useful but tedious business. In the mid-1970s dietary analysis was accomplished via mainframe computers for research purposes or by hand for clinical use. Because dietary analysis is basically a record-keeping function, the microcomputer industry quickly recognized the advantage of producing software to perform the various functions. The first software was quite simplistic and limited in capacity. Among the shortcomings were a limited list of foods, the inability to analyze "custom recipes" or those not named specifically in the computer list, the absence of record storage, and questionable methods of computing personal recommended daily allowances. Like many products, dietary analysis via microcomputers has advanced with time and field testing.

There are many useful programs available through commercial vendors. It is possible to create your own analysis; however, it is a time-consuming task and seldom necessary. Rather than one specific software package, a composite of various dietary analysis programs is presented. Athletic counseling, classroom instruction, adult fitness, and research are areas that benefit from the use of microcomputer analysis of dietary consumption. If time saving impresses you, consider that a one-day hand analysis for nutrients including vitamins, minerals, fats, protein, and carbohydrates can take about 1 hour. Computer analysis including boot-up, coding, and data entry may take only 10 to 12 minutes. A good diet analysis program can be run on 48K and a single disk drive; however, experience dictates that two drives are more efficient and avoid the constant switching from main program to food inventories found with the single drive. Generally speaking, the popular diet analysis programs present the user with three main programs (see Figure 11.13).

Recommended Dietary Allowances

Recommended dietary allowances (RDA) provide the nutrients necessary to maintain health free from obvious disease. Because nutrient amounts vary for sex, age, exercise level, and so on, questions are

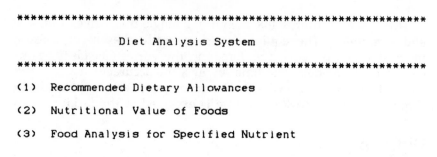

Figure 11.13 Main menu for diet analysis.

```
**********************************************************
              RECOMMENDED DIETARY AMOUNTS
**********************************************************

NAME:  Sample                    SEX:  Male
AGE GROUP:   23-50                 WEIGHT:   150 Pounds
HEIGHT:   72-79 IN                ACTIVITY LEVEL:  Very Active

Calories           2815  **      Carbohydrates     408 G *
Protein              55  G       Cholesterol       300 MG*
Dietary Fiber        28  G *     Fat-Unsat          63 G *
Vitamin A          5000  IU      Fat-Total          94 G *
Thiamine-B1         1.4  MG      Calcium           800 MG
Riboflavin-B2       1.7  MG      Copper            2.5 MG*
Pyridoxine-B6       2.2  MG      Iron               10 MG
Cobalamin-B12          3  MCG    Magnesium         350 MG
Folacin              400  MCG    Phosphorus        800 MG
Niacin             18.6  MG      Potassium        3750 MG*
Pantothenic Acid       7  MG*    Selenium          125 MCG*
Vitamin C            60  MG      Sodium           3000 MG*
Vitamin E            10  MG      Zinc               15 MG

     * No Specific RDA: Suggested Values.
    ** Average Value: Individual Needs May Vary.
```

Figure 11.14 RDA for an individual based on age, height, sex, weight, and activity level.

asked so the user may personalize the calculations. Figure 11.14 illustrates questions that may be asked to provide necessary information so that calculations may be performed to generate the RDA for a particular individual.

Nutritional Value of Foods

Food analysis for a specific nutrient is a program that allows the user to check specific foods for a specific nutrient. For instance, if you are concerned about cholesterol intake, you may wish to quickly look up a food you are considering eating to check its cholesterol content. Perhaps the thought of eating a butter cookie for a snack has you worried because of the association of cholesterol with the word butter. In Figure 11.15 the user is asked to indicate which nutrient is being requested. After deciding on a nutrient, the user is presented with a food code and quantity measure. When the requested information is entered, the microcomputer searches the food files for the food that was entered and selects the information stored for cholesterol.

```
****************************************************************
                  ANALYSIS FOR SPECIFIED NUTRIENT
****************************************************************
Nutrient Analysis                 Cholesterol
                                     (MG)
1 Ea   Butter Cookies               .72
                  Total             .72 MG
```

Figure 11.15 Analysis for cholesterol in a specified food.

Food Analysis for Nutrients

Perhaps the most frequently used feature of diet analysis is the capacity to search for foods and identify all the nutrients for that food. Figure 11.16 shows the foods entered for a single breakfast. The food code must be identified from a listing provided in the software manual. The quantity and units of measure may appear on the screen for selection or may be found in the manual. Typically, the code serves to identify the food item; the quantity is a multiple or fraction of a standard measure, and the standard measure may be slices, pieces, cups, and so on. After the last food item is entered, choices appear on the screen to display the results on the monitor, have them printed, or both. Notice in the current example the percentage of contribution to total calories from the three major food groups is presented. Most, but not all, programs will do this and provide useful information to the health professional.

Some diet analysis programs provide the user with storage capability so diet consumption may be compared at various times. A few diet analysis programs provide specialty items such as junk food menus, sample reducing diets with user-specified caloric limits, and even diets to gain weight in conjunction with exercise programs. A diet program that would list foods to meet a certain criteria in nutrients (e.g., vegetables low in sodium) would be useful; however, this fea-

```
****************************************************************
                  NUTRITIONAL VALUE OF FOODS
****************************************************************
NAME:   Sam

Items Analyzed:

Code            Qty        Meas       Item

315             1          Ea         Raw Apple (with skin)
628             19         Grm        CKD Pork Breakfast Strips
094             2          Ea         Fried Egg
151             2          Pce        White Bread (firm)
075             1          Cup        Frozen Orange Juice
```

NUTRITIONAL ANALYSIS

```
          WEIGHT:   564 GRAMS    (93.9 OUNCES)
```

Calories	626		Carbohydrates	82.0 G
Protein	24.1	G	Cholesterol	512 MG
Dietary Fiber	7.73	G	Fat-Unsat	12.3 G
Vitamin A	842	IU	Fat-Total	23.0 G
Thiamine-B1	.684	MG	Calcium	150 MG
Riboflavin-B2	.557	MG	Copper	.382 MG
Pyridoxin-B6	.381	MG	Iron	4.71 MG
Cobalamin-B12	1.49	MCG	Magnesium	60.9 MG
Folacin	182	MCG	Phosphorus	326 MG
Niacin	4.38	MG	Potassium	917 MG
Pantothenic Acid	2.43	MG	Selenium	30.5 MCG
Vitamin C	113	MG	Sodium	1019 MG
Vitamin E	2.24	MG	Zinc	2.61 MG

```
              Calories From:    Protein          15%
                                Carbohydrates    52%
                                Fats             33%
```

Figure 11.16   Input and output for nutritional value of foods.

ture may not as yet be available. Consider obtaining diet analysis software like shopping for a pair of pants; find one that is comfortable to use, meets your needs, and is compatible with the hardware.

Risk Appraisal

Risk appraisal refers to the attempt to categorize and quantify major health risks for the purpose of awareness and life-style intervention. Typically, the risk appraisal asks a variety of questions regarding personal health history, coronary heart disease, regular medical care, safety practices, psychological outlook, personal satisfaction, and miscellaneous items. Risk appraisals are available from a wide variety of sources both commercial and public. The sensitivity, validity, and usefulness of risk appraisals are not universally accepted. Some risk appraisals have considerable research behind them, and others are reflections of deductive thinking that may or may not agree with reality. Regardless of how credible the risk appraisals may be, they are used with increasing frequency in fitness programs, health enhancement programs, public health services, industrial wellness programs, and hospitals and clinics as the utility of preventive medicine gains a broader foothold. Risk appraisals may be completed by an individual and graded by the health professional. Those who are familiar with computers recognize that grading is a job that may be easily accomplished.

The system illustrated has been adapted from Sharkey (1984) and is in use in both the public and private sector in fitness and health enhancement programs. It is used as a screening and awareness tool and makes no claims relative to diagnosis or predictive powers.

A 48K microcomputer with a single disk drive, monitor, and printer is more than adequate to run this system. The numerical values for the answers for each question are programmed to reflect the relative degree of risk. This value may be changed to reflect modification of the risk appraisal or a shift in the thinking of the health professional who is grading the appraisal. The individual is presented the appraisal and completes it manually. The health professional codes the responses by indicating numerical values 1 to 5. The codes are transferred into values representing the degree of risk previously mentioned. An example of the questions, numerical values for risk, and numerical values for coding are shown in Figure 11.17.

The risk inventory is compiled and graded, and a summary report is presented to the health professional based on the findings. This summary may be further interpreted by the professional or sent directly to the individual. The summary identifies areas of risk and encourages intervention. As usual, the computer-generated report represents a means of making a slow, repetitive task much quicker and helps assure accuracy. Personal experience has shown that the procedure of grading and formulating a summary report takes about 20 to 30 minutes by hand, whereas computer grading and computer summary takes no more than 30 to 45 seconds. Ultimately, it is still up to the individual and health professional to develop a plan of action. An example of a printout is shown in a sample Risk Factor Analysis Summary Report located at the end of the chapter.

It has been stated previously that the use of microcomputer is limited only by your imagination. This is not quite true. Programming skills, knowledge of elementary electronics, and some spare time would certainly help. You can seldom copy existing custom hardware and use

RISK APPRAISAL

NAME _____ DATE _____ BIRTHDATE _____

Underscore choice which most nearly describes your situation in each of these areas.

Code	1	2	3	4	5
SMOKING	(+1) never used	(0) quit	(-1) cigar, pipe or a close family smoker	(-3) 1 pack/day	(-5) 2 packs/day or more
HEREDITY CHD—Coronary Heart Disease	(+2) no family heart disease	(0) 1 close relative over 60 with CHD	(-1) 2 close relatives over 60 with CHD	(-2) 1 close relative under 60 with CHD	(-4) 2 or more close relatives under 60 with CHD
BODY WEIGHT	(+2) 5 lbs. below desirable weight	(+1) -5 to +4 lbs. desirable weight	(0) 5 to 20 lbs overweight	(-2) 20 to 35 lbs. overweight	(-3) 35 lbs. or more overweight
SEX	(0) female under 45 years old	(-1) female over 45 years old	(-1) male	(-2) stocky male	(-4) bald, stocky male
STRESS	(+1) unhurried and generally happy	(0) ambitious but generally relaxed	(-1) sometimes hard driving, time conscious, competitive	(-2) often hard driving, time conscious, competitive	(-3) always hard driving, time conscious, competitive
PHYSICAL ACTIVITY (+3) high intensity 30 minutes long daily workout		(+1) intermittant 20–30 minutes 3 to 5 times/week	(0) moderate intensity 10–20 minutes 3 to 5 times/week	(-1) light intensity 10–20 minutes 1 to 2 times/week	(-3) little or none
EAT BREAKFAST	(+1) daily	(0) sometimes	(-1) nothing at all	(-2) only coffee	(-3) coffee and donut
REGULAR MEALS	(+1) 3 or more/day	(0) 2 daily	(-1) not regular	(-2) fad diets	(-3) starve and stuff
SLEEP	(-2) 6 hrs./day or less	(0) 6-7 hrs./day	(+1) 7-8 hrs./day	(0) 8-9 hrs./day	(0) 9 or more hrs./day
ALCOHOL	(+1) none	(+1) occasional social drink	(0) 1 to 2 drinks daily	(-2) 2 to 6 drinks daily	(-4) 6 drinks daily
MEDICAL EXAMS AND TESTS	(+1) regular tests. see Doctor when necessary	(+1) periodic medical exam and regular tests	(0) periodic medical exam	(0) sometimes get tests	(-1) no tests or medical exams
HEART	(+1) no history of disease—self or family	(0) some history	(-1) rheumatic fever as child, no murmur now	(-2) rheumatic fever as child, have a murmur	(-3) have ECG abnormality and / or angina pectoris
LUNG (including pneumonia, TB)	(+1) no problems	(0) some past problems	(-1) mild asthma or bronchitis	(-2) emphysema, severe asthma/bronchitis	(-3) severe lung problems
DIGESTIVE TRACT	(+1) no problem	(0) occasional diarrhea, loss of appetite	(-1) frequent diarrhea or stomach upset	(-2) ulcers, colitis, gall bladder or liver problems	(-3) severe gastrointestinal disorders
DIABETES	(+1) no problem or family history	(0) controlled hypoglycemia (low blood sugar)	(-1) hypoglycemia and family history	(-2) mild diabetes (diet & exercise)	(-3) diabetes (insulin)
DRUGS or MEDICATIONS	(+1) seldom take	(0) minimal—regular use of aspirin or other drugs	(-1) heavy use of aspirin or other drugs	(-2) regular use of amphetamines, barbituates, etc.	(-3) heavy use of amphetamines, barbituates, etc.

DRIVING IN CAR	(+1) 4,000 mi/yr mostly local	(0) 4000–6000 mi/yr local & highway	(0) 6000–8000 mi/yr local & highway	(−1) 8000–10,000 mi/yr highway & local	(−2) 10,000 or more mostly highway
USING SEATBELTS	(+1) always	(0) 75% of time	(−1) on highway	(−2) seldom (25% of time)	(−3) never
RISK TAKING BEHAVIOR (MOTORCYCLE, SKYDIVE, MOUNTAIN CLIMB, etc.)	(+1) some with careful preparation	(0) never	(−1) occasional	(−1) often	(−2) try anything for thrills
DIET	(+1) high complex carbohydrates and low refined sugar	(0) balanced moderate fat and refined sugar	(−1) balanced typical fat and sugar	(−2) fad diets	(−3) starve and stuff
LONGEVITY	(+2) grandparents lived past 90; parents past 80	(+1) grandparents lived past 80; parents past 70	(0) grandparents lived past 70; parents past 60	(−1) few relatives lived past 60	(−3) few relatives lived past 50
MARITAL STATUS	(+2) happily married	(+1) married	(−1) never married	(−2) divorced	(−3) other
EDUCATION	(+1) post graduate or master craftsman	(+1) college graduate or skilled craft	(0) some college or trade school	(−1) high school	(−2) grade school
JOB SATISFACTION	(+1) enjoy job, see results, room for advancement	(+1) enjoy job, see some results, able to advance	(0) job OK, see no results, no where to go	(−1) dislike job	(−2) hate job
SOCIAL TIES	(+1) have some close friends	(0) some casual friends	(−1) no close friends	(−2) stuck with people I don't enjoy	(−3) no friends at all
RACE	(0) white or Oriental	(−1) black or Hispanic	(−2) American Indian		
OUTLOOK ON LIFE	(+1) feel good about present/future	(0) satisfied	(−1) unsure about present/future	(−2) unhappy in present don't look forward to future	(−3) miserable, rather not get out of bed
DEPRESSION	(+1) no family history of depression	(0) some family history— I feel OK	(−1) family history and I am mildly depressed	(−2) sometimes feel life isn't worth living	(−3) thoughts of suicide
ANXIETY	(−3) everyone hates me	(−2) always anxious	(−1) often anxious	(0) occasionally	(+1) seldom anxious
RELAXATION	(+1) relax daily	(0) relax often	(−1) seldom relax	(−2) usually tense	(−3) always tense
FOR WOMEN ONLY					
HEALTH CARE	(+1) regular breast and pap exam	(0) occasional breast and pap exam	(−1) never examined	(−2) treated disorder	(−4) untreated cancer
THE PILL	(+1) never used	(0) quit 5 years ago	(−1) still use (under age 30)	(−3) use pill and smoke	(−5) use pill and smoke (over age 35)

BLOOD PRESSURE 120 / 80
Cholesterol 170 mg/dl

Figure 11.17 Risk appraisal sample questions, risk values, and coding.

it without modification because instrumentation is so diverse. The plain truth, however, is that many applications simply are not very difficult. The examples in this section are provided only to stimulate thought and encourage interested individuals to tackle a project of their own design.

References

Donnelly, J.E., & Sintek, S. (1986). Hydrostatic weighing without head submersion. In J.A.P. Day (Ed.), *Perspectives in kinanthropometry* (pp. 251-255). Champaign, IL: Human Kinetics.

Sharkey, B.J. (1984). *Physiology of fitness* (2nd ed.). Champaign, IL: Human Kinetics.

Risk Factor Analysis Summary Report

Name _____ Occupation _____
Date _____ Employer _____
Age _____
Sex _____

The results from your risk factor analysis are completed. It is possible to assign a numerical value to various conditions and forms of behaviors; however, no one can predict how well or how long you will live. The numbers represent a means to confront the theoretical consequences of your life-style. Major areas that affect your well-being and longevity have been grouped under the following categories:

1. Coronary Heart Disease Risk Factors
2. General Health Habits
3. Current Medical Status
4. Safety/Risk Taking
5. Personal Life
6. Psychological Outlook
7. Female Health Considerations

Your longevity may be estimated from your present age, and this estimation is then modified by the risk factor analysis as either negative or positive. For example, if your current age is 50, you could expect to live to about 76 years of age based on normal population samples. A poor life-style will reduce this expectancy and a healthy life-style will enhance your life expectancy.

Introduction to Risk Factor Analysis

The risk factor analysis is presented by major categories and components within categories. This analysis will allow you to identify specific strengths and weaknesses in your current health history and life-style. A negative number indicates a component that is diminishing your life expectancy, a positive number will increase your life expectancy, and a neutral analysis will exert little influence. To understand how the risk analysis works, consider the following example:

Category 6. Psychological Outlook
a. outlook on life +1
b. depression   −2
c. anxiety   +1
d. relaxation   +1
Total   +1

The analysis shows a positive total score (+1) but reveals that the individual is occasionally depressed (−2). The interpretation of Category 6 would be favorable; however, the individual should seek to resolve the cause of the depression. In other words, the analysis provides a general impression and specific details.

Results of Risk Factor Analysis

1. CHD Risk Factors
   a. Blood Lipids   _____
   b. Blood Pressure   _____
   c. Smoking   _____
   d. Heredity   _____
   e. Weight   _____
   f. Sex   _____
   g. Physical Activity   _____
   Total   _____
2. General Health
   a. Breakfast   _____
   b. Regularity of Meals   _____
   c. Sleeping Habits   _____
   d. Alcohol   _____
   Total   _____

(Cont.)

3. Current Medical Status
   a. Medical Tests, Exams   _____
   b. Heart Disease   _____
   c. Pulmonary Disease   _____
   d. Diabetes   _____
   e. Medications   _____
   Total   _____
4. Safety/Risk Taking
   a. Automobile   _____
   b. Seat Belt Usage   _____
   c. Risk Taking   _____
   Total   _____
5. Personal Life
   a. Routine Diet   _____
   b. Longevity   _____
   c. Marital Status   _____
   d. Education   _____
   e. Job Satisfaction   _____
   f. Social Ties   _____
   g. Race   _____
   Total   _____
6. Psychological Outlook
   a. Outlook on Life   _____
   b. Depression   _____
   c. Anxiety   _____
   d. Relaxation   _____
   Total   _____
7. Female Health Consideration
   a. Birth Control Pill   _____
   Total   _____

The bar graph represents a summary of the results. A bar that extends to the right represents a positive contribution to your health from that category, a bar to the left indicates a negative contribution, and the absence of a bar indicates a neutral contribution.

Example of Risk Factor Summary

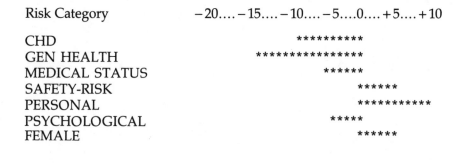

Risk Category	−20.... −15.... −10.... −5....0.... +5.... +10
CHD	**********
GEN HEALTH	****************
MEDICAL STATUS	******
SAFETY-RISK	******
PERSONAL	***********
PSYCHOLOGICAL	*****
FEMALE	******

Your life expectancy determined from your age is _____. From the analysis of your risk factors, this estimation has been

a. enhanced
b. reduced   from total score of risk analysis
c. unchanged

and is now estimated to be _____ years.

How to Interpret the Results of the Risk Factor Analysis

Of primary concern are the seven major categories in the risk analysis. A negative total score for any category should be interpreted as a strong warning and merits corrective action. A negative score within a major category may be interpreted as less severe by itself; however, you should attempt to reduce all risk factors.

A positive total score for any category indicates your behavior and life-style are enhancing the estimate of your longevity and should be maintained. Be certain to look at the components within a positive category for specific areas of concern that may be improved.

CHAPTER 12

Microcomputer Applications in Sport Psychology

Sharon Mathes
Richard Engelhorn

Sport psychology, which applies the principles of psychology to the understanding of sport behavior, like its parent, is composed of numerous subdisciplines (social, educational, experimental, personality, clinical, developmental, psychometric). Although somewhat different in perspective, all of these disciplines focus on how psychological factors affect performance or how sport experiences influence a host of psychological variables. Such psychological factors as motivation, competition, stress, anxiety, audience effects, group dynamics, concentration, self-confidence, and perceptual style all have been studied by sports psychologists to determine the impact of such factors on sport performance. In addition, the positive and negative influence of physical activity on performers' personality development, anxiety and stress levels, and psychological well-being have been topics of interest to sport psychologists.

Today, sport psychology is an exciting multidimensional field that addresses issues of interest to researchers, coaches, teachers, and athlete. Work in this area is helping bridge the gap between ill-defined concepts and misconceptions associated with terms such as ''psyched up.'' Through their research, writing, and consultation, sport psychologists are providing not only a data base and conceptual framework to explain once ambiguous concepts but also specific guidelines that assist athletes in achieving optimal levels of performance.

It might appear at first glance that microcomputers would have limited application to an area that focuses on understanding people and a host of seemingly intangible variables that may influence them in a sport performance setting. Most people, when they think of sport psychology, probably view it as an area in which a sport psychologist works one on one in a private, interpersonal way with an athlete whose goal is to enhance his or her performance or cope with a temporary crisis that is disruptive to performance. How could something as seemingly mechanistic and impersonal as a computer find application in such an individualized domain? It is true that sport psychology is concerned with athletes coming to know themselves and the factors that influence their behavior; however, this process can be enhanced by the use of microcomputers.

Athletes have experienced a host of psychological factors, and they are inherently interested in knowing more about themselves and these variables. Well-designed computer programs can provide an interesting, interactive, individualized laboratory in which students can do self-assessment, comparison, and training. Athletes and students may have read or heard about the importance in sport of concepts such as "concentration," but with the aid of microcomputers they can perform tasks that actually allow them to experience, evaluate, and even train attentional skills. Computers provide "hands-on" individualized learning experiences with immediate feedback and, therefore, are very engaging to athletes and students who want to know about themselves. In addition, the microcomputer laboratory experience is private, self-paced, always available, and endlessly repeatable. These characteristics make such experiences extremely attractive to students.

Motivation

A current area of great interest to athletes, coaches, and students alike is motivation. Numerous professional and trade books with titles such as *The Inner Athlete* (Niedeffer, 1976), *Athletes' Guide to Mental Training* (Niedeffer, 1985), *Don't Choke* (Scott & Pelliccioni, 1982), and *Sports Psyching* (Tutko & Tosi, 1976) illustrate that an increasing audience is interested in the psychological aspects of performance. The concept of motivation is complex, and in order to gain the underlying knowledge base associated with such concepts as "arousal," "anxiety," and "stress," it will undoubtedly be necessary to do some preliminary reading on one's own or receive instruction in a class setting. Microcomputers, however, can be very useful in providing experientially based tasks that illustrate basic concepts, provide self-assessment information, and even serve as training devices for the acquisition of certain psychological skills. In addition, the microcomputer can be utilized to catalogue and analyze information collected on oneself and others with regard to certain psychological constructs.

For example, the relationship between arousal or activation level and performance has traditionally been explored in sport psychology and motor performance courses. Students learn that as a person's level of activation changes in preparation for competition, concurrent physiological, perceptual, cognitive, and motor changes also occur that differentially impact on performance. Microcomputer programs can be very useful in assessing the changes that students have experienced and illustrating that such changes occur. Following are descriptions of some of the measurement and evaluation procedures often used by the sport psychologist. These are presented to provide an understanding of the breadth of the sport psychology area as well as to indicate possible topics to use in computer applications.

A commonly used device in the arousal area is the *Checklist for Tension and Anxiety Indicators* (Harris & Harris, 1984), which identifies various changes that accompany increased arousal levels (see Figure 12.1). At the simplest level students relate to the checklist by merely indicating how frequently they have experienced the behaviors specified. The checklist, therefore, provides basic diagnostic information about athletes' general precompetition behavior. The checklist also can be manipulated by asking students either to collect or to recall such information about themselves prior to, during, or after competition. This, in turn, provides information that is useful in differentiating whether the student is experiencing somatic or cognitive anxiety. In addition to providing a general picture of the behavioral changes associated with arousal, such a checklist may also serve as a benchmark for determining the areas in which students are experiencing the greatest difficulty.

A variation on this checklist is the *Muscle Tension Levels* (see Figure 12.2) described by Niedeffer (1985). This form assists athletes in identifying the levels of tension they experience in three major muscle groups during practice and competitive conditions. In order to increase their sensitivity to their optimal levels of arousal, athletes record their experienced levels of tension on a practice and/or competition checklist form.

In addition, they consider the influence of personality, skill, and situational factors by responding to questions based on these factors. Students answer a variety of questions such as the following: Does your level of tension vary with whom you are competing? Are you more or less tense when executing a particular skill (e.g., free throws vs. dribbling, batting vs. fielding)? Do certain situations make you more tense? Are you more tense at certain times (i.e., start, middle, end) during a performance? Do particular arenas or facilities create tension for you? (Niedeffer, 1985, p. 110).

Self-Assessment Diaries

Another example of the use of microcomputers in providing self-assessment information is associated with the concept of self-talk. Recently self-talk has received considerable attention as an important

Muscle Tension Checklist

SIGNS OF TENSION	CIRCLE FREQUENCY OF OBSERVATION		
	ALWAYS	SOMETIMES	NEVER
Facial grimaces, frowning	3	2	1
Clenching teeth, grinding teeth	3	2	1
General bodily restlessness	3	2	1
Moving body part continuously: foot, hands, knee ..	3	2	1
Headaches	3	2	1
Neckaches	3	2	1
Backaches	3	2	1
Diarrhea	3	2	1
Constipation	3	2	1
Irritable bowel	3	2	1
Indigestion	3	2	1
Irritable G. I. tract	3	2	1
Fatigue	3	2	1
Insomnia, disrupted sleep	3	2	1
Restless legs	3	2	1
Restless hands	3	2	1
Pulling, tugging on hair, moustache, eyebrows, etc.	3	2	1
Muscles twitches, spasms, cramps, tics	3	2	1
Excessive sweating	3	2	1
Cold, clammy hands and/or feet	3	2	1
Chewing fingernails	3	2	1
Chewing inside of cheek or lips	3	2	1
General irritability	3	2	1
Heart pounding or racing	3	2	1
Anger, hostility	3	2	1
Shaking hands, tremors	3	2	1
Irregular breathing rates, shortness of breath	3	2	1
Uncontrollable thoughts	3	2	1
Mental confusion	3	2	1
Forgetfulness	3	2	1
Skin rashes	3	2	1
Loss of appetite	3	2	1
Excessive eating	3	2	1
Unexplained fears	3	2	1

TOTAL SCORE_____

Figure 12.1 Tension and anxiety checklist. *Note.* From *Sport Psychology: Mental Skills for Physical People* (p. 182) by D. Harris and B.L. Harris, 1984, New York: Leisure Press. Copyright 1984 by Leisure Press. Reprinted by permission.

variable influencing athletes' attitudes toward themselves and performance. Various sport psychologists (Harris & Harris, 1984; Niedeffer, 1985; Scott & Pelliccioni, 1982) have suggested the need to examine the content of self-talk as well as techniques for positively enhancing such thoughts and behavior. Although the validity of analyzing what athletes say to themselves and when they say it might be more appropriately dealt with in readings or class discussion, students' awareness of their own behavior can be tapped by having them relate to

Muscle Tension Checklist

Practice	1	2	3	4	5	6	7	8	9	10
Total Relaxation					Average Tension					Very Tense

Face, neck,

jaw — — — — — — — — — —

Shoulders,

chest, arms— — — — — — — — — —

Calves,

thighs — — — — — — — — — —

Figure 12.2 Muscle tension checklist. Use the same chart, labeled competition, and fill one out for each practice and competitive condition likely to affect muscle tension. *Note.* From *Athlete's Guide to Mental Training* (p. 111) by R. Niedeffer, 1985, Champaign, IL: Human Kinetics. Copyright 1985 by R. Niedeffer. Reprinted by permission.

a Self-Talk Diary or Checklist available on microcomputers (Scott & Pelliccioni, 1982, p. 87). Students can be asked to record what they say to themselves before, during, and after competing and then to transfer this information to the microcomputer.

After students have added to this file for approximately 2 weeks, they can then be asked to analyze the statements recorded and indicate on the basis of the criteria provided whether or not the statements are self-defeating. *Self-defeating statements* can be designated as those that say something negative about the person and/or statements that put added pressure on the performer. Having identified and summed the number of self-defeating statements, the student can reflect on the quantity, quality, and timing of the statements. They can be asked to review the information recorded and determine whether negative statements or thoughts most frequently occur before, during, or after competition. Finally, students could be requested to select the most frequently given negative self-statements and to substitute coping statements. Once students have practiced modifying negative self-talk and practiced employing positive self-statements, the original diary form could again be employed. Eventually, it should also be possible to compare the type of self-talk in which students engage and their perceptions of the effect of such verbalization on their feelings of self-confidence, concentration, and performance. Obviously, students also may use the task described as the basis for various research experiments. For instance, students might collect self-talk data from athletes and compare it with athletes' affective feelings about performance or performance outcomes.

Stress Stimuli

In addition to various inventories that already exist, it is also possible to draw upon the work of others and devise variations of tools described in the research literature.

Kroll's (1982) research that identified that athletes' fears may be classified into five major categories (somatic complaints, fear of failure, feelings of inadequacy, loss of control, guilt) offers some interesting possibilities for extrapolation. Each of the major areas of fear are described as subscales with various behavioral attributes identified. It is possible, therefore, to employ these as the basis for the development of a checklist to which athletes might relate. For example, the Somatic Complaint Subscale (see Figure 12.3) contains 11 items that athletes report being concerned about prior to competition. These items could be provided and students asked to indicate if or how often they have experienced such physical changes prior to competition.

This same procedure could be followed for each of the other subscales. The information obtained from students relating to the subscales would provide an individualized anxiety profile, which would indicate the area(s) that the student finds most fear provoking as well as provide information regarding the appropriate anxiety remediation program. For example, a student might find that his or her major source of anxiety is fear of failure. On the basis of this finding, he or she might next prompt the computer to provide additional information about the nature of fear of failure as well as various coping techniques (cognitive restructuring, thought stopping, desensitizing) that might be appropriately employed for remediating fear of failure. The microcomputer, therefore, would provide information regarding the concept of fear of failure and enable the student to explore the characteristics and techniques of various cognitive coping strategies.

The use of paper and pencil tasks, inventories, checklists, and diaries in providing descriptive information about and to students appears to be limited only by the creativity of the authors in devising such tasks. The capability of the microcomputer to collect, save, analyze, and provide new information in a personalized dynamic setting makes such an experience interesting and exciting.

Somatic Subscale Example

Experienced	Very Often				Seldom
	5	4	3	2	1

1.Tightness in neck

2. Upset stomach

3. Nervousness

4. Awareness of heartbeat

5. Urge to urinate

6. Ringing in the ears

7. Yawning too much

8. Trembling

9. Throwing up

10. General body sweating

11. Sore muscles

Figure 12.3   Example of a Somatic Subscale. *Note.*   From "Competitive Athletic Stress Factors in Athletes and Coaches" by W. Kroll, 1982. In L. Zaichkowsky and W. Sime (Eds.), *Stress management for sports* (p. 3). Reston, VA: AAHPERD. Reprinted by permission of the American Alliance for Health, Physical Education, Recreation and Dance, 1900 Association Drive, Reston,VA 22091.

Psychological Instruments

In addition to checklists and other self-observation tools, classic psychological instruments also lend themselves to microcomputer applications. Psychological tests, such as the Rotter Scale for locus of control (Rotter, 1966), Life Change Index Scale (Holmes & Rahe, 1967), Hostility Inventory (Buss & Durkee, 1953), Taylor Manifest Anxiety Scale (Taylor, 1953), Body Cathexis Scale (Secord & Jourard, 1953), and the Social Desirability Scale (Crowne & Marlow, 1964), also lend themselves to being placed on the microcomputer. The use of such tests requires written permission, which can be obtained by contacting the publisher and author by letter in order to obtain a copyright release.

Another example of a well-known and respected instrument is the *Sport Competition Anxiety Test* (SCAT) developed by Martens (1977).

This test, which has an adult and children's form, has been widely utilized and has available means, standard deviations, and standard scores. As in the checklist previously discussed, students can respond with the aid of a microcomputer to the SCAT on a predetermined scale. Besides merely having personal descriptive information, however, students can compare their scores to the normed scores of other populations. Where the available norms are not appropriate, the student or program designer can also use this task as a research tool to collect information to develop new norms more suited for the specific populations.

Measuring Sport Anxiety

Assessing anxiety or arousal levels in a sport competition environment is an important area of interest for the sport psychologist. Understanding the procedure commonly used and the interpretations of the results of these evaluations are important concepts for the physical education student. The software to be presented in this section provides an example of a trait anxiety measure and its use in the sport psychology classroom and laboratory situation.

The SCAT is easily implemented on the microcomputer for use in a classroom or lab setting. With an interactive software version of the inventory, sport psychology students are able to learn about their own sport anxiety and, by thoughtful and logical experimentation, can gain an understanding of the types of response patterns leading to various SCAT scores.

The program provides an introduction to the instrument and specific instructions. It then presents each SCAT item (see Figure 12.4) and

```
COMPETING AGAINST OTHERS IS SOCIALLY
   ENJOYABLE.



        1 - HARDLY EVER

        2 - SOMETIMES

        3 - OFTEN


   INPUT CHOICE BY NUMBER  2
```

Figure 12.4 Example of SCAT response input screen.

waits for the subject's response before displaying the next item. After all 15 items have been presented by the computer, the total raw score is compared with normative data stored in arrays within the program. The results of the test and a brief explanation of the results are then displayed on the microcomputer video display (see Figure 12.5).

```
                    SCAT RESULTS


        THE ILLINOIS SPORT COMPETITION
        TEST IS AN A-TRAIT SCALE DESIGNED FOR
        MEASURING A PREDISPOSITION TO RESPOND
        WITH VARYING LEVELS OF APPREHENSION OR
        TENSION IN COMPETITIVE SPORT
        SITUATIONS.

        YOUR SCORE ON THE TEST WAS 21.
        SCORES MAY RANGE FROM 10 [LOW A-TRAIT]
        TO 30 [HIGH A-TRAIT].

        THE MEAN SCORE FOR YOUR AGE
        AND SEX IS 19.74

        YOUR PERCENTILE SCORE WAS 50 %.



        HIT ANY KEY WHEN READY TO PROCEED
```

Figure 12.5   SCAT results output screen.

The program listing (see Listing 12.1, located at the end of the chapter) is written in Apple BASIC and can be easily adapted to any microcomputer system. The hardware required consists of a typical microcomputer system: the 48K microcomputer, disk drive, and printer if hard copy is desired. The individual student's raw data and results can be printed or saved for future reference. If another set of inventory items is to be substituted for the SCAT items, they would be placed in lines 3970 to 4390 in the array Q$.

```
3970 Q$[1] = "COMPETING AGAINST OTHERS IS SOCIALLY        ENJOYABLE."
4000 Q$[2] = "BEFORE I COMPETE I FEEL UNEASY."
4030 Q$[3] = "BEFORE I COMPETE I WORRY ABOUT NOT          PERFORMING WEL
        L."
4060 Q$[4] = "I AM A GOOD SPORTSPERSON WHEN I COMPETE."
4090 Q$[5] = "WHEN I COMPETE I WORRY ABOUT MAKING         MISTAKES."
4120 Q$[6] = "BEFORE I COMPETE I AM CALM."
4150 Q$[7] = "SETTING A GOAL IS IMPORTANT WHEN            COMPETING."
4180 Q$[8] = "BEFORE I COMPETE I GET A QUEASY             FEELING IN MY
        STOMACH."
```

```
4210 Q$(9) = "JUST BEFORE COMPETING I NOTICE MY          HEART BEATS FA
     STER THAN USUAL."
4240 Q$(10) = "I LIKE TO COMPETE IN GAMES THAT DEMAND     CONSIDERABLE P
     HYSICAL ENERGY."
4270 Q$(11) = "BEFORE I COMPETE I FEEL RELAXED."
4300 Q$(12) = "BEFORE I COMPETE I AM NERVOUS."
4330 Q$(13) = "TEAM SPORTS ARE MORE EXCITING THAN        INDIVIDUAL SPO
     RTS."
4360 Q$(14) = "I GET NERVOUS WANTING TO START THE        GAME."
4390 Q$(15) = "BEFORE I COMPETE I USUALLY GET UP TIGHT."
```

Obviously, the number of items to be presented may change. If so, other lines would also have to be modified. The response choices can also be changed by substituting the new choices in lines 3850 to 3910 in array R$.

```
3850 R$(1) = "1 - HARDLY EVER"
3880 R$(2) = "2 - SOMETIMES"
3910 R$(3) = "3 - OFTEN"
```

Other simple changes may also have to be made if the new instrument is used without norms. However, if norms exist and are to be used, a much more complicated reprogramming that deals with the calculation of the percentile or normative scores would have to be completed. The functions of the various program segments are provided in the documentation within the program listing.

The program in Listing 12.1 searches the raw data scores for the correct one and then finds the percentile score at the same row position but in column 3 of the array. If the raw score was in array position (14,1), which is row 14, column 1, then the percentile score is found in array (14,3). The standard score is found in column 2 of the array but was not used in this example. The normative data are stored in data statements and read into the array in lines 1990 and 2140.

```
1990  DATA   719,698,677,655,634,612,591,570,548,527,505,484,
2020  DATA   463,441,420,399,377,356,334,313,292
2050  DATA   99,99,93,89,86,82,78,74,69,61,50,40,30,24,18,14,9,7,5,1
2080  DATA   652,631,611,590,570,549,529,508,488,467,447,426,406,
2110  DATA   385,365,344,323,303,282,262,241
2140  DATA   99,93,88,82,75,65,59,53,47,42,35,28,22,15,10,8,6,4,3,2,1
```

Other inventories applying a similar raw score to percentile table structure would be easily implemented with software similar to that used here. This example should provide ideas as to how other similar sport psychology inventories could be implemented and used. Students in a one-on-one interactive situation, for example, can use the inventories to find out about themselves as well as to gain an understanding of the information provided by the test to the sports psychologist.

Attention Grid Task

Besides having a multitude of applications for the utilization of inventories or intact psychological tests, as mentioned earlier, the microcomputer can also be helpful in illustrating certain behavioral changes. An example of this is the *Grid Task*. Harris and Harris (1984) suggest that this task has been used rather extensively in the eastern block countries prior to competition to select the best athletes to perform. They note that the task appears to be measuring athlete's level of concentration at the point in time in which it is administered. Athletes who are worried, anxious, or distracted are predicted not to perform well on the task. The grid task involves having students relate to 100 numbers randomly placed on a page within blocks. The task for the student is beginning with the number 11, to identify in sequential order as many of the numbers as he or she can within a 3-minute period.

This task can be adapted to the microcomputer, and software that does so is presented in the next section. This task provides performance information that obviously can be manipulated in a variety of ways. Students could be asked to do the task in a relaxed manner with no time limit, and this information could then be compared with information in which a time limit was set. They could also be asked to do the task in isolation or in competition with other students. The task could be conducted as well with varying auditory or visual distractors presented by the computer. Students also could be asked to repeat the task several times in succession in order to observe the effect of such demands on vigilance and fatigue. As with previously discussed microcomputer tasks, this one would certainly lend itself to the collection of information and various experimental manipulations.

Attention Grid Experiment

The concept of readiness to perform is of great interest to coaches. Is it possible to assess objectively the readiness of a performer prior to the competition? As described previously, a numerical grid task has been used by Eastern European gymnastics coaches to assess the readiness of their performers prior to competition. The grid task's implementation on the microcomputer is described in this section along with some potential classroom and laboratory applications. In addition to the readiness concept, it can also be used in the classroom or laboratory to illustrate concepts related to selective attention and the effects of sensory interference and anxiety on the gathering of environmental information.

The software in Listing 12.2 (at the end of the chapter) provides a simple version of the grid task. The software is written in Apple BASIC and makes use of a clock card. The Mountain Hardware clock was used in this program to provide the timing functions required for the experiment. The time, in seconds, that the student is allowed to search the GRID for numbers is input to the program at the start of the experiment.

Lines 200 to 460 of the software draws the grid on the screen (see Figure 12.6). As a number position is reached, a random number routine selects a number between 11 and 57 for display at that location. Another routine, lines 940 to 1000, checks to be sure this number has not been used previously in the grid. Every grid presented has a relatively random order of numbers in the grid. The student points to a number as it is found and simultaneously hits any key to update the count of numbers found. A more sophisticated program could employ a joystick to move a cursor around the screen to the next number in sequence and then hit the fire button on the joystick to indicate to the computer that the next number has been found. The software would then check to verify the correctness of the response and continue. An even better system would employ a light pen that the student would use to point out the next number in sequence. No

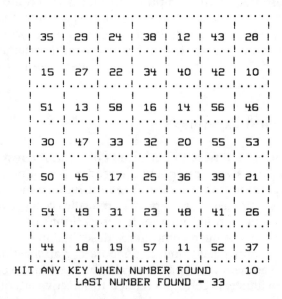

Figure 12.6 Example of attention grid output.

matter which method of selecting and pointing is employed, the task is appropriate for studying the relationship among the concepts of readiness, selective attention, and anxiety.

One use that can be made of this task is simply to use it to illustrate the difficulty one has in gathering information from the environment when the information is known to be present. In this case the next number in the sequence, which the student knows, is right in front of him or her on the screen. The task can at times be frustrating and very challenging to the student. This leads to a second application for the task. With the use of an A/D converter in the microcomputer, various physiological parameters could be recorded as the test is completed. If the task performance is made competitive, it may be interesting to have measures of the students' anxiety level before and during task performance.

Yet another application compares the students' ability to perform the task under quiet conditions versus a condition in which visual or auditory noise is present. The software, for example, could have certain numbers flashing off and on during the task to provide a possible visual distraction. This application of the task would illustrate the need to ignore extraneous information while searching for the relevant information, that is, selectively attending to appropriate stimuli only. Other uses could also be found for this task, but these examples should provide some ideas to those interested in this area of sport psychology and motor performance.

Another example of a concentration task that might be devised for the microcomputer is a variation of the classic visual afterimage phenomenon (Dember, 1966). With this task students are asked to look at the microcomputer screen, which appears all black with the exception of a 1- to 2-inch white square appearing in the center of the screen at eye level. Students are asked to sit about 2 to 3 feet away from the screen and to inspect the screen casually. Then they are directed to close their eyes for a few minutes and attempt to picture or visualize a black, velvety screen. Once they can visualize the black background without effort, they are directed to open their eyes and look at the white square on the black background. They are to continue looking at it without effort until they see an edge of color forming around the white square. When this occurs, they are to shift their view slowly to a white wall where an afterimage will occur. They are to attempt to hold this image as long as possible. On occasion a negative afterimage (i.e., black square with white background) may appear. According to Harris and Harris (1984), this exercise, with repeated practice, will help improve concentration and students' ability to transfer images viewed in the mind's eye. The development of such concentration skills should, in turn, facilitate students' ability to use imagery or mental practice. Exercises such as this one can be incorporated into larger, individualized student laboratory sessions with the use of microcomputers.

Biofeedback and Relaxation Techniques

In addition to illustrating and providing information about certain psychological factors that may influence performance, the microcomputer can also be helpful in learning certain mental strategies or techniques. For example, biofeedback and relaxation techniques quite readily lend themselves to use with the microcomputer. Biofeedback programs exist that require students to monitor certain physiological parameters and, based on the feedback provided, attempt to learn to control them. This type of task not only provides information to students about themselves but also provides an opportunity for them to practice the development of control over such things as body temperature, heart rate, galvanic skin response, and muscle tenseness. The microcomputer can become an ideal training device for such techniques.

Biofeedback

In addition to the evaluation of the state of arousal or anxiety of an athlete, the sport psychologist is also interested in intervention strategies that can be used to manipulate the anxiety level of an individual. Biofeedback, hypnosis, and relaxation techniques are three methods capable of affecting the anxiety or tension level of a performer. Various types of biofeedback devices that can monitor such physiological parameters as heart rate, respiration rate, skin temperature, electromyographic activity in muscles, electroencephalographic activity, and the galvanic skin response (GSR) are readily available. Using these devices, individuals are able to train themselves to control one or more of the above physiological parameters.

Feedback from the biofeedback devices may be visual or auditory, but in either case it will vary linearly with the level of the parameter being monitored. The microcomputer with an A/D converter is able to provide a similar, but often more sophisticated, biofeedback experience than the dedicated biofeedback units. The data collection phase of the biofeedback experiment is similar to that used in the motor-learning applications chapter. A voltage output proportional to the level of a particular physiologic variable is input to the A/D converter of the microcomputer. After sampling the input channel or channels, the relative level of the parameter is displayed on the screen and/or signaled auditorily to the subject. The auditory signal could be a tone of varying pitch or a frequency-coded series of tones or beeps. The visual display could take the form of a line graph, bar graph, numerical display, or other representation of the input data value.

Figure 12.7 illustrates a flowchart for a very simple program to display biofeedback data to the subject. One form of visual display is shown in Figure 12.8. In this display a vertical line with its length proportional to the input is drawn after every sampling period, which could be from a few seconds to a few minutes long. This information is then used by the subject to attempt to modify or control the pa-

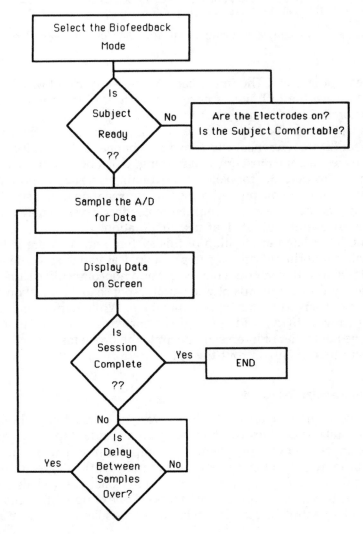

Figure 12.7 Flowchart for a biofeedback program.

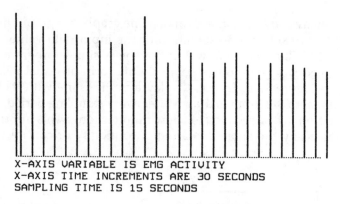

X-AXIS VARIABLE IS EMG ACTIVITY
X-AXIS TIME INCREMENTS ARE 30 SECONDS
SAMPLING TIME IS 15 SECONDS

Figure 12.8 An example of an output screen display for a biofeedback program.

rameter of interest. The immediacy of the feedback allows the subject to learn the techniques necessary to control the variable being monitored. The advantages of the microcomputer are that it allows for a flexible output display, provides a means for saving the data on disk for future reference, and allows for changes in the feedback timing to facilitate the most efficient training. One obvious disadvantage of the microcomputer for biofeedback training is its lack of portability. However, for the purpose of providing information to the sport psychology teacher, the microcomputer biofeedback system may provide the most useful and efficient instrumentation.

Another related application of this system and software is in the actual monitoring of one of the physiological variables while a student is involved in various competitive and noncompetitive situations. An example of a student's physiological response to the situation could then be observed by other class members. While performing in the competitive activity, students might be encouraged to attempt to control the parameter of interest to illustrate the problems of tension and anxiety that often confront the sports performer.

Neuromuscular Relaxation

Closely aligned to biofeedback are various relaxation techniques. Again, relaxation cues can be placed on an audio tape that can accompany a computer program. The computer program will monitor one or more physiological indexes and indicate the degree to which students are able to develop the relaxation skills. These skills can, in turn, be tied to other sport-related tasks. For example, students have learned to control their levels of relaxation consciously and can be asked to imagine that they are in certain sport situations (i.e., free throw shooting, pitching, serving a tennis ball, spiking a volleyball, fielding a ground ball, catching a pass). While imagining such situations, they can practice transferring their acquired relaxation skills. This task, somewhat like autogenic training, readily lends itself to microcomputer applications.

Relaxation Techniques on the Microcomputer

Closely related to biofeedback techniques are progressive relaxation techniques used to reduce tension or anxiety in a performer. The software described in this section allows a student to record the effects of various progressive relaxation strategies on one or more physiologic variables.

Several methods are commonly used for reducing tension and anxiety. A technique that can be easily implemented on the microcomputer uses a prerecorded audio tape to give directions for the subject to follow during the relaxation procedure. The computer controls the audio tape recorder through an interface that allows the computer to turn the recorder on and off. During the on cycle of the tape recorder, a message giving relaxation instructions to the subject is played. After the recorder has been turned off, the subject attempts to follow the directions given by the taped message.

The real advantage of the microcomputer in this situation is that during the implementation of the relaxation technique, the microcomputer can be sampling one or more physiologic variables to be saved and/or displayed following the completion of the relaxation session. As a result, students gain immediate knowledge of the effect of the session on the measured parameters and are able to understand, through their own experience, the benefits and changes elicited by the specific relaxation procedures.

The flowchart in Figure 12.9 illustrates the structure for the software that could be used to control the experiment just described. The hardware requirements for this project include a microcomputer system capable of a single-channel transistor-transistor logic (TTL) output (see chapter 1), an A/D converter, either a hardware or software timing capability, and an interface to control the tape recorder. The TTL output is usually easily available on microcomputers like the Apple II+ through the game port. Most audio cassette tape recorders have a remote jack through which the recorder can be controlled. The user plugs a push-button switch into this jack and controls the recorder with the switch. The microcomputer can also control the recorder with an electronic push-button switch. For a state-of-the-art system, the

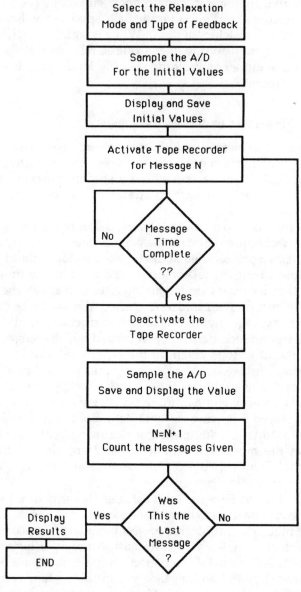

Figure 12.9 Flowchart for a progressive relaxation program using audio tape recorded commands.

user could employ a speech synthesizer and suitable software that would allow the computer to "speak" to the subject without the need for the tape recorder.

Other relaxation procedures could be manually implemented with the microcomputer simply providing the physiologic variable recording and display functions. Whatever the relaxation technique of interest, the microcomputer's advantage is the ability to display immediately the relative effect of the relaxation procedure on physiologic factors that reflect the tension level of the individual. By using the microcomputer in this way, the student is able to perceive the usefulness of progressive relaxation to reduce tension and anxiety and may be able to make comparisons among the different techniques commonly used.

In summary, microcomputers have almost unlimited potential in providing personalized laboratory settings in which students can explore in a private, self-paced environment a host of psychological factors that may influence performance. In an interactive setting, students can receive immediate feedback while they learn psychological concepts as well as engage in self-assessment, training, and even research activities. This chapter has focused primarily on the application of microcomputers in illustrating various factors associated with the construct of motivation. Clearly, however, various other psychological subdomains are equally as viable for the development of microcomputer programs and student experiences.

References

Buss, A., & Durkee, A. (1953). An inventory for assessing the different kinds of hostility. *Journal of Consulting Psychology, 21*(4), 522-528.

Cox, R. (1985). *Sport psychology concepts and applications.* Dubuque, IA: William C. Brown.

Crowne, D., & Marlow, D. (1964). *The approval motive.* New York: Wiley.

Dember, W. (1966). *The psychology of perception.* New York: Holt, Rinehart and Winston.

Harris, D., & Harris, B. (1984). *Sport psychology: Mental skills for physical people.* New York: Leisure Press.

Holmes, T., & Rahe, R. (1967). The social readjustment rating scale. *Journal of Psychosomatic Research, 11,* 213-218.

Kroll, W. (1982). Competitive athletic stress factors in athletes and coaches. In L. Zaichkowsky & W. Sime (Eds.), *Stress management for sports* (pp. 1-10). Reston, VA: AAHPERD.

Martens, R. (1977). *Sport competition anxiety test.* Champaign, IL: Human Kinetics.

Niedeffer, R. (1976). *The inner athlete.* New York: Thomas Y. Crowell.

Niedeffer, R. (1980). *The ethics and practices of applied sport psychology.* Ithaca, NY: Mouvement Publications.

Niedeffer, R. (1985). *Athletes' guide to mental training.* Champaign, IL: Human Kinetics.

Rotter, J.B. (1966). The causal dimension scale: A measure of how individuals perceive causes. *Journal of Personality and Social Psychology, 42,* 1137-1145.

Scott, M., & Pelliccioni, L. (1982). *Don't choke: How athletes can be winners.* Englewood Cliffs, NJ: Prentice-Hall.

Secord, P., & Jourard, S. (1953). The appraisal of body-cathexis: Body cathexis and self. *Journal of Consulting Psychology, 11,* 343-347.

Taylor, J.A. (1953). A personality scale of manifest anxiety. *Journal of Abnormal and Social Psychology, 48,* 285-290.

Tutko, T., & Tosi, A. (1976). *Sport psyching.* Los Angeles: Tarcher/St. Martins.

Listing 12.1 Input program for SCAT inventory.

```
100   REM   * * SCAT INVENTORY * *
130   DIM A$[15],ID$[5],Q$[15],R$[4],L$[5]
160   DIM SC[2,3,21],SM[2]
190   GOSUB 3220: REM  DISPLAY INSTRUCTIONS
220   D$ = CHR$ [4]
230   REM  READ NUMBER OF FILES ON DISK
250   PRINT D$;"OPEN CTSCAT"
280   PRINT D$;"READ CTSCAT"
310   INPUT COUNT: REM  COUNT IS THE NUMBER OF FILES ON DISK
340   PRINT D$;"CLOSE CTSCAT"
370   HOME
400   GOSUB 3700: REM  PUT DISPLAY STATEMENTS IN ARRAY
430   FOR I = 1 TO 5: REM  INPUT PERSONAL INFO
460   VTAB [10]: HTAB [4]: PRINT L$[I];: INPUT ": ";ID$[I]: HOME : NEXT I

490   IF ID$[2] = "M" THEN SX = 1
520   IF ID$[2] = "F" THEN SX = 2
530   REM  PRINT QUESTION AND DISPLAY CHOICES
550   FOR I = 1 TO 15
580   HOME : VTAB [6]: PRINT Q$[I]
610   VTAB [12]: PRINT  TAB[ 10];R$[1]
640   VTAB [14]: PRINT  TAB[ 10];R$[2]
670   VTAB [16]: PRINT  TAB[ 10];R$[3]
700   VTAB [20]: PRINT R$[4];: INPUT " ";A$[I]
730   IF  VAL [A$[I]] < 1 OR  VAL [A$[I]] > 3 THEN 700
740   REM  DO NOT SCORE THESE QUESTIONS
760   IF I = 1 OR I = 4 OR I = 7 OR I = 10 OR I = 13 THEN 970
790   XX =  VAL [A$[I]]
820   IF XX = 3 THEN 910
830   REM  CONVERT SCALE QUESTIONS 6 AND 11
```

(Cont.)

```
850  IF I = 6 OR I = 11 AND XX = 1 THEN XX = 3
880  GOTO 940
910  IF I = 6 OR I = 11 AND XX = 3 THEN XX = 1
940 PF = PF + XX: REM  CALCULATE SCORE
970  NEXT I
1000 GOSUB 1720: REM  CALCULATE PERCENTILE SCORE
1030 GOSUB 2650: REM  DISPLAY RESULTS FOR SUBJECT
1090 HOME : INPUT "SAVE THIS FILE ?? ";Y$
1120 IF Y$ < > "Y" AND Y$ < > "N" THEN 1090
1150 IF Y$ < > "Y" THEN 1510
1160 COUNT = COUNT + 1: REM  INCREMENT FILE COUNTER
1170 REM  UPDATE COUNT OF FILES STORED
1180 PRINT D$;"OPEN CTSCAT"
1210 PRINT D$;"DELETE CTSCAT"
1220 REM  SAVE STUDENTS DATA
1240 PRINT D$;"OPEN CTSCAT"
1270 PRINT D$;"WRITE CTSCAT"
1300 PRINT COUNT
1330 PRINT D$;"CLOSE CTSCAT"
1360 PRINT D$;"OPEN DSCAT,L200"
1390 PRINT D$;"WRITE DSCAT,R";COUNT
1420 FOR I = 1 TO 5: PRINT ID$[I]: NEXT I
1450 FOR J = 1 TO 15: PRINT A$[J]: NEXT J
1480 PRINT D$;"CLOSE DSCAT"
1510 HOME : INPUT "DO ANOTHER SCAT INVENTORY ";Y$
1540 IF Y$ < > "Y" AND Y$ < > "N" THEN 1510
1570 IF Y$ < > "Y" THEN 1690
1600 GOTO 190
1660 REM  OUTPUT
1690 END
1720 REM    READ NORMATIVE DATA
1750 RESTORE
1780 FOR J = 1 TO 2
1810 FOR K = 2 TO 3
1840 FOR L = 1 TO 21
1870 READ SC[J,K,L]
1900 NEXT L
1930 NEXT K
1960 NEXT J
1970 REM  STANDARD SCORES AND PERCENTILES
1990 DATA  719,698,677,655,634,612,591,570,548,527,505,484,
2020 DATA  463,441,420,399,377,356,334,313,292
2050 DATA  99,99,93,89,86,82,78,74,69,61,50,40,30,24,18,14,9,7,5,1
2080 DATA  652,631,611,590,570,549,529,508,488,467,447,426,406,
2110 DATA  385,365,344,323,303,282,262,241
2140 DATA  99,93,88,82,75,65,59,53,47,42,35,28,22,15,10,8,6,4,3,2,1
2150 REM  PUT RAW SCORES INTO ARRAY
2170 FOR J = 1 TO 2
2200 II = 0
2230 FOR L = 1 TO 21
2260 II = II + 1
2290 SC[J,1,L] = 31 - II
2320 NEXT L
2350 NEXT J
2380 REM  GROUP SCAT MEANS
2410 SM[1] = 19.74:SM[2] = 22.60
2420 RETURN
2440 REM    PERCENTILE CALCULATION ROUTINE
2470 PE = 0
2500 FOR I = 1 TO 21
2530 IF PF = SC[SX,1,I] THEN PE = SC[SX,3,I]
2560 IF PE < > 0 THEN 2620
2590 NEXT I
2620 RETURN
2650 REM    TEXT OF RESULTS OUTPUT
2680 HOME
2710 VTAB [1]: HTAB [14]: PRINT "SCAT RESULTS"
2740 VTAB [4]: PRINT "THE ILLINOIS SPORT COMPETITION"
2770 PRINT " TEST IS AN A-TRAIT SCALE DESIGNED FOR"
```

(Cont.)

```
2800   PRINT " MEASURING A PREDISPOSITION TO RESPOND"
2830   PRINT " WITH VARYING LEVELS OF APPREHENSION OR"
2860   PRINT " TENSION IN COMPETITIVE SPORT"
2890   PRINT " SITUATIONS."
2920   VTAB [11]: PRINT "YOUR SCORE ON THE TEST WAS ";;PF;"."
2950   PRINT " SCORES MAY RANGE FROM 10 [LOW A-TRAIT]"
2980   PRINT " TO 30 [HIGH A-TRAIT]."
3010   VTAB [15]
3040   PRINT "THE MEAN SCORE FOR YOUR AGE"
3070   PRINT " AND SEX IS ";SM[SX]
3100   VTAB [18]
3130   PRINT "YOUR PERCENTILE SCORE WAS ";PE;" %."
3160   VTAB [23]: PRINT "HIT ANY KEY WHEN READY TO PROCEED": GET A$
3190   RETURN
3200   REM    INSTRUCTIONS FOR THE INVENTORY
3220   HOME : PRINT "INSTRUCTIONS FOR SCAT INVENTORY": PRINT
3250   PRINT "BELOW ARE SOME STATEMENTS ABOUT HOW"
3280   PRINT "PERSONS FEEL WHEN THEY COMPETE IN "
3310   PRINT "SPORTS AND GAMES.  READ EACH STATEMENT"
3340   PRINT "AND DECIDE IF YOU 'HARDLY EVER',,"
3370   PRINT "OR 'SOMETIMES', OR 'OFTEN' FEEL THIS"
3400   PRINT "WAY WHEN YOU COMPETE IN SPORTS AND"
3430   PRINT "GAMES.  THERE ARE NO RIGHT OR WRONG"
3460   PRINT "ANSWERS.  DO NOT SPEND TOO MUCH TIME"
3490   PRINT "ON ANY ONE STATEMENT.  REMEMBER TO"
3520   PRINT "CHOOSE THE WORD THAT DESCRIBES HOW"
3550   PRINT "YOU 'USUALLY' FEEL WHEN COMPETING IN"
3580   PRINT "SPORTS AND GAMES."
3610   PRINT : PRINT : PRINT "HIT ANY KEY WHEN READY TO PROCEED": GET A$
3640   PRINT
3670   RETURN
3680   SETLABELS TO BE PRINT ED ON SCREEN FOR SUBJECT DATA
3700   L$[1] - "NAME "
3730   L$[2] - "SEX "
3760   L$[3] - "AGE "
3790   L$[4] - "TEAM OR INDIVIDUAL SPORT PLAYER "
3820   L$[5] - "NUMBER OF YEARS OF PARTICIPATION "
3830   REM    SET SELECTION ITEMS
3850   R$[1] - "1 - HARDLY EVER"
3880   R$[2] - "2 - SOMETIMES"
3910   R$[3] - "3 - OFTEN"
3940   R$[4] - "INPUT CHOICE BY NUMBER "
3950   REM    PLACE QUESTIONS IN ARRAY Q$
3970   Q$[1] - "COMPETING AGAINST OTHERS IS SOCIALLY      ENJOYABLE."
4000   Q$[2] - "BEFORE I COMPETE I FEEL UNEASY."
4030   Q$[3] - "BEFORE I COMPETE I WORRY ABOUT NOT        PERFORMING WEL
       L."
4060   Q$[4] - "I AM A GOOD SPORTSPERSON WHEN I COMPETE."
4090   Q$[5] - "WHEN I COMPETE I WORRY ABOUT MAKING       MISTAKES."
4120   Q$[6] - "BEFORE I COMPETE I AM CALM."
4150   Q$[7] - "SETTING A GOAL IS IMPORTANT WHEN          COMPETING."
4180   Q$[8] - "BEFORE I COMPETE I GET A QUEASY           FEELING IN MY
       STOMACH."
4210   Q$[9] - "JUST BEFORE COMPETING I NOTICE MY         HEART BEATS FA
       STER THAN USUAL."
4240   Q$[10] - "I LIKE TO COMPETE IN GAMES THAT DEMAND   CONSIDERABLE P
       HYSICAL ENERGY."
4270   Q$[11] - "BEFORE I COMPETE I FEEL RELAXED."
4300   Q$[12] - "BEFORE I COMPETE I AM NERVOUS."
4330   Q$[13] - "TEAM SPORTS ARE MORE EXCITING THAN       INDIVIDUAL SPO
       RTS."
4360   Q$[14] - "I GET NERVOUS WANTING TO START THE       GAME."
4390   Q$[15] - "BEFORE I COMPETE I USUALLY GET UP TIGHT."
4420   RETURN
```

Listing 12.2 Input program for grid task.

```
90   REM  GRID TASK PROGRAM
100  HOME : REM  CLEAR SCREEN
130  D$ = CHR$ (4)
160  DIM REP(59): REM  DIMENSION DATA ARRAY
190  GOSUB 1030: REM  START THE CLOCK
200  REM  DRAW GRID ON THE SCREEN
220  HTAB (3)
250  FOR J = 3 TO 38: PRINT ".";: NEXT J
280  PRINT
310  FOR I = 1 TO 7
340  FOR K = 3 TO 38 STEP 5: PRINT  TAB( K);"!";: NEXT K
370  PRINT
380  REM  PUT NUMBERS IN THE GRID
400  FOR L = 3 TO 33 STEP 5: GOSUB 850: PRINT  TAB( L);"!";" ";C;" ";: NEXT
     L: PRINT  TAB( 37);"!"
430  FOR K = 3 TO 37 STEP 5: PRINT  TAB( K);"!....";: NEXT K: PRINT "!"
460  NEXT I
490  GOSUB 1330
520  IK = 10
550  VTAB (23): PRINT "HIT ANY KEY WHEN NUMBER FOUND";
580  X = PEEK ( - 16384): REM   WAIT FOR A KEY PRESS
610  POKE  - 16368,0: REM  GET TIME AND DISPLAY
640  GOSUB 1240: GOSUB 1120
670  VTAB (23): HTAB (35): PRINT  INT (TIME / 1000)
700  IF TIME > 30000 THEN  GOTO 1420: REM  AFTER 30 SEC SIGNAL
730  IF X < = 127 THEN 580
760  IK = IK + 1
790  VTAB (24): HTAB (10): PRINT "LAST NUMBER FOUND = ";IK;: GOTO 580
820  END
830  REM  RANDOMIZE NUMBERS INTO THE ARRAY
850  C = INT ( RND (1) * 100)
880  IF C < 10 THEN 850: REM  PICK ONLY NUMBERS GREATER THAN 10
910  IF C > 58 THEN 850: REM  PICK ONLY NUMBERS LESS THAN 59
940  IF REP(C) = 1 THEN 850: REM  IF NUMBER ALREADY SELECTED GET ANOTHER

970  REP(C) = 1
1000 RETURN
1010 REM  CALCULATE THE CURRENT TIME
1030 X = PEEK ( - 16187): REM   START HARDWARE CLOCK
1060 PRINT D$;"BLOAD RCLK.OBJ": REM  START HARDWARE CLOCK SOFTWARE
1090 RETURN
1120 X1 = X1 - 176:X2 = X2 - 176:X3 = X3 - 176:X4 = X4 - 176:Y1 = Y1 - 1
     76:Y2 = Y2 - 176:Y3 = Y3 - 176:Y4 = Y4 - 176
1150 TIME = (X4 + X3 * .1 + X2 * .01 + X1 * .001) - (Y4 + Y3 * .1 + Y2 *
     .01 + Y1 * .001)
1180 TIME = INT (TIME * 1000) / 1000
1210 RETURN
1240 CALL 896: REM  READ CLOCK STARTING TIME
1270 X1 = PEEK (642):X2 = PEEK (643):X3 = PEEK (644):X4 = PEEK (646)

1300 RETURN
1330 CALL 896: REM  READ CLOCK CURRENT TIME
1360 Y1 = PEEK (642):Y2 = PEEK (643):Y3 = PEEK (644):Y4 = PEEK (646)

1390 RETURN
1400 REM  SOUND BUZZER WHEN TIME UP
1420 FOR I = 1 TO 20:X = PEEK ( - 16336): NEXT I
1450 HOME : REM  CLEAR SCREEN AND PRINT  NUMBER JUST FOUND
1480 VTAB (10): PRINT "    NUMBERS FOUND = ";IK - 9
1510 VTAB (15): INPUT "DO ANOTHER ?? : ";Y$
1540 IF Y$ < > "Y" THEN  END
1550 REM  RESET THE NUMBER ARRAY
1570 FOR I = 1 TO 59:REP(I) = 0: NEXT I
1600 HOME : GOTO 220
```

CHAPTER 13

Microcomputer Applications in Biomechanics

James G. Richards

During the past several years, the area of biomechanics has become more and more reliant on microcomputers. Virtually every facet of this interdisciplinary science is now in some manner dependent on the use of these machines. Experts in the area of biomechanics have been quick to realize the many benefits that can be gained through the acquisition and implementation of microcomputer technology. This holds true for researchers as well as teachers and technicians. In the long run, everyone from the administration to the students benefits from the carefully planned and implemented application of microcomputers.

Because biomechanics incorporates applications from the fields of engineering, physics, anatomy, and mathematics, research topics under the umbrella of biomechanics may bear little resemblance to one another. Researchers in this area are liable to have the interest and the capacity to work on a variety of research topics in a multitude of environments. For example, one researcher in biomechanics may have an interest in working on an experiment involving noninvasive ways to estimate red/white muscle fiber content in humans, whereas another may be involved in researching the effectiveness of running shoes in terms of shock absorption and rearfoot stability. Still other researchers may be investigating the effectiveness of an athlete's technique in throwing a javelin.

Because of the extremely wide variety of research conducted in the field of biomechanics, many different instruments are used by researchers. Much of this instrumentation has, in recent years, evolved into computer-compatible or computer-dependent equipment. Likewise, many of the researchers in this field have become equally dependent upon the computerization of laboratory equipment. This chapter explains the benefits of using a microcomputer in the biomechanics laboratory by presenting several common research applications and explaining how the microcomputer has changed the effectiveness of these applications.

Benefits of Microcomputers in the Laboratory

The researchers perhaps reap the largest rewards from the use of microcomputers. For their applications, microcomputers provide a degree of flexibility, accuracy, and speed that is rarely matched by other types of equipment. For example, consider applications involving communication between the microcomputer and other types of laboratory equipment. These applications always consist of a two-part interface. One part is the hardware interface, and the other is the software interface. Whereas the hardware interface usually determines the accuracy and speed of the system, the software aspect determines the functional characteristics. For instance, in collecting data from a force platform, software can be written that will produce X, Y, and Z direction force-time curves, a center of pressure path, a moment-time curve, or any other data manipulation function the user chooses, such as integration. The microcomputer provides flexibility far beyond that of standard data-recording equipment. Through the use of microcomputers, the researcher can tailor the system to perform any function of which the hardware is capable.

Level of Accuracy

Another benefit gained by the researcher is the level of accuracy achieved through the use of computers. For example, data obtained through the use of chart strip or other recorders requires manipulation by researchers in order to reduce the data to meaningful numerical form. This process is one that introduces a tremendous amount of error into the data reduction sequence because the analysis of chart strip output is, in part, subject to the skills of the analyst. If the analyst must determine exact values of specific points on the curve or on the baseline and possibly determine the area under the curve by tracing the waveform with a planimeter or digitizer, then the accuracy with which this process can be completed is determined strictly by the analyst's skills at tracing the curve.

Microcomputers circumvent the above problems by eliminating the need for manual analysis of the data and by operating at a known resolution, as determined by the hardware used to communicate with the computer. Data collected by a microcomputer are not subject to the skills of the analyst and can be presented in usable form to the researcher. Also, as you may suspect, the computer can perform this task in a very small fraction of the time required by the analyst.

Data Collection Speed and Storage

The speed at which data can be collected by microcomputers typically exceeds the capabilities of most dedicated recorders as well as the needs of the researcher. Analog input systems are currently available for some microcomputers that allow data to be collected at fairly high (12-bit) resolution at virtually any sampling rate. This rate is generally controlled through the software and may range from as low as 1 sample per second to over 1,000,000 samples per second.

Another tremendous benefit to the researcher is the microcomputer's ability to store large amounts of data, thereby providing a convenient method for the researcher to compare and analyze data. Information stored from one trial can be averaged or directly compared with data obtained from other trials. In addition, software modifications allow the researcher to manipulate data in different ways without having to go back through the process of collecting the data a second time or cross tabulating sheet after sheet of numeric information.

Control of Instrumentation

Microcomputers also provide the researcher with the ability to control certain types of instrumentation in the laboratory. Signals output from the microcomputer in either digital or analog form can be used to control motors, cameras, timing lights, and a multitude of other devices. This type of control gives the researcher the capability to perform such a task as synchronizing equipment with an extremely high degree of accuracy, thereby simplifying the data reduction process. On a higher level, several new instruments in the area of biomechanics rely solely on the microcomputer to control virtually all machine functions. An example of this is a device called the KIN-COM, which provides the ability to test joint functions in both eccentric and concentric forms. This unit controls its movement speed, range of motion, and data collection processes by software in the microcomputer system.

Cost Effectiveness

The principle advantage of laboratory microcomputers from an administrator's perspective is the relatively low cost of these units, especially compared with the retail cost of dedicated recording/analysis equipment. Since microcomputers can be adapted to perform almost any data collection/analysis role through the innovative use of software, fewer pieces of equipment need to be purchased and maintained.

Furthermore, dedicated equipment is often very difficult to adapt to changing situations and must be replaced as the needs of the researcher change. Microcomputers can almost always adapt to changing needs, and although it is possible for the researcher to outgrow the capacities of the microcomputer for specific project requirements, it more often than not will adequately meet necessary project specifications.

An additional advantage of microcomputers when more than one is being used in the laboratory environment is the noticeable decrease in downtime of the data collection equipment. Microcomputers are fairly durable units, but like all other instruments, they are susceptible to failure. When this does happen, a second microcomputer in the laboratory can usually be called upon to complete the necessary tasks. Although this flexibility is rarely needed or used, it can be a critical factor in the successful completion of projects dependent on time. This is one application where dedicated laboratory collection units are extremely limited.

Teaching Aids

Students also see a tremendous benefit from the use of microcomputers in a laboratory environment. Because the unit that collects the data from equipment is also used to analyze and present the data, much of the development work that occurs for the purposes of research can also be used in the biomechanics teaching laboratory. In learning the kinetics of gait, for example, the student can be given the opportunity to determine what effects on ground reaction force or center of pressure are generated with the use of different types of shoes. In this manner, systems that were initially designed for research can function beautifully in a teaching environment, and students can be given the opportunity to see and manipulate information that could previously only be explained crudely through illustrations and descriptions in textbooks. The hands-on experience makes the concepts presented in the classroom tangible to the student.

Another benefit that the students may see is in a nonlaboratory use of microcomputers. When not functioning as components of a laboratory system, the microcomputer can often be used by students and faculty for word processing or problem solving. These additional uses provide even greater justification for the use of microcomputers and may, in most cases, increase the productivity of both students and faculty.

Force Measurement

A substantial portion of current research topics in biomechanics centers on the measurement of forces involved in human motion. These forces may be involved in creating motions, such as those generated by the lower extremities in the sprint start, or in stopping or changing motions, such as those created in collisions. In either case, the researcher is usually attempting to determine both the magnitude and direction of the forces involved as well as several additional parameters, such as location of the center of pressure or total generated impulse.

Devices used to measure these forces are varied in design and are usually specific to the application. However, most force-measuring systems have a common set of components. Typically, these consist of a sensing device (e.g., a transducer or strain guages), an amplifier, and some type of recording unit. The particular application may call for one or several of these units and may be capable of producing several channels of data.

Advantages of Using a Microcomputer

The microcomputer fits into the force-measuring system either in place of the recording unit or as an addition to the recording unit. In this configuration, the microcomputer is given the capacity to collect, display, and store data collected from the force-measuring system. It offers several advantages over the traditional strip chart recorder, which is the mainstay of most force-measuring systems. First, the microcomputer gives the researcher a means to manipulate the collected data. For example, the researcher can average several force readings together. This is a very straightforward and simple process that cannot be done efficiently with data from chart strip recorders. Likewise, the researcher can also choose to analyze specific points on the curve or even to modify the time base if necessary. Second, the microcomputer gives the researcher a means to perform calculations on the curve rapidly and accurately, such as identification of peak forces, integration of the waveform, or calculations of moments about a specific axis. Third, use of a microcomputer for analyzing a force curve improves the accuracy with which the analyzation process can be performed. Measurement errors on the part of the researcher are virtually eliminated, and the level of precision of the computer is usually much greater than that of the researcher. For example, a researcher who is visually analyzing a force curve collected with a recorder may be capable of dividing the height of the curve into 100 parts. Thus if the total height of the curve represents 200 kilograms, the researcher can read the curve and be accurate to the nearest ±2 kilograms. A microcomputer employing a 12-bit A/D converter will be capable of dividing the same curve into 4,096 parts and, when reading a single point on the curve, be accurate to the nearest ±0.0048 kilogram. This represents a tremendous difference in resolution. Fourth, implementation of microcomputers as force-recording devices is often less expensive than the use of dedicated chart strip recorders or plotters. Microcomputers can readily adapt to most force-measuring applications with software changes, whereas chart strip recorders or plotters are usually dedicated to the system with which they are purchased.

Using Microcomputers With Forceplates

One of the most common applications of microcomputers in force data collection is in the collection and analysis of force platform data. *Forceplates* are devices capable of reading forces in three axes and typically produce data appropriate for the calculation of location of center of pressure and moments about each of the axes. Frequently found in gait analysis laboratories, these devices can be used to diagnose dynamic dysfunctions in gait caused by anatomical or functional abnormalities. They can also be used in such applications as determining the static balancing capabilities of an individual or teaching kinetic properties of gait.

Data collected from force platforms may consist of as many as eight channels of information: four in the vertical direction, two in the lateral direction, and two in the frontal direction. When data are collected from all eight channels and presented to the researcher in strip chart form, the researcher must manually perform a point-to-point comparison of each curve in order to find total force values or vectors as well as center of pressure locations and peak forces. In addition, each curve must be integrated in order to measure impulse values. This process, when performed manually, is extremely tedious and prone to error. As you might suspect, a properly configured microcomputer can accurately perform all of these functions in a very short period of time.

Figures 13.1 to 13.3 represent the output of an Apple IIe microcomputer that has been interfaced to an eight-channel Kistler force platform. The data was collected from a single step of a subject walking across the forceplate at a moderate walking speed. All software for

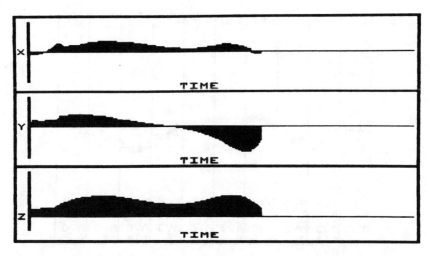

Figure 13.1 Raw data from a Kistler forceplate presented on the Apple II monitor.

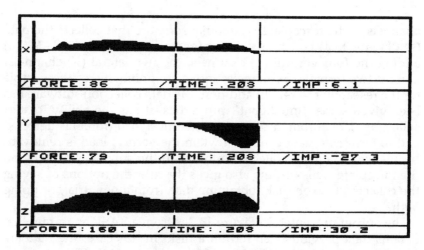

Figure 13.2 The same data from Figure 13.1 following analysis for peak force and impulse. The impulse value was obtained from the areas between the two vertical bars.

this system was written in BASIC with the exception of the data collection subroutine, which was written in machine language because BASIC is far too slow to enable the Apple to collect data at the required rate of 500 samples per second. The interface consists of an 8-bit A/D converter programmed to collect data from each of the eight

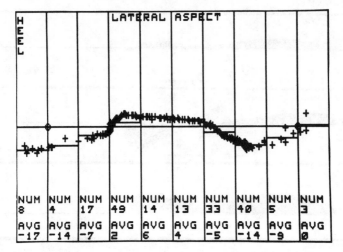

Figure 13.3   A sample center of pressure path obtained from a force platform.

channels of the forceplate. The initial software that collects the data (see Figure 13.1) is responsible for (a) storing the data in RAM; (b) adding the four vertical (Z) channels, the two lateral (X) channels, and the two frontal (Y) channels; and (c) graphing the resulting curve for the researcher to see. In addition, the data collection software has been given some "intelligent" properties. It has the ability to start collecting data automatically when a vertical load (force) is detected and to terminate data collection when the vertical load is removed. In this way, data are collected only when the subject is actually on the forceplate. This routine also gives the user the options of saving the collected trial on disk, obtaining data from a new trial, or doing both.

The output presented in Figure 13.2 is from a BASIC program that obtains data previously stored on a disk. In this case, the data are from the same trial as that presented in Figure 13.1. This program constitutes one data analysis program for these curves. The researcher can use the arrows on the keyboard to control a cursor that is presented as a plus sign (+) on the X-axis of each curve. When the cursor is in a desired position, the user can request information concerning the instantaneous force value of each curve as well as the time at which that force occurred. This is accomplished simply by pressing the space bar with the cursor in the desired position. The user can then move the cursor to another location on the curve and request the same information on the new location. In addition, the software provides the user with the ability to define the beginning and end of an area on the curve. Once this area has been defined, the software calculates the area under the curve and ultimately the impulse associated with that portion of the curve. It should be noted that this portion, if so desired, can consist of the entire force curve.

Figure 13.3 illustrates yet another set of calculations that the computer can perform on the same data. In this case, the calculations consist of a sample-to-sample determination of the location of the center of pressure. In this specific example, the horizontal line across the center of the graph represents the midline of the foot along the long arch. The two circular points on this line represent reference points that have been made on the bottom of the subject's foot at the center of the heel and the head of the second metatarsal. This line divides the center of pressure path into medial and lateral components, whereas the vertical lines divide the path into 10 transverse sections. The number of samples falling in each transverse band (NUM) is indicative of the relative amount of time that the center of pressure was located under that part of the foot, whereas the number labeled AVG indicates the relative distance of the average of the center of the pressure path within each transverse band from the midline of the foot. A positive value indicates that the average center of pressure location was on the lateral aspect of the foot, whereas a negative number indicates that the average center of pressure location was on the medial aspect of the foot.

It should be evident from these examples that data collected from a force platform by a microcomputer can be subjected to several types of analyses strictly by manipulation of the software. In fact, this is such a convenient method of analysis that force platform manufacturers such as AMTI are now selling their forceplates complete with computer interfaces and software for collection and analysis purposes.

Using Microcomputers With Isokinetic Dynamometers

Another type of force measurement data collected by biomechanists is that generated from *isokinetic dynamometers*. These are devices that measure torques about a joint axis at specific and constant movement speeds. Currently available are three isokinetic machines that can be considered true isokinetic dynamometers: Cybex II, KIN-COM, and BIODEX. The Cybex II has been available for many years, whereas the KIN-COM and the BIODEX units represent more recent developments in isokinetic technology.

Until very recently, data provided by the Cybex II consisted of a torque-time curve and a position-time curve presented in chart strip form. A sample waveform generated by the thermal recorder available with the Cybex II is presented in Figure 13.4. The user of such

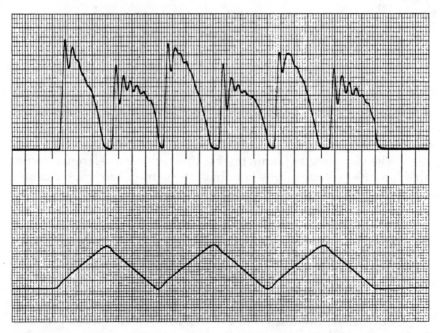

Figure 13.4 A sample torque/time curve from the Cybex II Isokinetic Dynamo-meter. The curve was collected from the right knee at 120°/s.

a device would then usually identify several parameters on the curves. In fact, a complete bilateral/ipsilateral analysis of a single joint at a single speed might consist of the following calculations:

1. The user identifies the peak torque for both joint actions (i.e., agonist and antagonist) and for both sides of the body by matching the peaks of the appropriate waveforms to a paper scale provided with the recorder.
2. With a second scale, the user then determines where in the joint range of motion these torques occurred by measuring the position-time curve values that correspond to the location of the peak torques.
3. The user next determines the corresponding work values generated by integrating each waveform with a planimeter or digitizer and then multiplying the area by the appropriate constant values. To determine power, these values are divided by the total time duration of the curve.
4. Finally, the user places these values in a table and makes the appropriate comparisons between actions (i.e., agonist vs. antagonist

groups on one side of the body, then agonist vs. agonist groups on opposite sides of the body, etc.). This process is performed for each of the values measured.

This entire process may take as long as 15 minutes to perform by an experienced user, and it is usually performed at more than one movement speed. Thus, a complete analysis of a single joint on both sides of the body might take 30 minutes or more to complete.

In an effort to streamline this process, a microcomputer was utilized to collect and analyze data from the chart strip recorder. In fact, numerous researchers have attempted this project in the past few years, and the result has been the development of several computer hardware/software systems capable of collecting, analyzing, and storing isokinetic data. The following description presents the main features of one microcomputer system that has been specifically programmed to analyze data from the Cybex II dynamometer.

Figure 13.5 shows the output from a sample data collection bout on the Cybex II. The data have been collected from the right knee at a speed of 120° per second, and the values above the curve indicate the results of the analysis performed by the computer at the time of the analysis. "Peak Torque" represents the maximum torque attained during any of the repetitions of extension and flexion. The values entitled "Work" represent the average work values achieved

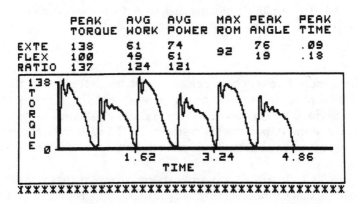

Figure 13.5 The same torque/time curve shown in Figure 13.4 as collected and analyzed by a microcomputer.

for each action in all three trials. Power values are calculated based upon the average work values. "Peak Angle" refers to the angle of the limb at the point where peak torque is generated, and "Peak Time" refers to the time elapsed between the start of the joint action and the detection of peak torque. ROM represents the maximum range of motion that was utilized by the joint structure during the data collection period. The user is given the option of printing the data as it appears on the screen, saving the data on a disk for further analysis, or abandoning the trial.

Figure 13.6 provides the results of a bilateral analysis. The output is strictly numeric and allows the user to make a direct comparison

```
            BIOMEK BILATERAL ANALYSIS
                     RICHARDS

   TEST    DATE          JOINT        SPEED
   ----    ----          -----        -----
    1      4/28/86       LT KNEE      120
    2      4/28/86       RT KNEE      120


ACTION: EXTEN
TEST TORQUE WORK POWER  ROM  ANGLE TIME
---- ------ ---- -----  ---- ----- ----
  1    166   66    84    89    62   .19
  2    138   61    74    92    76   .09
RATIO 120   108   113    96


ACTION: FLEX
TEST TORQUE WORK POWER  ROM  ANGLE TIME
---- ------ ---- -----  ---- ----- ----
  1    96    46    59    89     8   .09
  2   100    49    61    92    19   .18
RATIO 95    93    96    96
```

Figure 13.6   The results of a bilateral analysis performed by the microcomputer. The analysis compares right and left knees at 120°/s.

of all measured values between the right and left sides of the body. The ratios provided on the printout represent the ratios of the top values divided by the lower values and are expressed in percentage form. Once the data have been stored on the disk from the data collection process, the bilateral analysis requires approximately 2 minutes to complete.

Figure 13.7 illustrates an applications program that accomplishes an analysis that cannot be done by hand. This program isolates a torque curve from a single repetition collected during a single joint action and overlays it on a torque curve from another selected repetition.

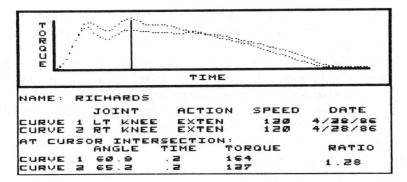

Figure 13.7 A sample graph from a waveform overlay program. This graph again compares data obtained from right and left knees (extensors) at 120°/s.

A movable cursor then provides the user with the ability to make point-to-point comparisons of torque values between each curve. In this manner, deficiencies at a single point on the curve can be quickly identified and quantified.

The illustration presented in Figure 13.8 provides the user with yet another method of analyzing the Cybex data. This software presents a "spectral" view of the peak torque values of two joint actions. Peak torque values from each joint action are plotted against the speed at which they were collected. Like the bilateral analysis, this program

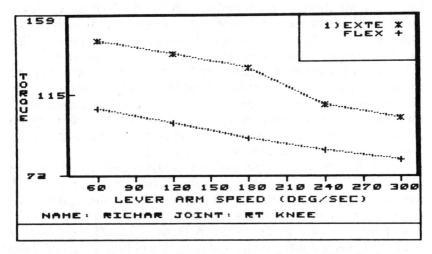

Figure 13.8 A "spectral" graph of peak torque plotted against the lever arm speed. The data presented was collected from the right knee.

can simultaneously plot curves from both sides of the body and provide the user with the ability to see how the torque output of a joint is affected by movement speed.

This application of microcomputer technology has streamlined the researcher's ability to collect and analyze isokinetic data. In fact, the KIN-COM isokinetic unit, a newcomer to the isokinetic market, was built around a microcomputer. All of its functions as well as its data-handling capabilities are directly controlled by the microcomputer, providing the user with a much more accurate means of controlling the measurement process.

Film Analysis

High-speed cinematographical analysis is one of the principal tools used in biomechanical research. This tool has been in use for decades and is familiar to every student of biomechanics. However, until very recently, detailed cinematographical analyses were restricted to institutions having access to mainframe computers that could be linked to digitizers. These links were somewhat cumbersome and quite expensive on both an initial and ongoing cost basis. In addition, the mainframes operated on a time-sharing basis; during times of heavy user loads, they could be very slow in responding. These features made development of film analysis systems prohibitive to many college-level biomechanics programs.

When inexpensive microcomputer technology emerged in the late 1970s, development of digitizing systems became a tangible objective for most institutions of higher education. As the technology developed, the sophistication of the software created for film analysis also increased, so that by the mid-1980s, virtually all two-dimensional film analysis routines could be implemented on microcomputers.

To date, many institutions have developed their own microcomputer software to handle the task of high-speed film analysis. Many similarities exist between these programs and a great deal of functional duplication has occurred. However, the objective of all of these programs remains the same: to produce linear and angular kinematic data on human motion that has been recorded on film.

One such system that accomplishes this task is described here. The film analysis hardware consists of a stop action projector, a 3- by 4-foot digitizing table, and an Apple II+ microcomputer system with two disk drives and a graphics printer. An overview of the capabilities of the software is illustrated in Figure 13.9. The software is completely menu driven and has the capability of producing both plots and complete listings of linear and angular kinematics (i.e., linear and

```
SELECT ONE OF THE FOLLOWING:


  1)DIGITIZER        6)LINEAR LIST

  2)SCALING          7)ANGULAR LIST

  3)PATH OF MOTION   8)STICK PLOTS

  4)LINEAR PLOTS     9)FORMAT A DISK

  5)ANGULAR PLOTS



   COPYRIGHT 1982 BY RICHARDS, WILKERSON
```

Figure 13.9 The main menu for the film analysis software. *Note.* Copyright 1982 by J. Richards and Wilkerson.

angular position, displacement, velocity, and acceleration) for all digitized points as well as the center of gravity, if applicable. In addition, all data are digitally filtered in order to remove as much extraneous error as possible prior to inclusion in calculations.

Figure 13.10 illustrates the topic of the displayed digitizing session. This is a sample output from the program entitled STIKPLOT on the menu page, and it presents data from the left side of an athlete performing a luge start. This program was designed simply to produce a visual representation of the data for qualitative purposes. It provides the user with the interactive ability to select endpoints for plotting as well as to define those points that constitute a given line segment. All data are automatically scaled to fit the screen in order to produce the maximum image size.

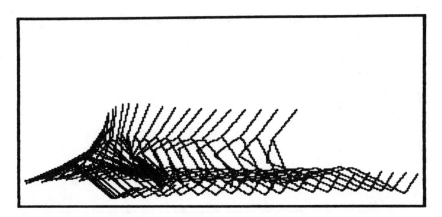

Figure 13.10 A stick plot of a sledder performing a start on the luge run.

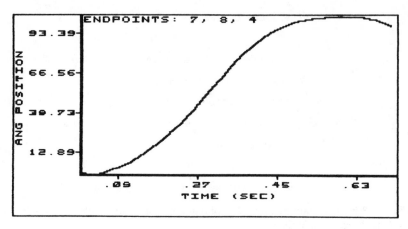

Figure 13.11   An angular position/time plot of the sledder's hip in the luge start.

A sample printout from the program entitled ANGULAR PLOTS on the menu is presented in Figure 13.11. The endpoints 7, 8, and 4 at the top of the graph indicate that the graph is an angular position-time curve of a luge sledder's hip. This program can plot the kinematics for any angle defined by three digitized points. Included in the available kinematics are angular position, angular displacement, angular velocity, and angular acceleration.

Figure 13.12 presents data from the program entitled LINEAR PLOTS on the menu page. Endpoint 10, evident on the top of the graph, indicates that this is a linear velocity-time curve of the luge sled during

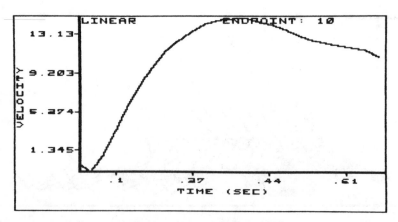

Figure 13.12   A linear velocity/time plot of the sled as it moves during the luge start.

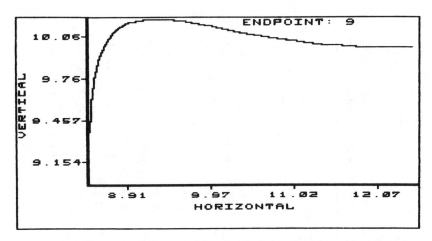

Figure 13.13 The path of motion of the sledder's head while performing a luge start.

the starting phase of the race. This program has the capacity to plot horizontal, vertical, and/or linear displacement, velocity, and acceleration.

The graph presented in Figure 13.13 depicts the path of motion of a sledder's head at the start of a luge race. This graph is generated from the program entitled PATH OF MOTION on the menu page. This is the path of motion the head follows when the sledder propels himself from the starting bars. The path is set to full scale in both the horizontal and vertical directions so that the vertical motion of the head appears somewhat exaggerated.

Both the LINEAR LIST and ANGULAR LIST programs on the menu page provide all kinematic data used to produce the plots in printed form to the user. In this manner, the user can more accurately identify kinematic parameters at a specific point in time. A sample printout from the LINEAR LIST program is provided in Figure 13.14. This represents the linear kinematic data on the sled in a luge start.

It should be apparent from these printouts that the capacity of the microcomputers currently available is equal to the capacity of many of the mainframe systems used to analyze film data just 10 years ago. It should also be noted that the system illustrated above was implemented on a 48k Apple II + computer, a machine with very limited storage capacity and speed. Despite this, the programs that were illustrated are complete and are presented to the user in an easily usable interactive format. This is documented by the fact that the system described here has been used regularly by undergraduate students for class projects since 1984.

FILENAME: FRANK1.DATA ENDPOINT: 10

FRAME	X	Y	TIME	HORIZ DISPL	VERT DISPL	LINEAR DISPL	HORIZ VELOC	VERT VELOC	LINEAR VELOC	HORIZ ACCEL	VERT ACCEL	LINEAR ACCEL
1	7.61	7	.03	.05	.01	0	1.78	.74	.12			
2	7.1	6.99	.03	.15	.01	-.03	5.05	.74	-.63	115.24	-2.89	8.06
3	7.04	7	.03	.19	.01	.03	6.65	.57	1.12	95.3	-4.22	31.53
4	7.16	7	.03	.22	0	.11	7.72	.34	3.78	71.33	-5.07	52.99
5	7.35	7.04	.03	.25	-.01	.19	8.65	.11	6.45	51.54	-5.07	66.33
6	7.65	7.03	.03	.28	-.01	.25	9.59	-.04	8.71	38.81	-4.15	69.75
7	7.9	6.99	.03	.31	-.01	.31	10.61	-.1	10.51	32.29	-2.59	65.03
8	8.19	7.01	.03	.34	-.01	.35	11.67	-.09	11.93	29.46	-.83	55.41
9	8.57	7.01	.03	.37	-.01	.38	12.69	-.05	13.03	27.66	.7	43.88
10	8.96	7	.03	.4	-.01	.41	13.6	.04	13.89	24.98	1.74	32.34
11	9.35	7								20.5	2.17	21.66

12	9.73	7	.03	.42	0	.43	14.35	.13	14.55	14.22	2.03	12.04
13	10.28	7.05	.03	.44	0	.44	14.86	.2	14.97	6.88	1.51	3.61
14	10.71	7.03	.03	.44	0	.45	15.03	.23	15.09	-.45	.82	-3.45
15	11.16	7.01	.03	.44	0	.44	14.92	.24	14.94	-6.75	.14	-8.89
16	11.57	7.05	.03	.43	0	.43	14.63	.25	14.63	-11.42	-.39	-12.62
17	12.01	7.06	.03	.42	0	.42	14.23	.22	14.23	-14.31	-.68	-14.75
18	12.44	7.05	.03	.4	0	.41	13.76	.18	13.76	-15.63	-.73	-15.57
19	12.82	7.05	.03	.39	0	.39	13.26	.14	13.27	-15.83	-.63	-15.51
20	13.21	7.05	.03	.37	0	.38	12.81	.14	12.82	-15.46	-.49	-15.03
21	13.57	7.08	.03	.36	-.01	.37	12.43	.15	12.46	-14.89	-.41	-14.45
22	13.93	7.06	.03	.35	-.01	.36	12.16	.15	12.18	-13.93	-.35	-13.52
23	14.23	7.08	.03	.35	-.01	.35	11.95	.14	11.98	-11.52	-.25	-11.21
24	14.56	7.08	.03	.34	-.01	.34	11.68	.11	11.7	-22.01	-2.34	-22.01
25	14.85	7.05	.03	.32	-.01	.33	11.02	.04	11.04			

Figure 13.14 A linear kinematic list of a point on the sled as it moves during the luge start.

Multiple Instrument Synchronization

Many biomechanical investigations involve more than one mode of measurement in order to obtain information necessary for a study. For example, a high-speed camera may be employed with a force platform in order to match specific points in an activity with recorded force data. An electromyograph may also be utilized to determine muscle activity during an endurance test on an isokinetic dynamometer. In situations such as these, different types of instrumentation must operate together within a specified period of time. The researcher, in order to analyze the data from both instruments, must be able to identify data from the same points in time on each instrument.

The process of synchronizing different types of equipment is frequently difficult to perform. How does a high-speed camera communicate with a force platform, or EMG, or isokinetic dynamometer? In the past, several methods of synchronization were employed, most of them involving the customized construction of controlling devices. One technique employed in an effort to synchronize a force platform and a high-speed camera consisted of placing a light in the field of view of the camera. When the subject contacted a switch mat, the light was turned on and a signal sent to the forceplate recorder. In this manner, the researcher could match the timing mark on the forceplate recorder with the appearance of the light on the camera. It was a crude method at best, but it worked.

Synchronizing Force and Film Data

The synchronization process has been refined tremendously with the intervention of microcomputers. For the example given above, the switch mat, the external light, and the controlling device have all been eliminated. Instead, a microcomputer controls a timing light inside the camera as well as the data collection process of the force platform.

Here's how this system actually works. Inside most high-speed cameras, the manufacturer has made provisions for an LED timing light that can be controlled either internally or externally. When controlled internally, the light places hash marks on the side of the film at set intervals (e.g., every 1/100th of a second). When controlled externally, the light becomes an event timer, capable of placing a single mark on the film at the point of a significant occurrence in the experiment. This timing light can usually be configured so that the computer becomes responsible for triggering the light. If the computer is collecting data from a device such as a force platform, it can send a timing signal to the camera every time it collects a sample from the forceplate. If the computer software has been designed to collect data from the forceplate at a rate of 500 samples per second and only when a load is available on the platform surface, then a timing mark will appear on the film every 1/500th of a second as long as the subject is on the forceplate. This application of microcomputer technology is an extremely important one because it results in a quite precise synchronization of two or more very different types of instruments.

Synchronizing Force and EMG Data

In another application of the microcomputer's ability to synchronize instruments, consider an experiment that involves collection of data from an isokinetic device and an electromyograph. Both machines would normally be configured to send data to recording devices, such as chart strip recorders. In this case, however, the output from both units could be fed into a microcomputer in place of the recorder. The computer can be programmed to collect data simultaneously from both devices through an A/D converter at a specified sampling rate and for a specified period of time. Because the sampling rate can be the same for both devices, the computer will read the data points from each device at the same time, plus or minus a few microseconds. Thus, when the software is created to perform a point-to-point analysis of the data, points that have been collected at the same time are automatically compared; that is, because the computer collected data from both devices at the same time, data from the devices have been automatically synchronized by the computer. This situation is equivalent to reading several channels of force platform data, where each channel is read at approximately the same time so that moments, vectors, and center of pressure locations can be determined.

Motion Sensing

It is occasionally desirable to obtain direct measures of motion rather than to film and analyze the data at a later time. For the most part, direct measures of motion are more accurate than those obtained from film and, once the equipment has been obtained, much less expensive to acquire.

Movement data that are measured directly are usually obtained through accelerometers or electrogoniometers. *Accelerometers* are devices that are very similar in nature to force transducers except that they detect motion instead of force. The strength of the signal obtained from accelerometers is directly proportional to the rate of acceleration of the device. *Electrogoniometers* are resistive devices capable of electronic determination of joint angles.

Accelerometers

Typically, output from an accelerometer is sent to a recording device such as an oscilloscope, and the user is presented with a photograph of the image. If a recorder with a fast enough response time is available, then the output is sent to the recorder instead. In either case, a tracing of the curve created by the accelerometer results. From this tracing, peak acceleration values can be obtained, but values at any point on the curve are subject to the same resolution problems as force curve data; that is, the accuracy with which the curves can be read is dependent upon the number of divisions the person analyzing the curve can visually distinguish.

If, however, the output is read directly into a computer via an A/D converter, the resolution level at which the tracing can be analyzed is tremendously improved. For example, if the data from an accelerometer that produces a full-scale deflection (5 V DC) at 5 g are read by a 12-bit A/D converter at a rate of 5000 samples per second, then the resolution with which the acceleration value can be read is ± 0.0002 g. The resolution of the time scale for this example would also be ± 0.0002 second. The advantage of reading accelerometer data into a computer is obvious.

Electrogoniometers

It was mentioned earlier that data from electrogoniometers consisted of joint position information in electronic form. When attached to a recording unit, these devices provide the user with a position-time curve for a given joint movement. By measuring the height of the curve at any point, the user can determine the joint angle. In addition, information on joint velocity and acceleration can also be obtained from this tracing. These values, however, require that the user digitize the waveform and then take the first and second derivatives using the points obtained from the digitizer. This process is very time consuming and prone to errors.

When a computer is used to collect and analyze the data from an electrogoniometer, the process is much quicker and more accurate. The computer communicates with the electrogoniometer via an A/D converter and can be programmed to collect the data for a specified period of time, calculate both first and second derivatives, and plot and/or list the results. The user is then presented with the position, velocity, and acceleration/time curves, which can then be further analyzed.

Timing Applications

Timing lights or photocells are frequently used by biomechanists to obtain quick measures of velocities and accelerations over specific distance intervals. Units that accomplish this task usually consist of a clock, two or more light sources such as infrared emitters or lasers, and two or more photocells or infrared detectors. These units are often designed and constructed to meet a specific need or are purchased from a manufacturer at a substantial cost.

Recently, researchers in our laboratory developed a need to accurately measure the speed of a lacrosse stick as it passed through an arc and impacted with "infinite" mass. The object of this experiment was to determine at what velocity different styles of sticks could travel and still hold a ball in the pocket at impact. The problem was to find a means of accurately measuring the linear velocity of the stick just prior to impact with the infinite mass. The path traveled by the stick in the laboratory was similar to that which occurs when a player cradles the ball on the field. In a field situation, the player attempts to keep the ball in the stick while opposing team members strike the stick in an effort to force the ball back into play.

Using two low-power lasers and an Apple II+ computer already available in the laboratory, plans were made to construct a photodetection system. Two photocell circuits were constructed with parts obtained at a local Radio Shack for $35. The electrical layout of the circuits

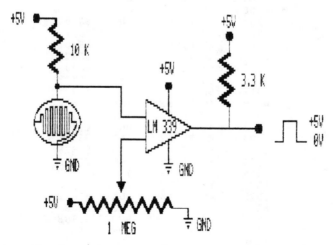

Figure 13.15 The electrical circuit used to create the photocell timing system.

is illustrated in Figure 13.15. The circuits were powered by the Apple II+ and connected to the computer through the annunciator inputs in the game port. A short program was written to determine the status of the photocell: either ON or OFF. The lasers were then aimed into the photocells. The sensitivity levels of the photocells were adjusted so that when the laser beam was broken, the cell would switch from the ON to the OFF position.

Once this was accomplished, BASIC and assembly language programs were written to measure the time between the two photocells (see Figures 13.16 and 13.17). The programs started counting when the beam to the first photocell was broken and stopped counting when the beam to the second cell was broken. Each count that the computer kept track of was determined to be equal to 1/20,000th of a second. Thus, the timing system was accurate to +0.00001 second. The lasers and photocells were aligned to produce a 2-centimeter distance between beams, and the program was modified to produce the time and the velocity at which the stick traveled through the two beams.

In a subsequent experiment, light from two high-intensity study lamps were substituted for the lasers with extremely positive results. No difference was found in the velocity of tennis balls ejected from

```
6300-    18              CLC
6301-    AD 61 C0        LDA     $C061
6304-    69 80           ADC     #$80
6306-    90 F8           BCC     $6300
6308-    18              CLC
6309-    EE 00 64        INC     $6400
630C-    D0 10           BNE     $631E
630E-    EE 01 64        INC     $6401
6311-    D0 10           BNE     $6323
6313-    EE 02 64        INC     $6402
6316-    D0 10           BNE     $6328
6318-    EE 03 64        INC     $6403
631B-    4C 2E 63        JMP     $632E
631E-    EE FF 62        INC     $62FF
6321-    B0 FE           BCS     $6321
6323-    EE FF 62        INC     $62FF
6326-    B0 FE           BCS     $6326
6328-    EE FF 62        INC     $62FF
632B-    4C 2E 63        JMP     $632E
632E-    18              CLC
632F-    AD 62 C0        LDA     $C062
6332-    69 80           ADC     #$80
6334-    90 D2           BCC     $6308
6336-    60              RTS
*
```

Figure 13.16 A listing of the assembly language program used to drive the photocell circuit in Figure 13.15.

```
10 SLOT = 4:D$ =   CHR$ (4)
12  FOR I = 25600 TO 25603
13  POKE I,0
14  NEXT I
15  HOME
17  VTAB 23: HTAB 10
18  PRINT "HIT ANY KEY TO START"
20  REM
70 X =  PEEK ( - 16384): IF X < 128 THEN 20
80  PRINT
90  HOME : VTAB 12
100  HTAB 11
110  PRINT "READING CELLS"
120  CALL 25344
130 TIME = 0
135  FOR I = 0 TO 3
140 TIME = TIME +  PEEK (25600 + I) * 256 ^ I
142  NEXT I
145 TIME = TIME / 21470
160 DIST = .1: REM  DIST BETWEEN CELLS IN METERS
170 VEL = DIST / TIME
200  HOME
210  PRINT "TIME = "; INT (TIME * 1000);" MSEC"
220  PRINT : PRINT "VELOCITY = ";VEL;"  M/S"
240  END
```

Figure 13.17 A listing of the BASIC program used to drive the photocell circuit presented in Figure 13.15.

a serving machine when high-intensity lamps were used in place of the lasers.

This application of a microcomputer has turned out to be a very functional one, both from an economic and an accuracy standpoint. The photocell system has since been used in a variety of other studies with a great degree of success.

Data Storage

Despite the number of functions microcomputers can perform in the research laboratory, they are not unlimited in their capacities. One type of application that microcomputers fail to satisfy are those requiring extremely fast sampling rates. Off-the-shelf A/D converters can usually sample data at a maximum sampling rate of approximately 12,000 samples per second for a single channel of data. If two channels of data are involved, then the maximum per sample collection rate becomes approximately 6,000 samples per second.

One specific application where this sampling rate has been found to fall far short of what is required is in the collection of ultrasound signals. The frequency of ultrasound transmitters is very high (i.e., greater than 20 kHz), and the computer must be able to collect data at a rate at least 2.5 times greater than the ultrasound frequency. This means that the computer may have to collect data at a rate as high as 1 mHz.

One solution applied to this problem is to interface the microcomputer to a digital storage oscilloscope. Several companies, including Tektronix and Nicolet, make oscilloscopes with the capacity to collect data at sampling rates as high as 100 mHz, store it in their own RAM, and then transfer it into a microcomputer via a serial or parallel interface. In this configuration, there are two options for handling the data. First, the user can use software written for the microcomputer to analyze data in much the same way forceplate or electrogoniometer data are analyzed. Second, the user can choose to send the data back to the oscilloscope at a later time and use the digitizing features of the oscilloscope to analyze the data. In this second approach to analyzing the data, the microcomputer acts simply as a mass storage device for the data and has very little to do with the analysis process. This method does, however, allow the user to store a very large number of waveforms for subsequent analysis at any preselectable sampling rate.

This solution to the problem of collecting data at a very fast rate is not an inexpensive one (i.e., the scope and interface cost approximately $6,000), but it does offer several advantages over a conventional A/D interface. First, the sampling rate of the scope can be altered by changing a switch on the front of the scope. This change requires no software modification and approximately 1 second to perform. Second, the sensitivity of the scope can be similarly adjusted to read in virtually any voltage range. In this manner, it will accept data from virtually any analog device without modification or addition of hardware. The scope can thus act as an A/D board that can be instantly modified to any data collection situation.

There is one limitation that exists in a configuration of this type, however. The largest number of channels that any of the available oscilloscopes can read is four, so such instruments as forceplates that generate six or eight channels of information are not good candidates for use with an oscilloscope.

Teaching

It was stated earlier that the field of biomechanics is actually a subdiscipline of several fields of study including engineering, physics, anatomy, and mathematics. Because of the integrated nature of the field, most of the principles that are utilized and taught in biomechanics are not intrinsic to the field of biomechanics but are principles adapted from other areas of study. At first glance, this situation may seem analogous to having a home without a country. However, when dealing with attempts to utilize such innovative instructional techniques as computer-based instruction, the situation may be a blessing.

A great deal of educational software has been developed to assist students in the disciplines from which biomechanics has evolved. Much of this software was initially developed on systems specifically designed to handle instructional applications. One such system manufactured by Control Data Corporation is referred to as PLATO and is currently used in many parts of the country. However, many institutions find such systems too expensive to acquire and maintain.

The microcomputer revolution has prompted many software developers to reevaluate which computers should be targeted for software support. As a result, much of the extensive library of software that was developed for the larger computers has been developed for machines such as the Apple II+ and the IBM PC. Students in biomechanics have been able to reap the benefits of these developments.

Lessons are available in trigonometry, physics (including projectiles and laws of motion), anatomy, and many other fields. Full-service computer stores are good places to locate the sources of this type of software, especially because it helps the stores sell computers. In addition, many publishing houses are starting to sell textbooks bundled with educational software. This is a trend that will probably continue for some time in the future.

The researcher in biomechanics is becoming more and more reliant upon the use of microcomputers for virtually all data collection and analysis applications. As long as the capacity of the microcomputers continues to increase and the price continues to decrease, this trend will continue.

Instructional software in biomechanics is not plentiful at the current time. However, two positive by-products of the microcomputer boom are impacting on CAI in this field. First, a great deal of educational software is being generated in such related areas as mathematics (trigonometry), physics, and anatomy. Much of this software is directly applicable to courses in biomechanics as they are currently taught. Second, because microcomputers frequently allow for the "instant" analysis of collected data, many of the instruments that were used solely for research are now being used effectively as part of the teaching laboratory. The students can see immediate results from a data collection session and, in many cases, can perform their own illustrative experiments with the equipment. For example, students may use a computerized forceplate system to investigate informally the effects of different heel heights on the path of the center of pressure during the walking gait.

Finally, it is becoming apparent that many equipment manufacturers are actively developing means of interfacing their instruments (i.e., hardware and software) to microcomputers in order to improve the data collection and analysis process. This is an indication that microcomputers will remain a major force in biomechanics laboratories for quite some time.

Software Directory

FileVision
Telos Software Products
1-800-554-2469
In Calif. 1-800-368-3813

MacWrite
Apple Computers
20525 Mariani Avenue
Cupertino, CA 95014

Megafile/Megamerge
Megahaus Corp.
5073 Oberlin Drive
San Diego, CA 92121

Market Computing
P.O. Box 6245
Huntington Beach, CA 92615

Overvue
ProVue Development
222 22nd Street
Huntington Beach, CA 92648

PFS: File
PFS: Software Publishing
1901 Landings Drive
Mountain View, CA 94043

SportsLog
27 Broadaxe Lane
Wilton, CA 06897

Super Text
Muse Software
347 N. Charles Street
Baltimore, MD 21201

Visicalc
Personal Software
Software Arts, Inc.
27 Mica Lane
Wellesley, MA 02181

Word/Multiplan/File
Microsoft Corporation
10700 Northrup Way
Bellvue, WA 98004

Glossary

Analog signal. A voltage which can take on any value within a specified range.

Anxiety. Perception that certain environmental stimuli are threatening or nonthreatening and the tendancy to respond with various levels of apprehension and tension.

Arousal. Activation of the central nervous system; alertness, activation, excitement.

ASCII code. A coding scheme for representing characters (letters, digits, etc.) in binary code.

BASIC. Beginners All-purpose Symbolic Instructional Code; a programming language for microcomputers.

Baud rate. The rate at which bits are transmitted across a serial interface.

Biofeedback. Information received about the body's autonomic or physiological responses that enables self-regulation of these processes.

Bit. An acronym for binary digit. A bit can take on a value of either logical 1 or logical 0.

Black box. An instrument dedicated to one test that cannot be altered.

Bus. A series of wires or lines which connect the various components of the microcomputer internally.

Byte. A collection of 8 bits, capable of representing virtually any letter or character.

Canned program. A program that is stored in the memory of the computer or on a floppy disk.

Chip. The jargon used to describe a complete circuit which has been imprinted on a silicon wafer.

Comparator. An electrical device capable of distinguishing which of two voltages is the larger.

Compiler. Software which enables a programmer to convert a program from a high level language such as BASIC to machine level language.

Computer incompatibility. The inability of one brand of computer to run the disk programmed on another brand of computer.

Conditional statement. A command that depends on a logical condition to determine if it will be executed.

CPU. An acronym for Central Processing Unit. This is the electrical "heart" of the microcomputer.

DATA statement. A command that identifies a computer line as containing numerical or string information.

Database. A program which allows for the storage of information and has the ability to arrange that information by "fields" or categories such as alphabetically, by topic, date, or any other desired factor.

DEF function. This command defines a function; usually used with a FN command.

DIM statement. A command that establishes space for a table to be included in a program.

DIP. An acronym for Dual In-line Package. This is the plastic and metal device used to house a chip.

Disk drive. An auxiliary device used to store large amounts of information, including programs, data, and text.

Do-until program. A looping program that executes an imperative statement first and then tests the completeness of the condition.

Do-while program. A looping program that executes a conditional statement before executing a conditional statement.

Experiencing. A category in the taxonomy of CAI utilizing programs that are high in student interest, thus enticing students to develop a deeper understanding.

Externally stored data. A file containing nothing but data.

Files. Used for storage of data or a program.

Fitness testing. More comprehensive than stress testing, it includes other fitness components.

Floppy disk. A magnetic medium for storing computer information.

Flowchart. A diagram or drawing of the way a computer program will perform.

FN statement. A command that defines an operation or programming step.

FOR-NEXT statement. A looping procedure that sets a limit on the number of times to repeat various calculations.

FORTRAN. An acronym for formula translation, a computer programming language.

GOSUB statement. A command that routes the computer to a designated subroutine in a program.

GOTO statement. A command that routes the computer to a new location in a program.

Graded exercise test (GXT). *See stress test.*

Graphics card. Expansion hardware which allows some computers such as the Apple to easily transmit graphic information to selected printers.

IF statement. A conditional statement usually followed by a mathematical operation.

If-then-else program. A combination of one conditional statement and two separate imperative statements.

Imperative statement. A command that must be executed by the computer.

Individualized exercise prescription. A data based exercise program designed for an individual.

Informing. A category in the taxonomy of CAI containing programs that provide information, sometimes by replacing the text or lecture.

Input device. Any peripheral equipment (such as a keyboard) which allows the user to give information to the computer.

INPUT statement. A command that allows the operator to insert a numerical value or literal string into the program.

INT function. A command that outputs the integer of the number contained in parentheses.

Integrating. A category in the taxonomy of CAI containing programs that require application of a previously learned idea.

Interacting program. A program that requires input from the operator at one or more steps in its execution.

Interactive video. A system for instruction that involves a computer-driven videotape or videodisk.

Interface. A hardware and software unit which allows the computer to communicate with peripheral equipment.

Internally stored data. The storage of data within the computer program.

Kilo. The prefix for 1,000.

Laser videodisks. Television programs that are encoded on 12-inch disks and played as phonograph records.

LET statement. A command that assigns a value to a variable.

Linear programs. Step-by-step programmed instruction that is not branched.

Live instruction. Traditional classroom teaching that uses a teacher to guide student learning.

Mainframe. A computer with very large memory, in the range of thousands of megabytes.

Management Information System. A systematic method of information retrieval designed to provide managers with the necessary data for making intelligent decisions.

Mega. The prefix for 1,000,000.

Microcomputer. A self-contained computer with a memory in the range of one megabyte or less.

Microprocessor. That portion of the microcomputer which is responsible for all mathematical and logical operations. This unit contains the CPU.

Minicomputer. A computer with memory in the range of 1 to 100 megabytes.

Modem. An acronym for modulator/demodulator: a device which allows the computer to communicate over telephone lines.

Monitor. The video screen on which information is presented to the user.

Motherboard. In computers such as the Apple and IBM PC, this is the circuit board which contains all of the main elements of the computer, including the CPU, ROM, and RAM.

Multi-use programmable system.   A versatile computer system which can be programmed to perform many functions.

Output device.   Any device which accepts information from the microcomputer, including the monitor and printer.

Parity.   A coding scheme whereby it is possible to detect if an error has occured in transmitting bytes from one point to another.

Perceived exertion.   A subjective estimate of the effort required to perform exercise.

PILOT.   A programming language for CAI that accepts free responses as well as multiple choice.

PRINT statement.   This command causes the computer to output to the screen or printer the value assigned to a variable or a literal enclosed in quotation marks.

Printer buffer.   A device which works between the computer and the printer. It accepts large amounts of information from the computer and independently transmits it to the printer, thereby freeing the computer for other tasks.

Program.   A logical set of instructions to accomplish a given task on the computer.

Programmer.   An individual who develops computer programs.

Project Evaluation and Review Technique (PERT).   A planning process where each step or task is identified, placed in sequence, and assigned a time allotment which directly calculates a critical path schedule.

RAM.   An acronym for Random Access Memory. This is the section of memory which is available to the user for holding data or programs.

Random access.   Reading data in any order, regardless of the order in which it is stored.

READ statement.   A command that causes the computer to assign numeric or string values to a DATA statement.

REM statement.   A remark statement placed in a program to identify specific steps or operations.

ROM.   An acronym for Read Only Memory. This is the section of memory containing programs which the computer needs in order to function.

RS-232.   One form of a serial interface.

Self-contained program.   A program that contains all the elements necessary for the computer to complete its operation and provide a solution.

Self talk.   Internal thought processing (oral, silent).

Sequential program.   A series of imperative statements where the execution of one command follows that of another.

Serial access.   A program that reads one data point immediately after another.

Serial card.   An interface used to transform electrical output from a testing instrument into meaningful values.

Software.   Any program that runs the computer.

Spreadsheet.   A calculation system which has the ability to create custom documents with formulas which can then be entered into the cells and direct a program to compute numerical analyses.

SQR function.   A computer command used to take the square root of the number in parentheses.

Stress.   Nonspecific biological responses to any demand.

Stress test.   An exercise test used to provide information regarding cardiovascular fitness.

Syntax error.   The incorrect use of the programming language.

TAB.   This command designates the number of spaces the computer is to skip on a given line before outputting a value.

Taxonomy of CAI.   A method for classifying types of computer-assisted instruction into the categories of experiencing, informing, reinforcing, integrating, and utilizing.

Tool software.   Computer programs that are used for a specific task such as word processing, database management, and spreadsheets.

User friendliness.   The ease with which an operator can understand and use a computer or computer program.

Utilizing.   A category in the taxonomy of CAI containing programs that serve as tools to solve complex real-life problems.

Word processing.   A program which functions very much like the typewriter and stores text information for ease of editing or repeated use.

Contributors

Jon B. Broyles
Department of Computer Services
Administration Building
Northeast Missouri State University
Kirksville, MO 63501

Dr. Joseph E. Donnelly
Director, Human Performance Laboratory
Department of Physical Education
Kearney State College
Kearney, NE 68849

Dr. Richard Engelhorn
Department of Physical Education and Leisure Studies
Iowa State University
Ames, IA 50011

Dr. Sharon Mathes
Department of Physical Education and Leisure Studies
Iowa State University
Ames, IA 50011

Dr. Jerry L. Mayhew
Director, Human Performance Laboratory
Northeast Missouri State University
Kirksville, MO 63501

Dr. James G. Richards
Human Performance Laboratory/Biomechanics
Department of Physical Education
University of Delaware
Newark, DE 19711

Dr. David K. Stotlar
Chairperson of Sport Management
United States Sports Academy
P.O. Box 8650
Mobile, AL 36689

Dr. Roger Volker
Department of Physical Education and Leisure Studies
Iowa State University
Ames, IA 50011

Index